The Making
of the
New Poor Law

The politics of inquiry, enactment
and implementation, 1832-39

Lord Althorp as Chancellor of the Exchequer, shown with his hand resting on the New Poor Law (from the portrait by Henry Bone, reproduced with the gracious permission of Earl Spencer).

THE MAKING
OF THE
NEW POOR LAW

The politics of inquiry, enactment
and implementation, 1832-39

Anthony Brundage

Professor of History
California State Polytechnic University

Hutchinson of London

Hutchinson & Co (Publishers) Ltd
3 Fitzroy Square, London W1P 6JD

London Melbourne Sydney Auckland
Wellington Johannesburg and agencies
throughout the world

First published 1978

Published in the USA by
Rutgers University Press
Copyright © 1978 by Rutgers,
The State University of New Jersey
Printed and made in the United States
of America

ISBN 0 09 133170 6

To Martha

Contents

Preface

There are two reasons for undertaking a history of the making of the New Poor Law. First of all, it has not been done. In the words of J. R. Poynter: "Despite the work of the Webbs and others a full-scale study of reform of the Poor Law in 1834 is still needed."[1] Related to this is the clear need for studying poor law reform in an explicitly political context. Poor law administration was pre-eminently a political process, involving a complex interplay of the poor, parish elites, county leaders, and Parliament. Changes in the poor laws can thus be studied in terms of the differing perspectives and power bases of local, county, and national leaders. The numerous studies of poor law history now available are heavily oriented to examining relief policies and techniques and make little or no attempt to connect them with political events or processes. This deficiency in the perspective of historians of social welfare is matched by that of political historians, who pay scant regard to the poor laws. Derek Fraser sums up the problem succinctly:

> Historical studies of the nineteenth century have committed the Poor Law to a non-political limbo. Political historians have assumed that politics was primarily concerned with parliamentary elections and have shown little interest in Poor Law affairs, except perhaps when they impinged on the wider political stage. Social historians interested in poor relief have concentrated heavily upon social administration and have ignored political dimensions.[2]

1. J. R. Poynter, *Society and Pauperism,* p. 317.
2. Derek Fraser, "The Poor Law as a Political Institution," p. 111.

The thread running through this book is the exercise or attempted exercise of power—the power of cabinet ministers, M.P.s, reformers, officials, magistrates, and landowners—in a variety of national and local contexts. An important feature of this approach is the use of such power to maintain the economic and social ascendancy of the landed interest.

When we keep the political aspect in focus, the New Poor Law appears far less revolutionary than it has been portrayed. From the perspective of numerous changes made over a long period before 1834 relating to such topics as the laws of settlement, magistrates, vestries, and unions of parishes, a very considerable degree of continuity in the 1834 statute is discernible. This very continuity, in turn, raises questions about the importance of the famous royal commission on the poor laws, and an analysis of its composition and operation in Chapter 2 reveals the complex political web in which reformers had to operate. Chapter 3 similarly views drafting and passage of the bill in relation to the interplay of political forces, including the press and public opinion. Understanding the implementation of the law requires an examination of the inner workings of the central commission as well as its relationship with the government, Parliament, and local leaders, which are examined in Chapters 4, 5, and 6. Such an assessment points up the need to reconsider the meaning and significance of the concept of centralization, a topic mentioned in various parts of the book but receiving its fullest treatment in the concluding chapter, where it forms a key part of the question of the relationship between the New Poor Law and the nineteenth-century "revolution in government."

A word of explanation seems in order regarding the selection of 1839 as a terminal point. If this book were a history of poor relief techniques, it might seem more logical to end with the poor law commission's major policy formulations of 1844 and 1852. If it were an institutional history of the poor law commission, a suitable terminus would be 1847, the year the agency was transformed into the poor law board. The purpose of the book, however, is to explore the political dimensions and consequences of poor law reform, and 1839 is an appropriate point to stop. The expiration of the poor law commission's initial term in that year occasioned a hard-fought struggle for its renewal, and the resulting debate well illustrates the political forces and tensions at work throughout the period. This debate came on the heels of the controversies over the New Poor Law generated by certain patterns of regional resistance, as well as those raised in the 1837 general election and investigated by a House of Commons select committee in 1837–38. The debate on the 1839 renewal bill is thus a culmination of the controversies of the first five years of the poor law commission. By this date, the New Poor Law had been implemented in more than 90 percent of the country. Relief policies, as well as the pattern of relationships between central and local authorities, were clearly established and were to undergo little change in the next half-century. Although there was an intensification of some aspects of the debate over the New Poor Law during the "hungry forties," the controversy remained firmly within the terms of reference developed by 1839.

Acknowledgments

I wish to thank the archivists and staffs of the following institutions for giving generously of their time and assistance: The Public Record Office, The Bedfordshire Record Office, The Bodleian Library, the British Museum, the House of Lords Record Office, the National Library of Wales, the Northamptonshire Record Office, the University of Durham (Department of Palaeography and Diplomatic), University College London, the University of London (Goldsmith's Library), and the West Sussex Record Office.

I am likewise grateful to Earl Spencer for his kind permission to reproduce Henry Bone's enamel portrait of Lord Althorp as the frontispiece of this book. I acknowledge with gratitude the permission of the trustees of the Goodwood Estate to quote from the duke of Richmond's correspondence.

For helpful criticism and advice at various stages of research, writing, and revising, I wish to thank Derek Fraser, D. Cresap Moore, Mark D. Neuman, David Roberts, and J. S. Taylor.

I reserve my deepest gratitude for my wife, Martha, who has provided unflagging inspiration and assistance in every possible way throughout many years of a fruitful partnership in studying the poor laws.

Abbreviations Used

B.M.   British Museum
HLRO. House of Lords Record Office
MH.   Ministry of Health Papers in the Public Record Office
NLW.   National Library of Wales
N.R.O. Northamptonshire Record Office
PLC.   Poor Law Commission
P.R.O. Public Record Office
UCL.   University College, London
UD.   University of Durham
UL.   University of London

Chapter I

Patterns of Power under the Old Poor Law

The passage of the Elizabethan Poor Law of 1597 and 1601 signaled the beginning of Parliament's long involvement with the fashioning of a national and secularized system of relieving the poor. The purpose of these acts, and of the many modifying statutes that followed over the next few centuries, was to relieve the aged, infirm, and impotent and to set the "industrious poor" to work. Through such public provision, funded out of local rates, it became possible to distinguish between those segments of the poor entitled to relief and the "sturdy rogues" and "idle vagabonds" whose alleged wilfull refusal to settle down and work in a disciplined manner could be countered by various penal measures. The political leaders of England, which is to say the peerage and gentry, fashioned the Old Poor Law into a method of controlling the poor well suited to the social and political structure of the country. The day-to-day business of dealing with applicants for relief was placed in the hands of annually named overseers, mostly drawn from the ranks of farmers and shopkeepers, who had a close knowledge of the character and needs of the parish poor. The gentry, in their capacity as magistrates, played a supervisory role and provided a place of appeal for the poor. Their greater leisure, experience, and education gave them a wider perspective than that of most overseers, while their involvement with parliamentary politics made it possible for them to devise and implement corrective legislation. The system thus not only controlled the poor but also enhanced the notion of hierarchy, bolstered the ethos of paternalism which was its corollary, and provided an efficient feedback into the national lawmaking mechanism.

It is, of course, misleading to describe the Old Poor Law as a "system" if this is taken to imply national uniformity. There were, from the beginning, marked differences in practice in various parts of the country, not simply local variations in applying statutory law, but—because much of the Old Poor Law was not statutory at all—a collection of customs and practices which, in the absence of a controlling central administration, sprang up and flourished in luxuriant profusion.[1] Nonetheless, in a broader sense, there was a recognizable pattern of hierarchical organization maintained by the partial overlapping of local elites supervising poor relief and members of Parliament legislating on poor relief. Despite many factors in preindustrial England that fostered regional and local particularism, sufficient points of economic and social interest were shared by most members of the parliamentary and magisterial classes to shape and direct the evolution of the Old Poor Law into particular channels. This is reflected in three facets of the law—the regulation of pauper settlement, the extension of the areas of management through unions of parishes, and the attempts to give greater power to the gentry on parish vestries and local boards through plural voting and other means.

The theory behind the laws of pauper settlement held that each parish was financially responsible for its own poor. Although parochial responsibility was explicit in the Elizabethan Poor Laws, considerable conflict arose in determining the basis on which a person was to be considered as "belonging" to a certain parish—was place of birth, residence, occupation, or some other factor paramount? Parliament attempted to deal with this problem by the Act of Settlement of 1662 (13 and 14 Car. 2, c. 12), which defined several "heads of settlement" for determining to which parish a pauper was chargeable (and hence removable if resident else-

---

1. An excellent survey of the complexities and variations of the Old Poor Law is Geoffrey W. Oxley, *Poor Relief in England and Wales 1601-1834.*

where). In subsequent years, many refinements were added, resulting in an increasingly complex code that did little to inhibit the burgeoning settlement litigation between parishes.[2] Reformers increasingly regarded the vexation and expense of the endless legal squabbles over pauper settlement as one of the chief failures of the system, and Adam Smith, in a well-known comment, indicted the settlement laws for impeding the free circulation of labor and as "an evident violation of natural liberty and justice."[3]

Parliament's tolerance for such a state of affairs resulted from neither negligence nor ineptitude: The laws of settlement were of considerable economic benefit to owners of large estates. By their control over housing in the parishes they owned, the gentry were able to keep the population and thus the poor rates down, while at the same time maintaining pools of laborers in adjacent parishes for whose relief they were not financially burdened. Landed magnates increasingly displayed a willingness to pull down cottages and prevent settlement by the poor. Other parishes, where land ownership was much divided, found such undertakings well-nigh impossible, and thus tended to become densely populated and heavily pauperised "open" parishes, in contrast to the "close" parishes controlled by one or a few landowners.[4] Although many parishes could not be so neatly classified, the great financial advantages of one close parish vis-à-vis a neighboring open parish encouraged the practice of clearing parishes. In 1801, Compton Wyniates, a parish in Warwickshire owned entirely by the earl of Northampton, had a population of 41 while the neighboring parish of Tysoe, owned by numerous freeholders, had 891 inhabitants.[5] Although Tysoe had a much greater geographic area, it was nearly five times as populous per acre. The most significant comparison is between the amounts expended for poor relief, which in 1785 were £469 for Tysoe and £9 for Compton. The laborers on the Compton estate lived mostly in Tysoe, whose ratepayers had to shoulder the

2. See P. Styles, "The Evolution of the Law of Settlement"; and Michael E. Rose, "Settlement, Removal, and the New Poor Law."

3. Adam Smith, *An Inquiry into the Nature and Causes of the Wealth of Nations* (New York: Random House, 1937; first published in 1776), p. 141.

4. B. A. Holderness, "'Open' and 'Close' Parishes in England in the Eighteenth and Nineteenth Centuries."

5. A. W. Ashby, *One hundred years of Poor Law administration in a Warwickshire village*, p. 5.

entire burden of relieving them. The earl of Northampton and his tenants paid only wages; the costs of supporting their aged, infirm, and unemployed laborers were borne by others.

The seventeenth and eighteenth centuries saw an increase in the size of landed estates, accompanied by the enclosure movement and by more rational, scientific, and capitalist attitudes and techniques. The laws of settlement, which might seem out of step with such tendencies, were in fact closely linked with them—a subbranch of the developing science of estate management. For large landowners, the system worked well: Much of the labor to work their estates came from adjoining open parishes, the latter being forced to maintain a large laboring population for the benefit of their wealthy neighbors.[6] If the ratepayers of an open parish, either in their vestry or through their overseers, tried to withhold relief from destitute laborers, the nearby squire, in his capacity as magistrate, could order the parish to grant relief. Under such a system, it was difficult to convince most gentry that there was that surplus population, exacerbated by the poor laws, to which Thomas Malthus began pointing with alarm at the end of the eighteenth century.[7] Indeed, at this very time, magistrates in parts of the south and the midlands were devising and issuing orders that tied a laborer's income (wages plus poor relief) to the price of bread and the size of his family. This policy was prompted not only by the high and widely fluctuating price of food but also by fear of "jacobin" uprisings among the poor. It must also be considered that the enclosure movement was near its peak and, as recent scholarship has demonstrated, heightened the demand for labor.[8]

The most widely copied model was an elaborate set of tables drawn up by a group of Berkshire justices at Speenhamland in 1795, but many areas, even in the south and midlands, never

6. It has recently been suggested that an analogous process was at work between industrializing towns and open rural parishes. The latter often had to support their settled laborers who had gone to work in the industrial areas but, for various reasons, lost their employment. It thus seems that the small rural freeholders and ratepayers paid a significant part of the costs of the Industrial as well as the Agricultural revolutions. See James Stephen Taylor, "The Impact of Pauper Settlement 1691-1834."

7. Thomas Malthus, *An Essay on Population* (London: J. M. Dent, 1952; the first edition appeared in 1798), 2:35-69.

8. J. D. Chambers and G. E. Mingay, *The Agricultural Revolution 1750-1880*, pp. 141-44.

adopted the practice.[9] The use of parish allowances in aid of wages (or in aid of large families) became known as the Speenhamland Plan, and came in for special criticism from Malthus and others, though it has been interpreted by Mark Blaug as a laudable attempt to deal with problems of structural and seasonal unemployment in a lagging sector of the economy.[10] One problem with Blaug's analysis is that it leaves out of account the difference between open and close parishes and assumes that each laborer worked in his parish of residence: "The Allowance System . . . added to the wages paid by farmers with one hand what it took from them in rates from the other."[11] In fact, the farmers of an open parish often supplemented the income of their settled laborers working in a nearby close parish, and thereby subsidized the running of some great landowner's estate. This situation persisted through the Napoleonic wars, but after 1814 a decline in agricultural prosperity and a reduced level of enclosure lessened the demand for labor. Moreover, the growing truculence of the peasantry, punctuated by outbursts of violence, affected close as well as open parishes and seemed to threaten the very survival of the social order. After 1815, more and more large landowners began to join in the Malthusian cry of rural overpopulation and point to the poor law policies adopted by their fathers a generation earlier as one of the causes of the countryside's troubles. More stringent policies were adopted by many magistrates, and by 1825 the average level of allowance scales had been reduced by one-third.[12]

Another development of the Old Poor Law that can be tied in part to the power of landed magnates and the increase in the size of estates is the expansion of the area of management.[13] Much of the early experimentation with unions of parishes, like the one created in Bristol by statute in 1696 (7 and 8 Will. 3, c. 32), was intended to

9. This was by no means the first scheme for an allowance system. See Sidney and Beatrice Webb, *English Poor Law History. Part I: The Old Poor Law,* pp. 177-79, hereafter cited as *The Old Poor Law.* Also see Mark Donald Neuman, "A Suggestion Regarding the Origins of the Speenhamland Plan."

10. Mark Blaug, "The Myth of the Old Poor Law and the Making of the New." For an insightful critique of some of the points made by Blaug, see James Stephen Taylor, "The Mythology of the Old Poor Law."

11. Blaug, op. cit., p. 176.

12. Ibid., p. 162.

13. See E. W. Martin, "From Parish to Union: Poor Law Administration 1601-1865."

establish more efficient workhouses in towns, though the creation of such institutions at the parish level predated the Bristol scheme by about sixty years.[14] The greater population and financial resources in unions of parishes made it possible to create larger and more efficient workhouses employing professional staffs. Although many union houses failed to advance much beyond the dismal level of most parish establishments, the financial savings prompted a number of local acts creating poor law unions in the early years of the eighteenth century. A general enabling act for building workhouses and grouping parishes was passed in 1722 (9 Geo. 1, c. 7), but relatively little activity ensued. Until midcentury, such amalgamations as did take place occurred in towns—in London, various commercial and textile centers, and agricultural market towns.

In 1756, the first rural incorporation was established by a local act in East Anglia, an area that saw a rapid extension of "incorporated hundreds" during the remainder of the century. Although there was some variation in the constitutions of these unions, it was common for magistrates, clergy, and substantial farmers to be named as "Guardians of the Poor." These in turn appointed a committee of directors to determine general policy and a group of acting guardians to superintend the parish overseers and the incorporation's house of industry.[15] Because this arrangement gave the local gentry a direct, corporate administrative role alongside the indirect, individual role of the Elizabethan code, a significant transformation was begun. Clearly, the gentry had found something amiss in allowing parish overseers to administer the system and decided to take a more active hand. A further step was taken by the passage of Thomas Gilbert's Act of 1782 (22 Geo. 3, c. 83), which permitted unions of parishes where "real power was taken out of the hands of the parish officers and entrusted to a committee of the neighbouring gentry."[16] This statute, which Gilbert had tried in vain to make mandatory, is of particular interest because its purpose was not to provide the basis for larger and more efficient workhouses. Rather, indoor relief was explicitly confined to the aged, the infirm, and children, thus eliminating the deterrent aspect for the able-bodied laborer. There has been a tendency for historians to

---

14. Oxley, op. cit., p. 80.
15. J. R. Poynter, *Society and Pauperism*, pp. 11-12.
16. Dorothy Marshall, *The English Poor in the Eighteenth Century*, p. 159.

regard this statute, in stark contrast to the New Poor Law, as inspired by humanitarian motives.[17] Despite important differences, the two acts were alike in placing administrative power in boards of guardians drawn from the principal landowners and occupiers. The reversal of the function of the workhouse between the 1782 and 1834 measures appears less important when the difference in the need for labor on landed estates between the two periods and the breakdown of social cohesion after 1815 are borne in mind: A system of poor law unions managed by the gentry was in existence by the latter half of the eighteenth century.[18] While considerable research on the policies pursued by these local authorities has yet to be done, it is not unreasonable to assume that they complemented the operation of the settlement laws and the allowance system for the benefit of the owners of landed estates. As conditions changed after the end of the Napoleonic wars, however, the Gilbert unions were saddled with a statutory mandate on the use of workhouses that no longer corresponded to conditions. The New Poor Law would utilize the principle of collective management of an extended district by a comittee of the local gentry and more affluent ratepayers, applied on a mandatory instead of optional basis, and combined with a deterrent workhouse.

Another constitutional device of the 1834 act developed in the last years of the Old Poor Law was the system of plural voting. Gilbert's Act provided that vestries of the parishes incorporated in a union were to set their policy not by a majority of ratepayers alone but also by a majority of the rates assessed. This introduced the principle of weighting the right to vote according to the amount of property occupied, a significant shift away from the traditional practice of permitting one vote to each ratepayer in parochial vestries. A further refinement stemming from the practice of plural voting according to the amount of stock held in the East India Company or other jointly owned companies, was introduced in 1807 in a bill by Samuel Whitbread, a wealthy brewer and Foxite M.P. The problem, according to Whitbread, was that every person

17. See, for example, Raymond G. Cowherd, "The Humanitarian Reform of the Poor Laws from 1782 to 1815." Humanitarianism as the dominant theme of the reforms of the latter half of the eighteenth century is also stressed by A. W. Coats, "Economic Thought and Poor Law Policy in the Eighteenth Century."

18. By 1834, there were 67 Gilbert unions incorporating 924 parishes, mostly in the rural midlands and east. Poynter, op. cit., p. 12.

rated to the poor's rate in the smallest sum had an "equal voice in the vestry with the proprietor who pays the highest proportion to the rate; and a very few inconsiderable renters sometimes have it in their power to dispose of the parish money against the opinion of the more substantial and better informed inhabitants."[19] Although Whitbread's bill was negatived, a sufficient shift of opinion was to occur in the next decade to make possible the adoption of the plural voting principle in the Select Vestries Acts of 1818 and 1819.

Before consideration of this legislation, it is necessary to examine the controversy and investigation that preceded it. Until 1815, there was relatively little concern about the alarming picture of imminent disaster painted by Malthus, and most magistrates and members of Parliament remained content with the "liberal" policies devised and enacted in the eighteenth century. By the end of the Napoleonic wars, however, the onset of a severe depression coupled with disquieting symptoms of rebellion among both rural and urban laborers rudely shattered this lassitude. In addition to reconsidering the arguments of Malthus and Whitbread, the country's leaders began to weigh the relative merits of schemes proffered by numerous reformers. It is obviously beyond the scope of this introductory chapter to indicate the richness and diversity of the reform literature that proliferated during these years, a task that is superbly performed by J. R. Poynter in *Society and Pauperism*.[20] But in the welter of arguments based on political economy, religion, humanitarianism, social control, or a discriminating charity movement, certain strands of opinion were common to most writers. These included the belief that both the poor rates and the discontent of the laborers had risen alarmingly, threatening the existence of the political, economic, and social order. Although many different reasons were adduced for this crisis, it was widely believed that one factor was the failure of the existing administrative framework. While abolition of the poor law, based largely on Malthusian principles, had powerful support, most writers and political leaders proceeded on the assumption that the poor law must be retained but substantially overhauled.

This was the consensus when Parliament turned its attention to

---

19. *Hansard's Parliamentary Debates*, 1st ser., 8(1807):896-97 (February 19), hereafter cited as *Hansard*.

20. My debt to Poynter's study of the period in much of the remainder of this chapter will be obvious and renders citations on every point unnecessary.

poor law reform in 1816. J. C. Curwen, a poor law pamphleteer and self-styled spokesman for the landed interest, moved for the appointment of a select committee in a speech notably tinged with abolitionism and rancor against the poor.[21] A committee was appointed but was unable to do any more during the remainder of the session than order the collection of returns, and Curwen moved for its reappointment in 1817. On this occasion, he urged the government to take charge of poor law reform, but Lord Castlereagh deftly sidestepped the burden. Castlereagh did tell the house of his own notion of poor law reform, which was to approximate the system in Scotland, where "the practice was for proprietors to assess themselves in what they deemed necessary for the support of those whom they themselves considered as entitled to it."[22] While Castlereagh admitted that such a step would be tantamount to abolishing the poor law and was therefore impracticable, the issue was raised again during the passage of the New Poor Law, which some of its proponents declared to be close in spirit to the Scottish system.[23]

The select committee was dominated by its chairman, William Sturges-Bourne, and by Thomas Frankland Lewis. Both men were Canningites and would become prominent figures in making and executing the New Poor Law—Sturges-Bourne on the royal commission of inquiry and Frankland Lewis as one of the three poor law commissioners. Neither was an abolitionist, and the select committee's inquiry was directed to methods of improving poor law administration, but the report was critical of compulsory assessment for relieving the poor and called for restoring descretionary power to parish elites:

> By following the dictates of their own interests, landowners and farmers become, in the natural order of things, the best trustees and guardians for the public; when that order of things is destroyed, and a compulsory maintenance established for all who require it, the consequences cannot fail in the end to be equally ruinous to both parties.[24]

21. *Hansard,* 1st ser., 34(1816):878-99 (May 28).
22. *Hansard,* 1st ser., 36(1817):523-24 (February 21).
23. See p. 62.
24. *Sessional Papers* (Commons), 1819, "Report from the Select Committee on the Poor Laws," 2:296. The report was first published in 1817 and reprinted in 1819. *(Sessional [Parliamentary] Papers* hereafter cited as *Sess. Papers.)*

The committee turned its attention to the operation of Gilbert Act unions, which were declared to be beneficial "in every case in which they have been superintended by the principal inhabitants of the united district; and that their success and advantage depends almost wholly on that circumstance."[25] One of their major recommendations was to make voting in the parish vestry dependent upon the amount of property held and to give such reformed parishes (or unions of parishes) a greater voice in poor law administration. The report declared that the best means of restoring sound practice was to confer authority on "such a part of the vestry as may bear some analogy to the heritors [landowners] and kirk session of Scotland." [26]

The legislative fruits of this investigation and report are to be seen in two statutes—An Act for the Regulation of Parish Vestries, 1818 (58 Geo. 3, c. 69), and An Act to Amend the Laws for the Relief of the Poor, 1819 (59 Geo. 3, c. 12)—together known as the Select Vestries Acts or Sturges-Bourne's Acts. The first of these established a plural voting system that regulated voting in a vestry according to the rateable value of a person's property on the following scale: one vote for property rated up to £50 and one additional vote for each £25 above that up to a maximum of six votes. This scale was later adopted in the New Poor Law for the election of guardians. The 1819 law added resident clergymen as ex officio members, and select vestries thus constituted were specifically enjoined to take the character of relief applicants into account and encouraged to distinguish between "the deserving and the idle, extravagant or profligate Poor." Such rigor was facilitated by provisions for salaried overseers, better kept accounts, and the building and enlargement of workhouses. Thus in those parishes which chose to adopt the Select Vestires Act, power was shifted away from the small farmers and shopkeepers whose ignorance, laziness, and jobbing ways, it was claimed, were a major cause of spiraling poor rates and pauper insubordination.

Besides transferring control of vestries to parish elites, the legislation also provided somewhat greater protection from magisterial interference. This observation at first seems paradoxical, since

25. Ibid., p. 306.
26. Ibid., p. 309.

magistrates were themselves the leaders of local elites. The problem arose because applicants refused relief by the overseers were free to appeal to any magistrate in the county. While a substantial portion of the magistracy had begun adopting a harsher policy toward pauper applicants, their greater corporate stringency could be nullified by a single "poor man's J.P.," whose generous proclivities quickly became known among the poor of a district. Such justices were, of course, firmly grounded in the traditional ethos of paternalism, which made their interference all the more difficult to combat. The proponents of strict relief policies were not yet prepared to endorse a major overhaul of the administrative structure that would end the considerable authority of individual magistrates, but a beginning was made in the 1819 act, in which two justices rather than one were required to overrule the decisions of a select vestry.

The 1820's saw a continuation of the debate on the poor law and attempts to reform it both within and outside Parliament. In a period beset by economic dislocations and the continuing furor over the resumption of specie payment in 1819, it is not surprising that acrimonious differences of opinion should arise or that unlikely political bedfellows should be paired. While many advocates of the existing system could be classified as Tory paternalists, they were joined by radicals led by Thomas Attwood of Birmingham, who argued that not the poor laws but the deflation brought on by the return to metallic currency in 1819 was the cause of distress. Radical followers of Cobbett and Hunt argued that poor relief was the birthright of the poor. On the other side, the abolitionist party comprised "theorists" like Malthus and James Mill and "practical" politicians like James Scarlett (later Lord Abinger), the jurist and M.P. who introduced abolitionist bills in 1821 and 1822. With such diversity in the extremes of opinion, it is not surprising that there were even greater variations among the majority who wanted stricter policies and lower rates without abolishing a system of compulsory relief.

In the absence of a government willing to take on the perplexing and thankless task of a major overhaul of the poor laws, magistrates and local reformers did what they could in their own districts. The reduction of allowance scales was one expedient, although this of course did not meet the problems posed by the poor man's J.P.s. Somewhat more effective in this regard were select vestries, which had been established in 2,868 parishes by 1827, though the number declined thereafter.[27] An extension of the benefits secured by the stricter practices of select vestries was difficult because the adoption of the act at the local level remained optional. There was growing sentiment for making the select vestry system mandatory, a step recommended by a committee of the Cambridgeshire bench in 1828.[28] The House of Commons Select Committee on Select and other Vestries, appointed in the final year of Wellington's ministry, urged the same thing in 1830.[29] Thus, even before the explosive Captain Swing riots of 1830-31 encouraged a disposition in favor of compulsory reform, opinion was moving in that direction.

During the postwar period, the deterrent aspect of the workhouse was stressed, and some notable successes in "dispauperising" certain districts were registered.[30] Usually, but not always, this policy operated in conjunction with the select vestry or union system. The degree to which the "offer of the house" before 1834 resembled the "workhouse test" of the law of 1834 is debatable. In the early period of workhouse building, the deterrent function was often overshadowed by a stress on the physical, moral, or educational benefits of institutionalization. Although the act of 1722 specifically provided for offering to admit the able-bodied into workhouses as a test of destitution, this was countered by subsequent legislation. Gilbert's Act of 1782 forbade such a function for Gilbert union workhouses while an act of 1795 (36 Geo. 3, c. 23) enabled justices to grant emergency outdoor relief even where a workhouse test was in effect. Even after 1815, when deterrence was emphasized once again, it is questionable whether it resembled the post-1834 workhouse system, which operated in harness with the "less eligibility" principle—that the situation of the able-bodied recipient of poor relief "on the whole shall not be made really or apparently as

27. Figures on select vestries were gathered by the Royal Commission on the Poor Laws of 1832-34, *Sess. Papers* (Commons), 1834, 27:115-17.

28. E. M. Hampson, *The Treatment of Poverty in Cambridgeshire, 1597-1834*, p. 199.

29. *Sess. Papers* (Commons), "Report from the Select Committee on Select and Other Vestries," 1830, 4:569.

30. The most widely publicized were those made by the "Nottinghamshire reformers"—Lowe, Becher, and Nicholls (the future poor law commissioner). See pp. 39-40.

eligible as the independent labourer of the lowest class."[31] The problem is to determine to what degree this formulation was implicit in the deterrent use of workhouses before 1834, and how much it resembles the kind of sentiment expressed in 1807 by Samuel Whitbread, who declared that one purpose of his bill was "to render dependent poverty, in all cases, a degradation and at all times less desirable than independent industry."[32] Such determination was increasingly widespread among practical men like the duke of Bedford's estate agent, who expressed his belief in 1830 that "all able bodied men must work hard for their allowance . . . at a price somewhat lower than an independent labourer earns—to make the condition of a pauper not desirable—but *mere maintenance*."[33]

J. R. Poynter has asserted: "Without the workhouse test as a practical instrument the principle of less eligibility might have remained a mere abstraction."[34] But it does seem that those in authority in the first third of the nineteenth century were coming increasingly to believe that it was possible to make the pauper's lot "less eligible" without the workhouse. Indeed, while the royal commission's report emphasized the workhouse test, some of the evidence revealed successful cases of the less eligibility principle without it, in the form of the "outdoor labor test," to which the economist G. Poulett Scrope called Parliament's attention during the passage of the New Poor Law.[35] And, as can be seen in the chapters on the implementation of the act, many boards of guardians would adopt this position, using the deterrent aspect of the workhouse only when it suited them and on a case-by-case basis. The problem was not so much one of the techniques of relief policy as it was one of administrative structure. The inability to stem the rising national tide of pauperism arose from the weakness of many parishes, attributable to their small size and dominance by ratepayers of modest means, and from the appellate system that lodged too much authority in solitary magistrates. The new local authori-

31. *Sess. Papers* (Commons), "Reports of Assistant Commissioners for Inquiring into the Administration and Practical Operation of the Poor Laws," 1834, 28:228.
32. Samuel Whitbread, *Substance of a Speech on the Poor Laws: Delivered to the House of Commons on Thursday, February 19, 1807*, p. 22.
33. W. G. Adam to Edward Crocker, February 22, 1830, Russell Estate Correspondence, R3/2861, Bedfordshire Record Office.
34. Poynter, op. cit., p. 315.
35. See pp. 60-61.

ties, the boards of guardians created throughout the country after 1834, were free from these defects and consequently able to apply the less eligibility principle on a pragmatic basis. Practically all the key components of the new system had been developed within and outside Parliament during the last fifty or so years of the Old Poor Law—the problem was to integrate them into a compulsory national pattern.

One further topic should be touched upon here—the question of centralization, which involves the issue of the influence of Jeremy Bentham's ideas on the 1834 reform. Relatively few proposals for a centralized control of the poor laws besides Bentham's were advanced, and none could compare with his in terms of bold and comprehensive analysis.[36] His insistence on central inspection alone seems to entitle him to the major credit for the creation of the poor law commissioners and their itinerant assistant commissioners. The key position of such Benthamites as Walter Coulson and Edwin Chadwick in making and implementing the reform strengthens this claim. But caution is needed: Most politicians and magistrates operated on terms of reference very different from those of the Benthamites. Because so much of the energy and talent of these practical men had gone into devising new local administrative structures—many features of which were incorporated into the New Poor Law—we should consider the creation of a central board in relation to this process. Historians of the New Poor Law have tended to treat the topic of centralization as if the Benthamite model were the only one available. They overlook an alternative model—one in which Parliament creates the central board of commissioners not to impose a new bureaucratic hierarchy or rigid uniformity, but in order to construct a network of powerful new local boards constituted according to the hierarchical social order of the countryside. This kind of "centralized" solution to the poor law crisis departs from the Benthamite model in structure, methods, and goals—a fact of which the Utilitarians associated with the reform were made painfully aware during the act's initial period of operation.

36. On the various plans for establishing central boards of commissioners, the earliest dating from 1796, see Sidney and Beatrice Webb, *English Poor Law History Part II: The Last Hundred Years,* 1:31-32n, hereafter cited as *The Last 100 Years.*

Chapter II

The Royal Commission of Inquiry

Considering the close connection for over two centuries between the poor laws and the social and economic well-being of the leaders of landed society, it is necessary to consider the fostering of a poor law amendment bill by the Grey ministry in the same light. Like its predecessor, the government was eager to find relief for the landed interest, and it was understood that this must involve a reduction of poor rates, which had caused outcries in every discussion of agricultural distress since the end of the Napoleonic wars. But lurking behind the financial concerns of peers and squires was the specter of social disintegration. The maladministration of the poor laws was seen to produce not only higher rates but a whole host of other evils, the most frightening of which were rural riots and incendiarism. The Swing riots were seared into the memory of many M.P.s, who consequently felt the need to restore the social fabric of the countryside.[1] This heightened awareness of the danger of continuing to drift made major amendment of the poor laws possible in the 1830's that had not proved possible in the preceding decade. On the other hand, if the government had a "mandate" to act from the landed interest, why did they not proceed to fashion a

1. E. J. Hobsbawm and George Rudé, *Captain Swing*, pp. 253-63.

bill in a cabinet committee and present it to Parliament? If, as has been suggested in the first chapter, the key reforms of the 1834 bill had all been adumbrated in previous discussion and enactments, the cabinet should have been able to produce such a bill out of its own deliberations. In short, why a royal commission? The creation of a royal commission suggests the systematic collection of evidence by extraparliamentary experts as the basis of a report to guide Parliament in drafting remedial measures. Inasmuch as such "scientific legislation" is rightly considered one of the hallmarks of Benthamism, it is not surprising that the New Poor Law has been considered a Benthamite measure. One noted work on royal commissions expresses the continuing view of many historians on the genesis of the 1834 act: "The Government accepted in large degree the recommendations which were deeply influenced by an ardent Benthamite [Edwin Chadwick] among the assistant commissioners, and the resultant statute was a revolutionary departure from the policy which had evolved since the time of Elizabeth."[2] The many questions begged by this bald assertion can only be investigated by examining the personalities and politics of poor law reform from 1832 to 1834, but first it is essential to consider why the government decided upon a royal commission.

It is, of course, impossible to define precisely what the "government" expected the commission to provide. Various ministerialists no doubt held differing views on the purpose of such a body. It is assumed that they all more or less expected the commission rigorously to investigate the administration of the poor laws, issue a report with evidence, and suggest certain changes in the law. This was the view of the marquis of Lansdowne, lord president of the council, who wrote to the lord chancellor, Lord Brougham, in the autumn of 1833 that the commission's report would

> act beneficially in two ways—by putting those who are willing to exert themselves to improve the administration under the existing law on the right methods—and by enabling us and members of Parlt. to come to the session with minds made up as to the extent of remedial interference necessary by amendment in the law itself.[3]

2. H. M. Clokie and J. W. Robinson, *Royal Commissions of Inquiry*, p. 103.
3. Lansdowne to Brougham, October 18, 1833, Brougham Papers, 38, 923, UCL.

But another key cabinet minister held a quite different opinion on the function of a royal commission. Sir James Graham, first lord of the Admiralty, expressed to Sir Robert Peel nearly ten years later his views on the reason for appointing a royal commission on the poor laws. He told Peel that a proposed commission on moral and religious instruction in the manufacturing districts would be a mistake because the government had to remedy already in mind: "A Commission is most useful to pave the way for a measure which is preconcerted; take for example the Poor Law enquiry." On another occasion, Graham told Peel that in the case of both the poor law and the municipal corporations, "the Government, which granted the Enquiry, contemplated and sought a specific change, and had the commission as a Pioneer for their measure."[4] Graham's statements raise some doubts about the government having to turn to a royal commission out of inability to devise a remedy of its own.

These doubts are reinforced by considering a statement made by Brougham in the House of Lords in June 1831. The earl of Winchelsea, in introducing an employment of laborers bill, had asked if the government had any plan "for the purpose of affording agricultural relief, by providing for the surplus population, by home colonization or otherwise."[5] After a noncommittal reply by the home secretary, Lord Melbourne, Brougham rose to declare that he had studied the poor laws carefully since 1816 and "at length, he believed, he saw daylight amidst the darkness which had hitherto enveloped the subject." Brougham declined to reveal the nature of his plan, disclosing only that it would be brought forward before the end of the next session, and "was intended to be prepatory to another measure for the consolidation and simplification of the existing Acts on the subject of the Poor-laws."[6] The ultimate measure indicated by Brougham's allusion was considered too potentially controversial to be dealt with as an ordinary bill, for the chancellor of the Exchequer, Lord Althorp, in stating the government's intention to appoint a royal commission on February 1,

4. Graham to Peel, December 26, 1841 and September 17, 1842, Peel Papers, B.M. Add. MSS, 40,446, fo. 253; 40,447, fo. 163.
5. *Hansard*, 3rd ser., 4(1831):261 (June 23).
6. Ibid., pp. 263-65.

hat because of the magnitude and complexity of the nember of the government, or of the House, would .ustified in bringing forward a measure that would apply generally to the whole collective system of the Poor Laws of this country." The royal commission would investigate and report upon the various systems of poor relief in practice, so that ministers "would then be able to determine whether they would propose any measure on the subject."[7]

The same reasoning evidently applied to the intermediary measure mentioned by Brougham, for there was no government bill forthcoming as a stopgap measure. But the bill that Earl Winchelsea introduced in the upper house—the employment of laborers bill—was enacted and gave legislative sanction to the poor relief expedient known as the labor rate. This act (2 and 3 Will. 4, c. 96), which expired on March 25, 1834, allowed a majority of three-fourths of the ratepayers in a parish, voting according to the Sturges-Bourne plural voting system, to adopt a labor rate, providing it was sanctioned by the justices at petty sessions. Upon adoption of the rate, the total labor bill of the parish was computed by multiplying the number of settled able-bodied laborers by their supposed market value and requiring each employer to hire a quantity of labor based on his rateable value or acreage. Ratepayers declining to hire their quota of laborers were assessed the difference at the regular parish poor rate. Such a scheme, which avoided many of the demoralising effects of the roundsman system, was favored by many large landowners and tenant farmers who employed considerable amounts of labor.[8] However, it was denounced by the royal commission for eliminating the distinction between free and pauper labor and for freezing existing patterns of parish settlement.[9] At least two members of the government strongly favored the labor rate—the marquis of Lansdowne and the

---

7. Quoted in George Nicholls and Thomas Mackay, *A History of the English Poor Law,* 2:214.

8. For a discussion of the roundsman system and labor rate, see Webb and Webb, *The Old Poor Law,* pp. 189-96. For contemporary descriptions of the operation of both measures, see Michael E. Rose, ed., *The English Poor Law 1780-1930,* pp. 56-58.

9. The commission investigated the subject at Althorp's request. The radical leader, Francis Place, claimed credit for publicizing the commission's denunciation of the labor rate, thus ensuring the defeat of the renewal bill in 1833. See Webb and Webb, *The Old Poor Law,* pp. 195-96n.

duke of Richmond. When the renewal bill of 1833 had been voted down, Lansdowne wrote Richmond:

> In the parish in this neighbourhood where it was most essential to have a labor rate to tide over next winter, the farmers have met and agreed unanimously, so that I hope we shall make our own law in spite of the H. of Commons.[10]

Lansdowne, Richmond, Winchelsea, and most other partisans of the labor rate would soon recognize that the comprehensive reform of 1834 was much more effective than the labor rate in reducing rates and restoring the social fabric of the countryside. But the bill is of interest both for being the only proposed reform of the period enjoying fairly widespread support within the landed interest, and because it adopted the plural voting system. It was left to the royal commission to frame a bill which would incorporate that system into a thoroughgoing reform.

The idea of a royal commission and the first suggestion for its personnel apparently came from Thomas Hyde Villiers, brother of the fourth earl of Clarendon, friend of John Stuart Mill, and secretary of the board of control. On January 19, 1832, he sent his recommendations to Lord Howick, the son of Earl Grey and undersecretary of the Home Department.[11] Considering Villiers' friendship with the younger Mill, it is not surprising that he recommended James Mill, the leading philosophical radical of the day, as one of the five commissioners. He also suggested another well-known figure, the Oxford professor of political economy, Nassau Senior. But the other three were neither economists nor utilitarians—Bishop Sumner, the Reverend Thomas Whately, and T. L. Hodges. John Bird Sumner, bishop of Chester, while noted for theological writings of an evangelical cast, was no expert on the poor laws or any other economic or social question. Whately and Hodges were both men of practical experience in poor law administration—Whately as a reformer of the parish of Cookham in Berkshire and Hodges as an active magistrate in Kent (as well as a Liberal M.P. for west Kent).

10. Lansdowne to Richmond, September 3, 1833, Goodwood MSS, 1439, fo. 225, West Sussex Record Office. The two peers also approved of creating allotments for their laborers. Lansdowne to Richmond, December 18, 1833, 1470, fo. 236.
11. Webb and Webb, *The Last 100 Years*, 1:47.

Brougham, the member of the cabinet given special cognizance of the poor law question, had begun to solicit advice and information even before Villiers' letter to Howick. One of those he consulted was Charles Mott, a wealthy London food wholesaler and contractor to the Lambeth workhouse, who was to become a paid assistant commissioner under the New Poor Law. Mott's reply to Brougham's letter of January 14 attacked drink, pawnbrokers, and profuse workhouse diets and called for abolishing all money relief and appointing paid magisterial superintendents in large parishes.[12] Brougham also contacted Nassau Senior, whose reply of January 27 indicates that the lord chancellor had accepted the wisdom of appointing a royal commission. The three names submitted by Senior include only one Benthamite—Walter Coulson, newspaperman, barrister, and amanuensis to Jeremy Bentham. Next was the Reverend Henry Bishop of Oriel College, who "resided for some years in a country parish in Oxford sh., much exerted himself there, and has valuable practical experience." The third name was Henry Frankland Lewis, the son of the future poor law commissioner, Thomas Frankland Lewis. The younger Lewis was known as a translator of German works, which Senior noted approvingly as "sufficient proofs of his diligence."[13] The royal commission appointed by the government a few weeks later contained seven men—two of them suggested by Villiers (Senior and Sumner) and two suggested by Senior (Coulson and Bishop). The other three were Bishop Blomfield of London, Henry Gawler, and William Sturges-Bourne, of whom only the last had any reputation as a poor law reformer. Edwin Chadwick (promoted from the ranks of the assistant commissioners) and James Traill were added the next year, and Chadwick's appointment brought one of the ablest and most energetic Benthamites to the commission. Senior and Chadwick were its most active members, and an examination of the inquiry and report must focus primarily on their ideas, strategies, and interrelationship.

Twenty-six assistant commissioners, each paid a daily allowance, were sent out to collect evidence in various parts of the country. Apart from Chadwick, none of those appointed in 1832 achieved great notoriety in poor law work although there were

12. Mott to Brougham, January 21, 1832, Brougham Papers, 37,691, UCL.
13. Senior to Brougham, January 27, 1832, Brougham Papers, 13,648, UCL.

indeed some notable figures among them, such as the jurist Charles Hay Cameron, the architect Redmond Pilkington, and the scientist John Wrottesley (second baron Wrottesley). The rest appear to have been an assortment of barristers, retired military officers, or men from prominent families. The best connected of the last was C. P. Villiers, another younger brother of the fourth earl of Clarendon, and a future president of the poor law board.

Senior's original ideas on the functions of the assistant commissioners was that they were to go forth on their travels with only the most general instruction: "To enquire into the effects of the present system of poor laws in England and Wales, to report the results after enquiries, and to suggest such measures as may appear to them advisable."[14] But the full commission had other ideas—the assistant commissioners were to be issued a set of quite specific instructions to guide their inquiries. These instructions were printed with the 1834 report, and they indicate some clear preconceptions about the nature of any reform. One in particular deserves attention. In addition to being instructed to confer with magistrates, overseers, and rectors and to examine parish books, each assistant commissioner was told to

> collect facts and opinions as to the practicality and probable effects of allowing a landlord, though not rated, to vote in the vestry in person or by proxy; and if so allowed, what influence should be given to his vote, compared with that of the tenant, and how far that influence ought to depend on the amount of his property.[15]

Considering Senior's proclivity for granting the assistants complete freedom in their inquiries, it is highly unlikely this instruction was his work. It bears the stamp of William Sturges-Bourne, whose select committee investigation of 1817-18 and Select Vestries Act of 1818-19 concerned themselves chiefly with questions of this nature. And since one of the key elements of the New Poor Law was the inclusion of just such a power for landlords, there is an evident continuity with previous reforms built into the very structure of the royal commission's inquiry. Another issue that figured

14. Ibid.
15. *Sess. Papers* (Commons), "Report of His Majesty's Commissioners for inquiring into the Administration and Practical Operation of the Poor Laws," app. A, Part 1, p. 252, 1834, 28:156, hereafter cited as "1834 Report."

in the instructions to the assistants was magisterial interference. The phrasing of this instruction strongly suggests that although any reform would strike at magisterial interference, this was to be interpreted as interference by those magistrates lacking some natural connection to the community in question.

> Where he finds such interference, he will inquire whether the magistrates who are most active or ready in such interferences are or are not resident within the parish in whose concerns they interfere, or within what distance; whether they contribute to its rates and attend its vestries; whether any and what profit arises to their clerks from summons and orders.[16]

Most of the other instructions involved digging up evidence on the allowance system, the labor rate, the roundsman system, workhouse diets, and so forth, from which it is possible to discern the general outlines of both the exposition of the evils of the existing law and the remedial measures of the 1834 report. Similar questions appear in the rural and town queries sent out to parishes throughout the country, which were filled in by overseers, magistrates, or rectors in approximately 10 percent of the 15,000 parishes. Respondents were asked numerous questions about the poor relief in their parishes and the nature of the local administrative system. The assistants were ordered to follow up on the questionnaires already returned from their districts, as well as to prod other parishes to fill theirs out and return them.[17]

Soon after the assistants were sent out to their districts in the autumn of 1832, their reports began flooding back upon the commission and upon Lord Brougham, who insisted on seeing the reports himself as they came in. As the publisher Charles Knight recalled:

> The Chancellor took an especial interest in the inquiries that were then proceeding under a Royal Commission as to the administration

16. Ibid.
17. Responses to the rural and town queries fill seven of the fifteen volumes of the report: *Sess. Papers,* 1834, vols. 30–36. The misleading manner in which some of the questions were phrased and the biased interpretation of the responses by the commission, particularly on the subject of allowances, has been demonstrated in two articles by Mark Blaug, "The Myth of the Old Poor Law and the Making of the New," and "The Poor Law Report Re-examined."

and operation of the Poor Laws. Evening after evening would his Dispatch-box bring down some Report of the Assistant Commissioners. He occasionally gave me the task of looking over these voluminous papers, and marking papers for his more careful perusal.[18]

What Brougham (as well as the commissioners) had access to were the weekly diaries sent in by the assistants, none of which is extant. Apparently, they were all destroyed after the assistants had written their final reports, those intended for publication. The latter are written in uniformly stiff and dull style, redolent of the spirit that informs the instructions from the commission. The diaries were no doubt written in a more lively style and would probably provide a much better feel for the actual condition of the poor and the state of prevailing opinions on poor relief. A glimpse is afforded by a private letter of one of the assistants, R. W. Pilkington, though it was written eight months after the promulgation of the report. Describing to Chadwick the situation near Hatfield, where Pilkington himself was a landowner, he wrote:

Of our Political Economy the following is a literal specimen—the Speaker a Farmer a tenant of my own a rate payer, and therefore with a right of voting in the Vestry—"Poor folk have as much right to bread as the rich, and that they never can have, till every man has land enif to keep a coo—How is a poor man, let me ax, to have a wife and eight children on his wage?" "But why," I ventured to suggest, "do men marry and get eight children without any likely means of keeping them?" "Why do folks marry!! thou maught as well ax why they catch smallpox or ought of that—what wouldst thou do I would like to know if left alone for half an hour with that ere lass?" turning to a girl who, for the benefit of his illustration, was at work close by. The girl simpered so prettily that it was impossible to particularize what I would *not* do—so my friend triumphantly continued—"Nay, sir, that's a matter of God's own ordering and man can't mind it—his very first command was 'Increase and multiply,' and there's no going agin it."[19]

Pilkington's mention of the fact that his ignorant tenant was a member of the vestry gives a political point to the anecdote which found more extensive expression in the official reports of some of

---

18. Charles Knight, *Passages of a Working Life during Half a Century*, 2:197-98.
19. Pilkington to Chadwick, October 20, 1834, Chadwick Papers, UCL.

the assistants. C. P. Villiers, in his report on Warwickshire, Worcestershire, Gloucestershire and north Devon, criticized the personnel of parish vestries as well as overseers, alike drawn from "farmers, tradespeople, and other persons who are . . . from their occupations, want of experience, and their local interests, totally disqualified for the duty."[20] On the issue of magistrates, Villiers noted great evils from their interference, especially where borough magistrates interfered with country parishes, as in the Coventry area.[21] Captain Chapman, reporting on Somerset and Devon, found magistrates eager to assist in reforming the system, noting that cases of magisterial interference resulted not from sinister motives but from lack of coordination: "Hitherto they have acted without method or system, or cooperation; it only requires to regulate and direct their exertions, and I have no doubt that they will give valuable and zealous assistance in promoting the object in view."[22] Assistant commissioner George Taylor, who was given the task of preparing a special report on magistrates and vestries, asserted that overseers were generally much more likely to exercise vigilance and economy than magistrates, to whom "local interests are of minor import, local circumstances little known, and to whom, even where personally concerned, the difference in the payment of petty charges is of little consequence."[23] Taylor found that select vestries functioned much more efficiently than others because of plural voting and the clergyman acting as chairman but saw their effectiveness undermined by the fact that each open vestry (often dominated by small ratepayers) had to vote to establish a select vestry— an impossibility in most cases.[24]

Material such as this clearly pointed to some sort of major reorganization of local government, and the cabinet was anxious to keep informed of the state of the inquiry. In December 1832, the commissioners were busy preparing "some cases of good and bad management" which the home secretary, Lord Melbourne, had requested.[25] Whatever the shape of the plan formed or developing in the minds of commissioners and cabinet ministers, it seems that Nassau

20. *Sess. Papers* (Commons), 1834 Report," app. A, pt. 2, pp. 49–50 (1834, 29:53–54
21. Ibid., p. 54 (29:58).
22. Ibid., app. A, pt. 1, p. 476 (28:480).
23. Ibid., app. C, p. 79 (27:83).
24. Ibid., p. 91 (27:95).
25. Senior to Brougham, December 16, 1832, Brougham Papers, 44,440, UCL.

Senior's plan for a highly centralized administration was finding little favor. On December 6, 1832 and January 10, 1833, the Political Economy Club, to which several cabinet ministers belonged, discussed some propositions put by Senior—whether the assessment, collection, and distribution of poor relief should be placed in the hands of government officers or left to parochial authorities; whether the fund should be a county, district, or national charge. There was a consensus in the club against a national system.[26] This negative reaction was evidently a disappointment to Senior, for on January 7, 1833 he wrote rather defensively to Brougham: "I still adhere to the opinion that the best plan will have to be a central administration in London and paid inspectors with magisterial authority over each district." His scheme called for three central inspectors and a corps of 200 paid magisterial inspectors, each presiding over a district averaging seventy parishes. In addition, paid overseers were to be appointed for each three parishes: "So that instead of our present establishment of more than 2000 magistrates and 30,000 overseers, we should have 3 central inspectors, 200 magisterial inspectors and about 4700 overseers." The only mention of any kind of representative local authority was that every parish was to be required to establish a select vestry which would meet thirteen times a year "for the purpose of making the poor rate and auditing the overseer's accounts,"[27] Such a solution would have been much closer to Benthamite nostrums than the bill that finally emerged from Chadwick's hands a year later, and no doubt went considerably beyond the ideas of most of the other commissioners. Possibly Senior believed that a quick enactment would be more likely to incorporate his views, for in March 1833 he wrote to Brougham suggesting that it would be possible, if the government decided to carry a measure that session, for the commission to issue a report in four to six weeks.[28] Although he recognized that a hastily drawn report issued prior to the volumes of evidence would carry less weight, he averred that if there was a prospect of a bill in the present session, "we ought immediately to

26. Marian Bowley, *Nassau Senior and Classical Economics* (London: Geo. Allen & Unwin, 1937), p. 286.
27. Quoted in S. Leon Levy, *Nassau W. Senior 1790-1864*, pp. 255-62. Sturges-Bourne, to whom Senior's plan was submitted in September 1832, did not approve of the form of central control. M. Bowley, op. cit., p. 319.
28. Senior to Brougham, March 9, 1833, Brougham Papers, 44,843, UCL.

set to work on our report, and write, which we could well do, from our general knowledge of the evidence, without referring to specific parts of it." This seems much more like an urging on Senior's part to act immediately rather than a prudent attempt to be ready for a sudden government move, for there is no evidence to show that the cabinet contemplated any reform that session, and the poor law had not been mentioned in the king's speech. In the same letter, Senior included a six-point outline of his intended reform, which he said could be in several bills. The first was the "substitution of paid officers for magistrates, with a central controlling power." Then followed better keeping of accounts, ending relief to the able-bodied and their families except in the workhouse ("and *that* workhouse as disagreeable as it can be made"), provision for emigration, changes in the laws of settlement, and a "system of police and secondary punishment by which the present semi-Irish system of intimidation may be checked."

It was probably the same desire for a quick enactment, plus the need for a vigorous colleague on the board, that led Senior three weeks later to press for Chadwick's appointment to the commission. He told Denis Le Marchant, Brougham's secretary, that Chadwick had been the most effective assistant commissioner and "his service therefore would be of the highest value in drawing up that part of our report which will point out the actual details (as far as we can actually enter into them) of our principal improvements."[29] So Chadwick, who was still hard at work as one of the royal commissioners on factories, was brought into the commission for the express purpose of drawing up the remedial measures, leaving Senior to the exposition of existing evils—a division of labor that would also save time, making an enactment in 1833 still possible. But Senior's hopes for a speedy report and bill were soon dashed. At the end of June, he was complaining to Le Marchant that Hansard had delayed printing the evidence which they had since February, although they had printed the greater bulk of the factory commission's evidence which had come to them four months after the poor law materials. Obviously feeling that the government was not giving sufficient backing to the commission, he concluded bitterly:

29. Senior to Le Marchant, April 1, 1833, Brougham Papers, 43,840, UCL.

> In fact they feel, like the rest of the world, that poor law amendment
> is nonsense and is to be postponed to everything else. Now we can
> make no use of the evidence in MSS., and write a report without it. . . .
> At the present rate of Hansard's proceeding, I think our appendix will
> be in print in the year 1843.[30]

The next day, however, he made one more effort to convince the
cabinet to slip a bill (or bills) through in the final weeks of the
session. In an unusually optimistic (and unrealistic) mood, he told
Le Marchant:

> I really think that a poor law bill erecting a central board, with power
> to appoint assistants, to make rules for relief both outdoors and in
> workhouses, audit accounts, direct the appointment of assistant over-
> seers, and supersede them, and compel parishes to use workhouses,
> might be carried if introduced without notice, or parade, as a mere
> tentative and not very important measure.

He added: "No time need be lost, as Chadwick has the bill in his
head, and could best form his own instructions."[31] In the event, no
bill was forthcoming, so that the public's only knowledge of what
the commission was up to was derived from the volume of extracts
from the evidence published in February 1833 in response to Melbourne's request for illustrative material. The lengthiest and most
impressive of the assistant commissioners' reports in this work was
Chadwick's on Berkshire and London. Considering the development of Chadwick's thinking on the nature of a proposed reform
during the remainder of 1833, it is interesting to note that the
administrative recommendations which close his report mention
only a central authority "with extensive powers." No local authority is discussed—only "paid officers acting under the consciousness
of constant superintendence and strict responsibility."[32] The bill
"Chadwick has in his head" was apparently much the same, at
that time, as Senior's plan.

Failing to get the government to push through a bill in the 1833

30. Senior to Le Marchant, June 27, 1833, Brougham Papers, 45,713, UCL. But
John Revans, the secretary to the commission, had written Le Marchant on June 15
that the reports of six assistant commissioners had "already been printed in antic-
ipation of a call from the House of Commons." Brougham Papers, 45,698, UCL.
31. Senior to Le Marchant, June 28, 1833, Brougham Papers, 10,857, UCL.
32. *Extracts from the Information Received by His Majesty's Commissioners as
to the Administration and Operation of the Poor Laws* (London, 1833), pp. 338-39.

session, Senior and Chadwick strove to finish the report and remedial measures during the recess so as to be ready for the opening of
Parliament in February. As we have seen, Senior had urged Chadwick's appointment, apparently in order to strengthen his position
and facilitate his labors, but according to Chadwick, he was appointed because Senior's plan of reform had been rejected while his
had found favor. In 1841, in one of his frequent reiterations of past
services in a vain attempt to gain a seat on the administrative poor
law commission, he told Lord John Russell:

> After Mr. Senior's very different plan had been set aside and mine
> which differed in its essential features from all others adopted, an
> application was made to have me added to the Royal Commission, as
> they could not in honour invest themselves in my plumes, or accept of
> services belonging to a principal unless I were made one.[33]

It is unclear from this who allegedly "adopted" Chadwick's plan—
the royal commission or the cabinet—and it is prudent to treat
Chadwick's assertions about his services with caution, but if there
is any substance to this claim, it shows that cabinet members or
royal commissioners (or both) were averse to Senior's highly centralized scheme. What did Chadwick have that was different? In a
memorial to Russell (by then Earl Russell) in 1866 entreating
appointment to the civil class of the Order of the Bath, Chadwick
declared:

> In my Reports alone I apprehend will be found set forth the principles
> of the combination of the parochial means in Unions, and of the
> combination of the principles of central control with local action,
> stated by Mr. John Stuart Mill the Author of the Elements of Political
> Economy as the best administrative combination of the kind exis-
> ting.[34]

Thus Chadwick's chief contribution, by his own claim, concerned
reorganization of local government, but this was not the plan he
had expounded in his report in the "Extracts."

Whatever effect these differing plans of reform may have had on
the feelings of Senior and Chadwick toward each other during the

---

33. Chadwick to Russell, n.d. [1841], Chadwick Papers, UCL.
34. Chadwick to Russell, July 2, 1866, Chadwick Papers, UCL.

writing of the report, there was at least surface harmony. By November, both men were being pressed hard by the cabinet to get the report into print and submit recommendations for a bill, as the government planned to commit itself on the question in the king's speech at the opening of Parliament.[35] Responding to Le Marchant's urging, Senior assured him that he and Chadwick were hard at work (to such an extent that Senior was unable to sleep) and hoped the report would "be in a sort of shape in a fortnight."[36] Chadwick replied to Le Marchant in a similar vein, adding that "the difficulties in the way of digest and exposition of a plan founded *on evidence* I do assure you are very severe."[37] Since the cabinet wanted the complete report with evidence, Senior's desire to slip something through quietly would have to give way to full public and parliamentary discussion of a bill that would at least apparently be founded directly on massive volumes of evidence. Meanwhile, consultation with others was altering Chadwick's views on the administrative system. This outside advice took the form of comments on some legislative proposals he had begun to circulate at about the time of his appointment to the commission.

Early in 1833, Chadwick drew up a set of proposals entitled "Notes for Heads of a Bill" which he planned to lay before the commissioners and the cabinet. Seeking expert criticism beforehand, he consulted, among others, Alfred Power, a young barrister serving as an assistant commissioner of inquiry who was later to be appointed an assistant commissioner under the New Poor Law. In the "Heads of a Bill" appears the first mention of unions of parishes under the control of boards of guardians, but Power offered no direct criticism in regard to them. His comments about the proposed central board, however, probably influenced Chadwick to alter the composition of his local boards. In light of the subsequent history of the measure, it is interesting to note Power cautioning Chadwick about the necessity of the right persons being appointed to the central board:

Suppose the Government should appoint Lord Godolphin as chairman, and a few noblemen and gentlemen whom I could mention, as

35. *Hansard* 3rd ser., 21(1834):1-5 (February 4).
36. Senior to Le Marchant, November 28, 1833, Brougham Papers, 13,486, UCL.
37. Chadwick to Le Marchant, November 1833, Brougham Papers, 19,798, UCL.

members of your Board, the poor laws would have little chance of
undergoing any improvement as regards their administration. You
go on the principle that, either there is no difference of opinion as to
the modes of administration to be recommended or that the right
opinions will find their way into the Board.[38]

Power also expressed apprehension over the central board's power
of making parishes into unions, "one of the most useful and important claimed for your Board, but one which Parliament will never
consent to delegate or at best ought not." Another commentator on
Chadwick's early draft was William Day, a young and vigorous
squire from Sussex who also became an assistant poor law commissioner. In his reply, Day was less critical than Power but called
Chadwick's attention to the fact that the section on boards of
guardians did not specify the mode of election. He urged that it be
changed so that "the votes are taken according to the Vestry Act,
and also that the qualification of the Guardians is made sufficiently high to secure their respectability."[39] Considering Sturges-
Bourne's presence on the commission, this was probably not the
first broaching of the subject of adopting the plural voting system
from the Select Vestries Act, but it was apparently the first time it
was brought forcibly to Chadwick's attention.

Since Day seems to have had considerable influence over Chadwick, on this point as well as others, it is time to examine his career
and ideas on poor relief more closely. A Tory squire, protégé of Lord
Liverpool, an active and concerned magistrate in a heavily pauperized district, Day approached the Old Poor Law from much the
same social and economic vantage point as others of the landed
interest, but he differed in his passion for comprehensive administrative reform.[40] In a pamphlet written in 1832, revised the next
year, and published as an appendix to the royal commission's
report, he described the reforms he had carried out in Sussex and
set forth his views on reforming the poor laws. Any good system,
according to Day, must be "self-acting. To be effective, it must
depend only on itself, and not on the benevolence, activity, or
caprice of individuals; and presuming it to be good, it should be left

38. Power to Chadwick, March 31, 1833, Chadwick Papers, UCL.
39. Day to Chadwick, n.d., Box 18, Chadwick Papers, UCL.
40. See R. A. Lewis, "William Day and the Poor Law Commissioners."

uncontrolled and uncontrollable by any party whatever in a parish."[41] He called for abolishing outdoor relief to the able-bodied and their families for those born since 1800, though in certain cases magistrates might take only part of a laborer's family into the workhouse.[42] Day had achieved striking reforms in the parish of Mayfield (population 2,738 in 1831) by attending vestry meetings regularly, starting in 1826, and convincing the parishioners to apply the workhouse test rigorously. The result was a decrease in the rates from nearly £4500 in 1826 to about £3000 in 1828. But when Day discontinued regular attendance after 1828, the rates rose to over £4000 in 1832. The problem with vestries, even select vestries, according to Day, was that they were controlled by occupiers—landlords should have votes "co-extensive" with their tenants and be allowed to vote by proxy.[43] In a postscript to the second edition, Day described how much more strongly physical intimidation was felt in the countryside in 1833 than in 1826. On the door of the first vestry he attended was affixed a notice that "they intended washing their hands in my blood. In 1826, a threat of that kind was readily disregarded—at present, it would be consummated in a riot or fire." Day's conclusion about this, which was probably echoed by many of the gentry throughout the country, denotes the shift in attitude necessary to carry poor law reform: "But if the alteration be the act of the legislature, it assumes a different aspect. It comes with the sanction of the law, and however it may be murmured at, the odium is removed from the obnoxious vestryman or the individual magistrate."[44] Finally, Day called for using the parliamentary constituencies under the Reform Act as the new relief districts, building "*de novo* a house of industry for the reception of the able-bodied paupers in each."[45]

Another of Chadwick's correspondents at this time was the tireless Charles Mott, whose early advice to Brougham on the poor laws has already been recounted.[46] His influence on both Brougham and Chadwick seems to have been resented by Senior,

41. William Day, *An Inquiry into the Poor Laws and Surplus Labour,* 2d ed., enlarged, p. 14.
42. Ibid., pp. 15-16.
43. Ibid., pp. 17-18.
44. Ibid., pp. 68-69.
45. Ibid., pp. 76-77.
46. See p. 20.

who told Brougham: "Mr. Mott is apparently a very sensible man, but I suspect that he will admire more than anybody else his own opinions when in print."[57] For his part, Mott was not enthralled with all of the ideas on reform set forth by Senior in his memo of March 1833. One of the six points was an emigration scheme, but Mott told Chadwick that "it is only the Industrious, hard working Labourer than can be induced generally to emigrate in the hope of bettering his condition whilst the Lazy and worthless able bodied Pauper remains at home quite satisfied 'with things as they are.'"[48] On perusing Chadwick's "Heads of a Bill," Mott commented that "a large majority of *the most respectable Housekeepers* would approve of the Central Board—but a different reception would await the proposal from the *small Housekeepers* and *persons interested in the present system.*"[49]

The advice offered by the three future assistant commissioners—Power, Day, and Mott—amounts to an increased emphasis on the constitution of boards of guardians. These were included in Chadwick's first draft, but Day suggested the voting system of Sturges-Bourne's Acts be applied. Power, while saying nothing directly about the local authorities, warned Chadwick that the appointment of unfit persons under the new law (a not altogether unlikely step by the Whig government) would render the central board virtually useless. The way to counteract this was to ensure that the local boards directly reflected the power of men of property and thus the coincidence of self-interest and efficient government which was the essence of Benthamism. This was reinforced by Mott's assertion that men of property were friendly to the idea of a central board, while the jobbing small fry were the real champions of a chaotic localism.

In the Chadwick Papers, there is a box containing three printed versions of a poor law bill; all are undated but internal evidence makes it possible to arrange them in sequence and thus trace the development of the measure.[50] The earliest of them is entitled "Measures proposed with relation to the Administration of the Poor Laws"; and inscribed on the back is "1st proof-uncorrected." It is

47. Senior to Brougham, January 4, 1833, Brougham Papers, 44,437, UCL.
48. Mott to Chadwick, March 23, 1833, Chadwick Papers, UCL.
49. Mott to Chadwick, April 27, 1833, Chadwick Papers, UCL.
50. Box 18, Chadwick Papers, UCL.

much the same as the "Heads of a Bill" and the only one of the versions that does not include a printed footnote: "See Report, Part II, Remedial Measures." It establishes a three-man central commission with power to appoint nine assistants and an unqualified power to prohibit outdoor relief. On the constitution of boards of guardians, there is no provision for plural voting and no mention of ex officio guardians. The second version (of which there are two copies) bears the same title, and "Poor Law—Original Draft of Remedial Measures by E.C. prepared for the Cabinet" is inscribed on the back. It differs from the first in requiring treasury sanction for the nine assistant commissioners; it reflects Day's influence in using the select vestry plural voting system for the election of guardians and in calling for resident clergymen as well as magistrates to be ex officio guardians. Finally, the third version (two copies) is entitled "Measures submitted by the Poor Law Commissioners to His Majesty's Ministers." It retains the plural voting system and ex officio membership for magistrates and clergy on boards of guardians; but it differs from the first two in weakening the power of the central board to abolish outdoor relief by adding the proviso "with such exceptions as shall be thought necessary." Instead of nine assistants, it provides only for "a certain Number"; and in the section on forming unions it permits the central board to unite only "such Parishes as shall not dissent therefrom." The last provision seems an incredible abandonment of an essential power. Chadwick must have realized that permitting parishes the option of not participating would preserve many a secure nest of pauperism and jobbery. Power's warning about the power to unite parishes may have begun to loom larger in Chadwick's mind as the time to present the bill to Parliament approached—"one of the most useful and important claimed for your Board, but one which Parliament will never consent to delegate." He might have hoped that such a massive concession would ensure the bill's passage and that once "voluntary" poor law unions had shown their effectiveness, other parishes would want to come in—or Parliament would then make the power mandatory. Whatever the explanation, the facts are clear—during the course of 1833 and the early part of 1834, Chadwick's bill was altered in two important ways: (1) The powers of the central board were pruned drastically, even beyond the limitation of its powers enacted in 1834; and (2) The composition of the local boards went from a democratic system to one based on property, compounded by making resident magistrates and clergy ex officio guardians.

When we compare this development with the remedial measures proposed in the report, the situation appears puzzling. Chadwick began work on these at the end of 1833, but they indicate nothing of the shift that was occurring in the several versions of his bill. There are twenty-one recommendations in all, interspersed throughout one hundred pages of discussion of the remedial measures.[51] The central board's powers are still intact in the remedial measures. As to local authorities, there is not even a mention of any specific kind of board, elective or otherwise. Following the enumeration of the powers of the central board (described as a "small and cheap agency"), it is stated that "the management, the collection of the rates, and the entire supervision of the expenditure . . . shall continue in the officers appointed immediately by the ratepayers."[52] This indeed implies the existence of some kind of local boards, but the total omission of any specifics as to their constitution is in stark contrast to the details of Chadwick's bill. A particularly careful reader might have been able to infer from this and from a few other passages [53] that the reform would foster considerable local powers, but it is not surprising that most readers (including historians) have viewed the remedial measures as embodying an extremely centralized system.

While the remedial measures do not accurately reflect the nature of Chadwick's bill, his 200-page report as an assistant commissioner does. This was printed two months after the report, as part of the voluminous appendices. In the most strongly promagistrate statement to appear in all the assistant commissioners' reports, Chadwick included his vital recommendation:

> Although in the performance of my duties I have met with instances of very great ability in persons of all ranks, yet the greater proportion of witnesses of the most distinguished ability in the rural districts, were undoubtedly found amongst the magistrates, as might be expected from their superior education and leisure. I need not enforce

51. *Sess. Papers* (Commons), "1834 Report," pp. 99–198 (1834, 27:103–202).
52. Ibid., p. 166 (27:170).
53. Ibid., pp. 166–67 (27:170–71).

the importance of retaining the beneficial services of such individuals. I submit that the course of change indicated by the evidence, is a
change of the position in which they will superintend the management of the rates, and that that change should be from the seat of
justice to the board of guardians for the administration of the relief to
the poor. In the confidence that in the latter position they would
render the most valuable services, I have ventured to suggest that the
magistrates should be rendered *virtute officii* members of all local
boards of guardians in any newly incorporated districts, where, with
the advantage of rules deduced from the greatest extent of experience
and observation, not of any one district, but of the whole kingdom,
they would doubtless act with the same public advantage with which
men of their information and rank have been accustomed to act, as
members of the boards of the incorporated hundreds; as well as in the
vestries of the parishes which they have dispauperised.[54]

That such a significant passage did not take its rightful place
among the remedial measures and that even this passage did not
mention the plural voting system is probably attributable to
several factors. First, the undemocratic constitution of the local
boards would not endear Chadwick to the radicals, a number of
whom (like Francis Place) otherwise supported the principles of the
reform.[55] Chadwick had in fact already been denounced privately
by Albany Fonblanque, the radical editor of the *Examiner,* for his
"partial arguments against the People."[56] Related to this was
Chadwick's desire to appear as a consistent, centralizing reformer

54. Ibid., app. A, pt. 3, p. 168 (29:420). Chadwick's attitude toward magistrates is
further revealed in an article ("The New Poor Law") he wrote for the *Edinburgh
Review* two years later in which he explained that one of the major fallacies
exploded by the royal commission was that removing the justices' power to interfere
would solve the problem: "On examination, it was proved that in whole districts this
was done—that the power of the magistrates was never exercised—and that these
districts were amongst the most degraded and pauperised." (p. 503). He went on to
point out that the New Poor Law, far from being a measure of centralization,
actually created local government where none had existed before and secured the
direct services of men "of education, interest in good management, and station." (pp.
519-26).

55. Writing to Sir John Cam Hobhouse in 1830 about the latter's vestry bill, Place
declared that in questions of poor law administration, "none are so likely to fall into
error as Noblemen and Gentlemen—few of them have any habits of business, and
scarcely any of them take a view of the whole matter in any case in which they
interfere." Place to Hobhouse, March 22, 1830, Place Papers, B.M. Add. MSS, 35,154,
fo. 125.

56. S. E. Finer, *The Life and Times of Sir Edwin Chadwick,* p. 78. Fonblanque was
particularly well known for his attacks on the unpaid magistracy. See Webb and
Webb, *The Parish and the County,* p. 602n.

in the remedial measures, the work by which posterity would judge him. Many years later, he claimed that he had intended the local executive functions to be carried out exclusively by the paid officers, with the boards of guardians exercising only a general superintendence:

> The functions assigned to the unpaid guardians were not executive, but solely supervisory; they were analogous to those of the visiting justices of the prisons. I failed, however, in getting the administrative principle, as set forth [in the remedial measures] acted upon, or in preventing the rules and orders being so couched; I failed also to take from the unpaid officers the responsibility of the executive details, those being left to be disposed of by the unpaid guardians at their weekly meetings—often in crowds of cases in large towns—perfunctorily and most objectionably.[57]

While this assertion is compatible with the administrative recommendations in the remedial measures, it is clearly belied by the attention given to boards of guardians in Chadwick's bills and especially by the quotation from his report as an assistant commissioner. In that report, he unequivocally declared that the services rendered by magistrates on the new boards of guardians would be the same as their services on "the boards of incorporated hundreds; as well as in the vestries of parishes which they have dispauperised." Such "dispauperising" labors were nothing if not executive in nature, and Chadwick's claim to have fostered a centralized reform which was thwarted by others cannot be sustained.

Finally, there was the need to save face for Nassau Senior. Since Senior's much more centralized plan had been set aside in favor of Chadwick's scheme, there was a strong desire to understate the differences in the remedial measures. Although, as we have seen, the impression created in the capitalized recommendations is of a strongly centralized system, this is subtly undercut by the accompanying text. To have included a specific recommendation on boards of guardians would have upset this balance and might have provoked Senior. We know that Senior did take an active part in working on the remedial measures, despite the division of labor

---

57. Quoted in Thomas Mackay, *A History of the English Poor Law* 3:93-94. (The first two volumes of this work are by George Nicholls.) Mackay's criticism of the New Poor Law focused largely on the discretion allowed to boards of guardians.

between him and Chadwick, and there were disagreements between the two men. In forwarding a proof of the first page of the
remedial measures to Le Marchant in December 1833, Chadwick
declared that he wanted to retain certain passages that Senior
insisted on striking out. The latter, with his abolitionist background, had eliminated a statement setting forth the necessity for a
poor law. Chadwick declared that although the passages were not
indispensable, "at the same time I think that we should keep to the
windward of the humanity mongers: and that this is done in the
first part of the report as it originally stood: the relief of the poor
being set forth at the same time as a matter of expediency and not
as a matter of right."[58] This letter illustrates Chadwick's more
cautious approach to the public, and in this case he prevailed over
Senior. The passages in dispute appeared on the first page of the
remedial measures:

> If we believed the evils stated in the previous part of the Report, or
> evils resembling or even approaching them, to be necessarily inciden-
> tal to the compulsory relief of the able-bodied, we should not hesitate
> in recommending its entire abolition. But we do not believe these evils
> to be its necessary consequences. We believe that, under strict regula-
> tions, adequately enforced, such relief may be afforded safely and
> even beneficially. In all extensive communities, circumstances will
> occur in which an individual, by the failure of his means of subsis-
> tence, will be exposed to the danger of perishing. To refuse relief, and
> at the same time to punish mendicity when it cannot be proved that
> the offender could have obtained subsistence by labour, is repugnant
> to the common sentiments of mankind; it is repugnant to them to
> punish even depredation, apparently committed as the only resource
> against want.[59]

Having assuaged the "humanity mongers," Chadwick no doubt
felt more disposed to yield on mentioning the boards of guardians:
They were in the bill he had drawn up for the cabinet and in his
reports as an assistant commissioner, so there was little harm in
keeping them out of the remedial measures. But to make certain the
cabinet was aware that the boards of guardians were still mentioned to the public, Chadwick sent Le Marchant the proofs of his

58. Chadwick to Le Marchant, "Saturday" [December 1833], Brougham Papers,
27,617, UCL.
59. *Sess. Papers*, (Commons), "1834 Report," p. 128 (1834, 27:132).

own report along with the proofs of the remedial measures, noting "the new provisions, as they are not likely to appear in the report in a connected form, and I would submit them as deserving the Lord Chancellor's attention." In the following month, a few weeks before the publication of the report, Chadwick wrote Le Marchant: "I think it would be of use to intimate that we intend no mischief to the magistrates and shall adopt no measures that have not the sanction of some of the most eminent of their body."[60]

Chadwick's attachment to the reforming segment of the rural magistracy is illustrated by his handling of the dispute between John Walter, *The Times* proprietor, and Henry Russell of Swallowfield. As part of his investigation as an assistant commissioner in Berkshire, Chadwick came across a bitter dispute on the Berkshire bench concerning poor relief. Henry Russell of Swallowfield, a reforming magistrate anxious to reduce rates and restore social discipline, had convinced the majority of the magistrates to support reform-minded vestries and overseers and actively participate in their own parishes. But Walter was a poor man's J.P. who had partially frustrated Russell's efforts by giving judgments in favor of the paupers who appealed to him.[61] In his report, Chadwick described the attempted reforms and the obstacle to them, quoting Russell's charges against "a neighbouring J.P.," but refraining from mentioning Walter by name. Walter somehow got hold of a proof of Chadwick's report and demanded a chance to reply. Chadwick agreed and began a correspondence with Russell on the issue, with a view to printing Walter's and Russell's letters with his report.[62] This occurred during the period when he and Senior were working on the remedial measures, and at one point Chadwick had to apologize for delaying a reply to Russell: "I have been engaged in an arduous contest to preserve some organic portion of the remedial measures."[63] Despite his labors on the remedial measures, however, Chadwick was determined to give his fullest support to Russell, recognizing in him a potent ally. On one occasion, he sent Russell a

60. Chadwick to Le Marchant, "Friday" [January 1834], Brougham Papers, 27,618, UCL.

61. See Mark Donald Neuman, "Aspects of Poverty and Poor Law Administration in Berkshire, 1782-1834," pp. 249-55.

62. Chadwick's letters to Russell, from December 7, 1833 to January 21, 1834, are in the Bodleian Library, MS. Eng. Letters, c. 175.

63. Chadwick to Russell, "Saturday" [December 7, 1833], fo. 103.

copy of William Day's pamphlet, along with Day's comments on Russell's report.[64] Anxious to make Russell appear the victor in the printed exchange of letters, Chadwick urged him in regard to one of Walter's replies: "If you can avoid inserting new facts pray do so, as I may then close the correspondence with your rejoinder."[65] Chadwick's plan to employ an editorial guillotine was frustrated by Walter, who "has access to persons of influence in authority and having called at the commission office the other day he was enabled to see your letter before I could return it to you for modifications." Then another stratagem occurred to Chadwick—the very length of the correspondence was now such as to offer an excellent excuse for "the prevention of its insertion." But Russell's side of the story could still be publicized—Chadwick sent him one hundred printed copies of it: "The more you can circulate them amongst influential persons who are members of the legislature the better. Our franks shall be at your service for the purpose."[66] The ethos of impartial investigation was not the only casualty in this skirmish—the potential good will of the most powerful newspaper in the country was forfeited, though Chadwick may have reasoned that, given Walter's background in poor law administration, he was extremely unlikely to support the pending reforms. The only recourse open to Walter was to insert the exchange of letters with Russell and Chadwick in his pamphlet against the report and the bill, which he addressed to the electors of Berkshire and published in April 1834.[67]

Another occasion in which the royal commissioners found themselves caught up in a local squabble concerned the so-called "Nottinghamshire Reformers." This involved the conflicting claims of George Nicholls, (a former overseer at Southwell and a future poor law commissioner), the Reverend J.T. Becher, and the Reverend Robert Lowe of having developed the "Anti-Pauper System."[68] One of the assistant commissioners to report on Nottinghamshire was Major William Wylde, the deputy visitor of the Thur-

64. Ibid., December 11, 1833, fo. 52.
65. Ibid., January 7, 1834, fo. 107.
66. Ibid., January 21, 1834, fo. 114.
67. John Walter, *A Letter to the Electors of Berkshire on the New System for the Management of the Poor, proposed by the Government.*
68. See J. D. Marshall, "The Nottinghamshire Reformers and Their Contribution to the New Poor Law."

garton incorporation, who gave the credit to Becher, (the visitor of that Gilbert Act union), and criticized Lowe's administration at Bingham.[69] But another assistant commissioner, J. W. Cowell, ignored Becher's claims, giving the credit to Lowe and Nicholls.[70] The result was a second edition of Becher's pamphlet, released just after the publication of the royal commission's report, which pointed out the discrepancy and asserted Becher's claims.[71] A pamphlet by assistant commissioner Cowell followed, refuting Becher and claiming that the improved condition of Becher's territory (centered at Southwell) "owes everything to the plan of Mr. Nicholls and to his meritorious exertions, and nothing, as far as I could perceive or learn on the spot, to anyone else."[72] Cowell gave Lowe the credit for originating the antipauper system and included a letter from Nicholls corroborating this.[73] The seeds of future conflict over the implementation of the New Poor Law in Nottinghamshire were sown in this exchange, but it would have been difficult to issue any report on the county that did not create offense in certain quarters. The episode shows that Chadwick was not alone in running afoul of men of influence. The publication of the hostile pamphlets by John Walter and the Reverend Becher certainly damaged the credibility of the commission's investigation, but to some extent, this was an unavoidable result of exposing local differences to national view. Still, the incidents were greatly exacerbated by those connected with the commission. In the Berkshire dispute, Chadwick's blatantly partisan approach to the Russell-Walter feud further alienated the latter. In Nottinghamshire, the initial error was to appoint William Wylde, a local man and a disciple of Becher, as assistant commissioner. This was compounded by printing both Wylde's report and that of Cowell, which came to opposite conclusions.

An appraisal of the views and activities of Senior and Chadwick during the tenure of the royal commission points to a number of

69. *Sess. Papers* (Commons), "1834 Report," app. A. pt. 2, p. 105 ff., (1834, vol. 29).
70. Ibid.
71. J. T. Becher, *The Anti-Pauper System*, 2d. ed. (London, 1834).
72. J. W. Cowell, *A Letter to the Rev. J. T. Becher* (London, 1834), p. 37. In his article on the Nottinghamshire reformers, J. D. Marshall states that Becher "got the last word" (op. cit., p. 395) in his second edition, but Cowell's pamphlet is clearly a rejoinder.
73. Nicholls gives a further account of the reforms in *History of the English Poor Law*, 2:227-36.

conclusions bearing on the final shape of the New Poor Law. To begin with, Senior, the erstwhile abolitionist, remained the most ardent centralizer throughout the enquiry, yielding reluctantly to Chadwick and insisting on some face-saving expedients in drawing up the remedial measures. Chadwick, whose views as an assistant commissioner seemed to coincide with Senior's, was brought in because he had a plan for reorganizing local government acceptable to the other royal commissioners and the cabinet, although it is not clear that Senior was aware of this. He was, moreover, much more sensitive to public opinion and political realities than Senior, watering down his bill in response to outside advice and apprehension over getting any measure through Parliament. There was an unmistakable thread of deviousness in Chadwick's strategy— making private representations to Brougham about the "real" reform while allowing his official work on the commission to convey a quite different impression (not least of all to Senior) and taking a rather shabby part in Russell's fight against Walter. It is easy to conclude that Chadwick was an adroit political manipulator whose motives were unworthy, considering he undoubtedly desired to be a paid commissioner under the new law. But it would not be accurate to depict Chadwick as a betrayer of Benthamism: Chadwick was never in any position to force a fully centralized measure on the commission or the cabinet. Realizing this, he developed a workable and brilliant reform, the constitutional provisions of which were geared to the economic and social structure of English society. Chadwick had provided the full elaboration of a measure that was, in Sir James Graham's expression, "preconcerted." At the same time, there is no reason to doubt his sincerity about the social, economic, and moral benefits he anticipated from it. Nor is there anything to indicate real bitterness on Senior's part, although there was an unseemly squabble between the two in later years about which of them was responsible for various parts of the report.[74] Senior, nevertheless, most strongly urged Chadwick's appointment as a paid commissioner under the act.[75] And Senior came to recognize the wisdom of strengthening local government in the manner of Chadwick's bill, for in a letter to Lord Howick two years later setting forth his abolitionist arguments against the

74. M. Bowley, op. cit., p. 287.
75. See p. 77.

proposed Irish poor law, he explained the factors which made public provision for the poor workable in England: "The abundance of comfort is higher, the desire of improvement (of bettering ourselves, as Smith calls it), more active and diffused and the rural aristocracy more numerous and better fitted for local government than in any part of Europe."[76]

The report was published on February twentieth, but the appendices were not completely printed for several months, and the public's initial impression of the proposed reform had to come through the remedial measures. Since these conveyed a strongly centralized spirit, hostile reaction was inevitable, but it was expected that this would dissipate when all of the evidence was before the public, and the cabinet brought Chadwick's bill before Parliament. *The Times*, while withholding detailed criticisms until the bill appeared, attacked the workhouse system and asked sarcastically: "Why not at once have the boldness to declare poverty 'penal'?"[77] Considering his previous dealings with Walter, Chadwick had anticipated this, and wrote complacently to Le Marchant:

> The opinion of the Times is Walter's opinion and not deduced from a conception of what will be the opinion of the people at large. The report itself will produce a very different impression to the mere enumeration of the propositions, which however have been received in a much better manner than we expected. In fact all that we hear from other quarters than the papers is favorable.[78]

Chadwick did attempt to get Walter to soften his stance somewhat, but Walter replied icily: "I see some of the principles which are apparently adopted by the Commissioners are so different from mine, that I fear I cannot render much service."[79] An unfavorable reaction was expressed by some Conservative politicians, for in early March, Sturges-Bourne wrote Chadwick that he was "sorry . . .

76. Senior to Howick, January 8, 1836, Grey MSS, Department of Palaeography and Diplomatic, UD.

77. *The Times,* February 25, 1834. S. E. Finer unaccountably asserts that *The Times* was uncommitted until the thirtieth of April. Finer, op. cit., p. 99. Although Finer was referring to Walter's reaction to the bill, there could have been little doubt as to what it would be, considering the leading erticle in February against the report.

78. Chadwick to Le Marchant, February 27, 1834 Brougham Papers, 27,619, UCL.

79. Walter to Chadwick, February 28, 1834, Chadwick Papers, UCL.

to hear that there should have been such a concurrence of opinion at the Carlton Club." He promised to speak to the duke of Wellington at the first opportunity, but believed the chief cause of the problem was the failure to print the appendices at once: "It was unfavourable to the Report that its Recommendations should be submitted to the Public without the accompanying reasoning and evidence."[80]

An attitude generally unfavorable to the royal commission was also taken by the Tory *Quarterly Review:* A month before the publication of the report, the M.P. and economist G. Poulett Scrope reviewed the "Extracts" of 1833.[81] Scrope was a leading anti-Malthusian and advocate of an outdoor labor test, but not an opponent of some kind of central board. He praised Chadwick's report but severely criticized Senior's alleged abolitionism and highly centralized plan of reform. He expressed his approval on hearing that Chadwick was to draw up the remedial measures, believing that the proposed central board would leave ample discretion for magisterial authority. In a pointed reference to Senior's rejected plan, he continued:

> There have been rumours of an intention to recommend the appointment of special salaried commissioners, sitting each in his peculiar district, for the decision of poor law cases, in place of the existing magistracy, Some such suggestion may have entered the head of a briefless barrister, to whom a snug commissionership of this nature would be exceedingly agreeable, but can hardly be entertained for a moment by any other person.[82]

In August, Scrope reviewed the full report in the *Quarterly Review.* He criticized the abrogation of magistrates' powers and the plural voting system for boards of guardians, but called for magistrates to take an active hand in establishing the new law.[83] His posture did not reflect the attitudes of most Tories in Parliament, as is reported

80. Sturges-Bourne to Chadwick, March 6, 1834, Chadwick Papers, UCL.

81. [G. Poulett Scrope], "The Poor Law Question." A tentative attribution to Scrope is made in Walter Houghton, ed., *The Wellesley Guide to Victorian Periodical Literature* (Toronto: University of Toronto Press, 1966), 1:714. The views expressed in the article all conform to Scrope's known positions on the poor laws, for which see M. Bowley, op. cit., pp. 248n., 283n.

82. [Scrope], op. cit., pp. 365-66.

83. [G. Poulett Scrope], "The New Poor Law."

in the next chapter—the initial unfavorable response in the Carlton Club was to change quickly. Scrope himself, though he introduced a motion in the House of Commons to retain outdoor relief, did not vote against the bill,[84] and later took a positive part in implementing the law.[85]

Moreover, as Chadwick had pointed out, the general reaction was better than expected. Most papers took a muted line on the report, waiting until the appendices and the bill were brought forth. The *Morning Chronicle,* enumerating the recommendations in the remedial measures to create a central board, to group parishes for workhouse purposes, and to apply the workhouse test and the principle of "less eligibility," commented that these provisions "seem to us calculated to produce a great good throughout the country."[86] Besides, the government had at its disposal the services of Harriet Martineau, the popularizer of economics, whose *Poor Laws and Paupers Illustrated* (1833) was based on the reports of the assistant commissioners, which Brougham turned over to her as they came in.[87] Her *Illustrations of Political Economy,* published between 1832 and 1834, included some lively tales illustrating the evils of the existing poor laws and no doubt proved convincing in certain quarters.[88]

Those connected with the government, however, were not necessarily pleased with her radical views, especially her vigorous denunciation of magistrates. Lansdowne wrote Brougham that her work was "tainted . . . with prejudices of her own quite as strong as

---

84. See p. 63.
85. See p. 165.
86. *Morning Chronicle,* February 25, 1834.
87. *Harriet Martineau's Autobiography,* ed. Maria Weston Chapman, 1:167-68. The publisher, Charles Fox, sustained a loss of £380 on this project (R. K. Webb, *Harriet Martineau,* p. 129). Martineau herself never received the subsidy of £25 per number promised by Brougham, which accounts in part for her estrangement from the lord chancellor after 1834 (*Autobiography,* 1:166-67); and she presented a very unflattering account of Brougham's careeer in her *Biographical Sketches,* pp. 153-64.
88. Harriet Martineau, *Illustrations of Political Economy.* This cheap duodecimo edition contained twenty-five tales that could be purchased separately or in a boxed set. The Quaker reforming circle, centered on Elizabeth Fry and her brother J. J. Gurney, were allegedly convinced of the need for drastic poor law reform by reading Martineau's "Cousin Marshall" (*Autobiography,* 1:173-74). The fullest treatment of the publicity accompanying the reform is R. K. Webb, *The British Working Class Reader,* chapter 6, "The New Poor Law."

those she imputes to others, and very ill executed."[89] Lord Howick, after meeting her, noted in his journal that "she is certainly rather too much elated by the position into which she has been suddenly brought and I think she has in consequence become a little disposed to pronounce positive and precipitate opinions upon subjects she has only imperfectly enquired into." Before closing the entry, however, Howick conceded that "her mistakes are evidently the result of a sincere and ardent desire for the public good."[90] These criticisms remained strictly private, for the government realized that the mobilization of favorable public opinion in the towns, and especially in London, required such allies. This consideration loomed larger as the time for introducing the reform to Parliament and the country approached.

89. Lansdowne to Brougham, December 17, 1833, Brougham Papers, 38,924, UCL.
90. Howick's Journal, December 12, 1833, Grey MSS, Department of Palaeography and Diplomatic, UD.

Chapter III

Drafting and Passing the Bill

Because the poor law amendment bill of 1834 was framed and passed without apparent trouble, historians have ignored the politics of the process. The Webbs, devoting only a few pages of their monumental work to an account of the parliamentary proceedings, comment that the bill

> slipped through both Houses of Parliament, in an exceptionally broken and tempestous session, notwithstanding the intervention of two severe political crises, a change in the Prime Ministership, and two successive cabinet reconstructions, within four months of its introduction, without adequate discussion of principle, or detailed examination of details.[1]

Nonetheless, an examination of the discussion of the bill and the changes made in it both by the cabinet and by Parliament further illuminates the purposes of the measure and demonstrates the alignment of forces for and against it.

Considering Chadwick's role, during his tenure on the royal commission, in working up a bill suited to the taste of cabinet ministers and M.P.s, it is surprising to find him all but excluded from the process following the publication of the report. The final negotiations with the cabinet were entrusted to Nassau Senior and

1. Webb and Webb, *The Last 100 Years*, 1:101-102.

Sturges-Bourne, and the understandable resentment on Chadwick's part led him to dissociate himself briefly from the measure.[2] Senior and Sturges-Bourne, informed at the beginning of March that the cabinet wished to confer with them, requested the parliamentary solicitor, John Meadows White, to draw up an abstract of the principal clauses to be considered by the cabinet. These were to be based on a bill that White and others were already drafting "in pursuance of the recommendations of the Report."[3] Exactly when White had been ordered to draft a bill is unclear, but it seems likely that it was before the end of February, when Chadwick finished the last of his three bills. This indicates that the cabinet was not willing to allow the bill to emanate from a single source. Despite Chadwick's cooperative attitude as a royal commissioner, ministers were determined to have alternative versions to consider. It should be recalled, too, that Chadwick's final measure greatly weakened the central board and allowed parishes the option of not participating in unions. Since the White bill was based upon the remedial measures, it seems likely that it provided for a more powerful central authority. The bill that finally emerged in April provided for a stronger board than did Chadwick's measure but in other respects was based closely upon it, indicating a likelihood that White drew on many of the provisions of Chadwick's bill.[4] The cabinet, however, had begun deliberations even before Chadwick completed his versions and at least three weeks before the publication of the report. At the end of January, Lord Howick noted that ministers had met to confer on poor law reform at Lansdowne House, a meeting he regretted his son Henry could not attend "as it is the most interesting of all subjects."[5] That Senior was asked to confer with the cabinet no doubt helped to assuage any lingering resentment he may have felt at having his original scheme superseded by Chadwick's. Morever, Senior was anxious to procure a lucrative mastership in chancery from the government, an employ-

2. Finer, op. cit., p. 96.
3. Nassau Senior's MS Diary on the Passing of the Poor Law Amendment Act, MS Diary 173, Goldsmiths' Library, UL.
4. When Chadwick had consulted White, he responded with an outline for a centralized measure in which each new power was made "to follow almost of necessity out of the next preceding clause." White to Chadwick, May 25, 1833, Chadwick Papers, UCL.
5. Howick's Journal, January 31, 1834, Grey MSS, Department of Palaeography and Diplomatic, UD.

ment which he told Le Marchant would give him "a couple of hours a day and all my Sundays for political economy, or any other useful employment."[6]

Senior and Sturges-Bourne held their first meeting with all fourteen cabinet members on March seventeenth. At this session, which lasted nearly three hours, the first twelve clauses of White's bill were discussed.[7] A clause enabling the central board to commit to prison for disobeying their orders was deleted, while one allowing the board to issue general and special orders aroused "much discussion" and was put over for further consideration. Also struck from the bill was a clause giving the central board all poor relief powers previously vested in any other body. A clause preventing the adoption of Gilbert's, Sturges-Bourne's, or Hobhouse's acts without the consent of the central board was directed to stand over, but one giving the board the power to unite parishes for workhouse purposes and issue regulations for their management was approved. The most controversial clause was the one allowing the commissioners to rate parishes for the building of workhouses. Althorp objected to it on constitutional grounds and was seconded by the duke of Richmond; Lords Lansdowne and Ripon supported it; and the rest of the cabinet seemed undecided. When Sturges-Bourne and Senior asked what could be substituted for the workhouse system, Althorp suggested removing all magisterial interference, with which the entire cabinet concurred. He further suggested forbidding allowances in aid of wages, requiring labor in return for relief, and giving all relief by loan. Senior effectively countered some of these alternatives by asking Althorp "whether we could safely say to every able bodied applicant you shall work hard from 6 to 6, and at the end of the day I will lend you a shilling?" Richmond's plan was simply to abolish all magisterial interference and give the commissioners the power to incorporate parishes into large unions "for all purposes whatever and to issue rules for the regulation of workhouses, and this being done he believed that the

6. Senior to Le Marchant, January 28, 1834, Brougham Papers, 46,993, UCL. Senior was appointed master in chancery on June 10, 1836 and held the office until its abolition in 1855, when he retired on full salary. *Dictionary of National Biography*, s.v. "Senior, Nassau William."

7. All accounts of cabinet deliberations up to the introduction of the bill in the House of Commons on April seventeenth are based on Nasssu Senior's MS Diary, cited in note 3.

mere circulation of the Report would do the rest." In his attitude toward the central board, Richmond was representative of many landed magnates who supported poor law reform. The board would be useful for creating new poor law unions and regulating work-houses, but the real control of relief should be in the hands of the new local authorities in the unions, who would be freed from the troublesome interference of individual magistrates.

At the end of this first meeting, Lord Grey asked Senior to make such changes in the bill as he thought "most likely to suit the views of the Cabinet." Three days later, he and White went to see Mel-bourne and suggested several changes that met some of the objec-tions raised earlier, such as providing for ratepayer approval of any ordered construction of a workhouse when the outlay exceeded a certain percentage of the rates. While the home secretary ex-pressed his approval of this and other changes, he told Senior that the bill would be referred to a cabinet committee consisting of Richmond, Lansdowne, Althorp, Melbourne, Russell, and Graham. Two days later, Senior and White met with the committee, the bill was read clause by clause, and some minor changes made. A more important gathering took place the next day (Sunday, March twenty-third) at which the whole committee was present. Senior was relieved to find approval for his suggestion that ratepayer approval for building a workhouse be sought only when the sum exceeded one year's rates, which "would in almost every case be sufficient." At the time, Senior thought Richmond the only dissent-ing voice, but he discovered later that Althorp also disapproved: The issue was to reemerge in later meetings. Clauses empowering the commission to order the appointment of officers and to remove them were approved. Richmond reiterated his argument that dras-tic expedients like the workhouse were unnecessary because the report itself had already opened people's eyes—a view shared by Graham. Senior replied that the agents of central government would have to take an active part in effecting the reform: Because of the climate of intimidation in the countryside, "the enforcement of improvements must devolve upon those who had no stacks to be fired." The session coming to an end as other ministers began to arrive for a general meeting, another meeting was arranged for the following Wednesday. Althorp instructed Senior to prepare for this session by drawing up a clause that enabled parishes to suspend any outdoor relief order, state their objections to it, and allow the commissioners to withdraw, modify, or confirm it.

Senior brought the amended clause to a meeting on March 27, but Althorp was not present. Richmond still objected to granting prohibitory powers to the commission, however qualified they might be. Ripon and Graham accepted the clause, provided that parishes be enabled to object to a prohibitory order on the grounds of the special circumstances not only of the parish, but also of the individual applicant. This was approved by the others on the committee except Richmond, who continued to object to the entire clause. He again returned to the charge that all the mischief had been done by interfering magistrates and would cease when their control was removed. Senior replied that magistrates had originated the evils forty years before "but that at present their opinions were much changed and that the great sources of mischief were the public authorities." Richmond retorted that the clause would pass the House of Lords "as the Lords were all landlords, but that in the Commons they would excite a burst of indignation which no ministry could withstand." At this, Lansdowne declared solemnly that it was their duty to do what was right and not worry about the consequences. The question was thus settled on the basis of the proviso of Ripon and Graham, which in effect reintroduced the principle of deciding each case on its merits, a practice the report had so strongly condemned. Senior clearly recognized the danger of this principle, but in the political context could only feel relief that Richmond's views were not accepted.

At Senior's last meeting with the committee, which occurred on March 30, only Richmond, Melbourne, Lansdowne, and Graham were present. After much discussion of the settlement clauses, the entire bill was finally gotten through. Graham asked Senior what he thought of the changes, and he answered that little harm had been done. The next three days were spent in completing the bill according to the instructions of the committee, which received the finished product on Friday, April fourth. A cabinet council was held on April twelfth to consider the bill, at which none of the royal commissioners or solicitors were present. When the cabinet council met again the following day, Senior and White were directed to attend. Arriving at the appointed time, 2:00 P.M., they had to wait three hours while the cabinet continued its deliberations. When at last they were ushered in, they learned that three new provisions had to be added: (1) the central board would have no power to order the building of workhouses without the consent of a majority of the parishes in a union; (2) parishes would be authorized to unite themselves for all purposes; and (3) severe penalties would be provided for the misbehavior of workhouse masters. Naturally, the first of these propositions most alarmed Senior, who had thought the issue safely disposed of at the meeting on March 23. He told Lansdowne that it was so injurious to the bill that he would beg the cabinet to add a proviso that consent of the parishes to enlarge their workhouses would not be required when the sum involved was less than one-tenth of the annual rates. This small concession did not change the need for majority consent for the original building of a workhouse, but Senior saw it was the best he could hope for. Lansdowne and Althorp accepted the change and the committee approved. The second provision—permitting parishes to join together for other functions—raised no dispute, but it does indicate that the cabinet saw the potential of the new boards of guardians as all-purpose local authorities.

A few days after these last changes were incorporated, the government was ready to submit the bill to Parliament. Until the seventeenth of April, when Althorp introduced the measure to the House of Commons, the country still did not know what sort of bill to expect. By this time, however, all of the appendices of the report were in print, and those who read them carefully could surmise that the reform would not be as centralized as had appeared from a perusal of the remedial measures. On the tenth of April, Sir Francis Baring, one of the lords of the treasury, told Althorp that the magistracy awaited the bill with generally positive feelings:

> I have been at Quarter Sessions partly to hear what is said about the poor law Report—Being myself a great coward on the question. I find on the whole that the great unpaid look upon the Report with more favorable impressions than I had expected and tho' I do not consider that there was an adherence to all the propositions of the Report yet that any attempt of Gov't to bring in a measure on the subject would meet a very favorable audience.

He cautioned Althorp, however, that the farmers and laborers had not read the report and that unless their minds were prepared, the bill "will be accompanied with disturbance."[8] The introduction of the measure on the seventeenth went quietly and smoothly. Althorp castigated the allowance system and the 1796 statute permitting magistrates to order outdoor relief and pointed out reformed systems of administration in various parts of the country, notably Nottinghamshire.[9] In the short debate that followed, no important statement was made in opposition, those who disliked the bill saving their fire for the second reading. Althorp's speech was considered effective and conciliatory, and he received a note from the king congratulating him "on this first Result of his Labours."[10] The king also had his secretary, Sir Herbert Taylor, inform Brougham of his satisfaction at the introduction of the bill and of his belief in "the necessity of establishing that which shall remove the Evils which at present affect more or less all Classes of Society in this Country."[11] But the prime minister, after telling Brougham of "the testimony of every body who heard it, to the excellence of Althorp's speech," cautioned him that "we are doomed, even when things appear to go best, to meet with crises."[12] No crisis materialized, but there were ominous rumblings from some of the London radicals, which would require all the ministry's skill to assuage. Francis Place wrote to Joseph Parkes on the twenty-first (the day the bill was printed) that the government had "castrated the Poor Law Bill, and will make it one which no man who thoroughly understands the subject will, as a Commissioner, undertake to put into execution."[13] It is interesting to speculate about the attitude of Place and his friends toward Chadwick had they known that the bill was largely his work and that in fact the one introduced by Althorp was stronger than Chadwick's final version. Unlike Chadwick's, the government's bill neither gave parishes the power to opt out of unions nor gave ex officio status on the board of guardians to the rector, vicar, or curate of each parish within a union. The last provision would have been particularly galling to the radicals, most of whom were Dissenters.

8. Baring to Althorp, April 10, 1834, Spencer Papers, Box 10.
9. *Hansard*, 3rd ser., 21(1834):878-79 (April 17).
10. William IV to Althorp, April 18, 1834, Spencer Papers, Box 12.
11. Taylor to Brougham, April 18, 1834, Brougham Papers, 39,055, UCL.
12. Grey to Brougham, April 18, 1834, Brougham Papers, 39,098, UCL.
13. Place to Parkes, April 21, 1834, Place Papers, B.M. Add. MS 35,154, fo. 193.

On April 27, Althorp summoned Senior to discuss several proposed alterations, the most important of which limited the life of
the commission to five years and exempted the metropolis altogether. On the first point, Senior countered by proposing that the
commissioners be prohibited from sitting in Parliament. This was
accepted, but in tandem with the five-year limit, not as a substitute.
The proposal to exempt the metropolis proceeded from the desire to
pacify both the London vestries and radical opinion, both of which
were adverse to the principle of plural voting. Senior contended
that a change in the plural voting clause to limit all occupiers to a
single vote would satisfy much of the opposition, to which Althorp
agreed. Thus, whereas the second and third versions of Chadwick's
bill, as well as that introduced by Althorp, had given plural votes to
owners and occupiers alike, this amendment restricted each occu-
pier to a single vote. In London, where occupiers far outnumbered
owners, this move would virtually democratize poor law elections.
The effect on rural parishes would be slight because of the relatively small number of occupiers. As Senior put it:

> we introduced such powerful conservative elements by giving votes to
> the owners, in writing and by proxy, that equal votes might safely be
> conceded to occupiers, voting by property being preserved to the
> owners or their votes would be of little use, as a whole parish is often
> owned by one or two persons.[14]

To further forestall any opposition from London, the government
called upon Chadwick to lobby assiduously for the bill, a task he
took up with characteristic energy. He was able to report to Le
Marchant early in May:

> I have today been amongst the City parishes and in several instances
> have succeeded in stopping petitions against. From all I can learn
> great numbers are waiting for the debate on the second reading and
> will be determined by it pro or con. There has been much approbation
> of the measure in several of the Vestries where hostile proceedings
> are taken. It is agreed that the speeches in the house on friday will be
> of the utmost importance and will be the only effectual means of
> stopping the misrepresentation of the Times and other papers. I
> would urge therefore that some good speeches be got up or as many
> popular or radical members got to speak as possible.[15]

14. MS Diary 173 (April 27, 1834).
15. Chadwick to Le Marchant, May 1834, Brougham Papers, 27,620, UCL. The

Clearly, Chadwick's sulking in his tent after being superseded in the final drafting of the bill was now at an end. He even volunteered to hand out pamphlets to M.P.s in the lobbies on the night of the second reading, for which he was soundly berated by *The Times*.[16]

After such careful preparations, the second reading proved anticlimactic. Competent speeches were made on both sides, but none of the spirited opposition that was to erupt in subsequent years was evident. The relative handful who spoke in opposition dwelt on the alleged unconstitutionality of the central board and the harsh spirit of the measure. Colonel William Evans, a Liberal M.P. for Leicester, declared that the government should take in hand abolishing the Corn Laws and providing moral education for the poor. The ending of outdoor relief, he continued, would amount to a revolution. Some metropolitan opposition materialized when Sir Samuel Whalley opposed the central board and spoke fondly of his parish, St. Marylebone, as "a little kingdom—aye, a little kingdom."[17] But other metropolitan M.P.s spoke in favor of the bill. Lord Howick noted approvingly in his journal that useful speeches were made by George Grote (City of London), William Clay (Tower Hamlets), Benjamin Hawes (Lambeth), and Joseph Hume (Middlesex), "the last really was very good and remarked very happily on the violent and unfair articles with which the Times has lately been filled, in answer to Walter."[18] The concerns of many rural leaders were summed up by R. A. Slaney, the Liberal M.P. for Shrewsbury, who declared he supported the bill because "no village, hamlet, or parish was safe from the work of the incendiary; and when the flames were raging at the highest, the labourers, instead of helping to extinguish them, were seen silently looking on."[19] It was clear from the debates that the opponents would be in a small minority,

---

Marylebone vestry voted seventeen to eleven to petition against the bill, despite the strenuous exertions of Chadwick and Joseph Hume. Sir Samuel Whalley carried the vestry by attacking the plural voting clause, "by the force of which one or two great landed proprietors with their tenants might take the whole of the management of the poor rates into their own hands." *The Times*, May 2, 1834.

16. Finer, op. cit., pp. 104–105.

17. *Hansard*, 3rd ser., 23(1834):809 (May 9).

18. Howick's Journal, May 10, 1834, Grey MSS, Department of Palaeography and Diplomatic, UD.

19. *Hansard,* 3rd ser., 23 (1834):821 (May 9). Another who felt the bill was too weak was Althorp's father, Earl Spencer. He published a pamphlet calling for greater restriction on outdoor relief, gaol-like workhouses, and the whipping of male vagrants. Webb and Webb, *The Last 100 Years*, 1:100n.

but few could have anticipated the overwhelming government victory—a vote of 319 to 20. The twenty-two opponents (counting the tellers, Evans and Whalley) included only two knights of the shire—Major A. W. Beauclerk (East Surrey) and John Walter (Berkshire). Of the remainder, nine were Irish M.P.s and eleven represented English boroughs: Birmingham (both M.P.s), Whitehaven, Brighton, Oldham, Wolverhampton, Tynemouth and North Shields, Bristol, Leicester, St. Ives, and Marylebone.[20] Although both Attwoods were among the minority, neither of them spoke and the currency issue was not raised. The government could be well pleased with the pathetic size of the minority; and there had been but a single defection from the ranks of the metropolitan members. Furthermore, no party spirit manifested itself—only three of the English opponents were Conservatives: Mathias Attwood (Whitehaven), James Halse (St. Ives), and Sir Richard Vyvyan (Bristol).[21]

Despite the resounding victory on the second reading, ministers realized that subsequent stages of the bill were likely to be contested hotly. Among the majority, many had misgivings on such provisions of the bill as the commission's powers, the electoral system, the settlement clauses, or bastardy; and they were awaiting the committee stage to make their views known. The government continued to be most concerned about holding the metropolitan members in line. Indeed, in supporting the bill, George Grote put ministers on notice that London would not supinely acquiesce in the erosion of local authority: "If the Commissioners make any regulations which annoy or oppress the parish, still more if any exercise of their authority should fall hardly or cruelly upon individuals, the Vestry will serve as a rallying point for all well-grounded discontent."[22] The day after the second reading, Althorp again summoned Senior and presented him with two alterations. The first put a limit of £50 on the enlargement of a workhouse the commissioners could order without consent of the guardians or parishes. Senior saw this as a further erosion of the commission's power, since the previous limit—one-tenth of the annual rate—would almost always be greater than £50, but he was unable to

20. *Hansard*, 3rd ser., 23(1834):842-43.
21. John Walter stood as a Liberal in 1832, and in the 1835 election he called himself a Liberal-Conservative. Only in subsequent elections did he style himself a Conservative. Charles R. Dod, *Electoral Facts from 1832 to 1853 Impartially Stated.*
22. *Hansard*, 3rd ser., 23(1834):815 (May 9).

dissuade Althorp. The second proposal was more serious—to exempt all parishes with a population of more than 70,000 from compulsory unionization. When Chadwick was told of it, he described it as "ruinous," and "employed himself all Sunday Morning in writing a long protest against it." After arguing fruitlessly with Althorp on the proposal, Senior asked him to read Chadwick's paper before making a final decision. Althorp replied that the alteration would remove all further metropolitan resistance and that if Chadwick's arguments were no stronger than Senior's he would not change his mind. But the next day Senior received a note from Althorp declaring that Chadwick's paper had convinced him—there was to be no exemption for London.[23] The metropolitan parishes began to bestir themselves: Heated discussions took place in many vestries, and some petitions opposing the bill were passed. Sturges-Bourne worked to prevent an unfavorable petition to Parliament in his vestry (St. George's, Hanover Square) and succeeded in getting his fellow vestrymen "to suspend the declaration of any opinion on a subject of such vital importance to the country . . . until it shall have been more fully discussed in its progress through the legislature."[24]

The press also fully discussed the bill. To no one's surprise, *The Times* had come out strongly against it on April 30. Also expected was the support of the Liberal *Morning Chronicle,* which had lauded the report on its appearance. But the manner in which it supported the bill not only indicates a desire to pacify the London vestries but also reveals what seems to have been the attitude of many proponents of the bill in town and country:

There can be no question as to the fact that those to whom the property of a parish belongs must be better able to decide as to the proper method of managing the poor than any set of gentlemen resident in London can be, and if we once succeed in destroying the allowance system, and making the labourer an independent man, the Board may become unnecessary, and parishes, or such unions of parishes (for many parishes in England are too small, if some be too large, for a proper management of the poor) as may be formed, may be safely left to pursue the course dictated by their own interests.[25]

23. MS Diary 173 (May 10, 1834).

24. *Newcastle Courant,* May 17, 1834. For accounts of the heated discussions in a number of the London vestries, see *The Times,* May 2 and 5, 1834.

25. *Morning Chronicle,* April 25, 1834.

Shortly afterward, the *Chronicle* was purchased by John Easthope, a wealthy Liberal businessman temporarily without a seat in the House of Commons. Easthope, who was made a baronet in 1841 for his services to the government, kept the paper in a strongly pro-reform posture, and a running battle with *The Times* was the result. In this struggle, Chadwick was often caught in the crossfire, Walter assuming (incorrectly) that he was responsible for various strongly worded pieces in the *Chronicle*.[26] Elsewhere in the country, newspapers began taking definite stands, often on party lines. A Tory paper in the west country declared that the bill was brought forward for the patronage it would afford and labeled the central board a "new High Commission Court."[27] A similar line was taken by the Tory *Leeds Intelligencer*, which declared that "this Board affords nice bits of patronage; excellent temporary provision for the young Whig-lawyerings who are training up to do other work for Lord Brougham in due season."[28] The Liberal rival to the *Intelligencer* was the *Mercury*, edited by Edward Baines, Jr., son of the Leeds M.P. who was unhappy about some parts of the bill and ended up voting against it at the third reading, but the *Mercury* took a generally supportive line: "A Central Board possessing great powers we believe to be absolutely necessary, if any reform is to be effected in a system so rife with abuse as the administration of the Poor Laws." But it concluded by pointing out that some of the powers seemed unconstitutional and hoped they would be moderated.[29] At the end of August, the *Mercury*, stung by a charge in *The Times* that it had understated its opposition, replied: "some person connected with that paper has gone mad on the subject of the Poor Laws Amendment Bill, and the man runs on half blind, foaming at the mouth, and biting every one that comes in his way."[30] The most striking feature of northern newspaper response to the measure was moderation, even by those who opposed it. A number of northern Liberal papers, led by the *Manchester Guardian*, supported the

---

26. Finer, op. cit. pp. 100–105, *The Morning Chronicle* savagely reviewed Walter's pamphlet against the New Poor Law on the eighth of May; on the twelfth, it began referring to Walter as "the poor man's Magistrate."
27. *Salisbury & Wiltshire Herald*, April 19 and 26, 1834.
28. *Leeds Intelligencer*, April 26, 1834.
29. *Leeds Mercury*, May 17, 1834.
30. Ibid., August 30, 1834.

bill.[31] There was little to portend the clamorous northern opposition of subsequent years.

The bill entered committee in the House of Commons on May 14, but a spirited opposition took some time to develop. On the first day, Sir James Scarlett, a Conservative M.P. for Norwich who had worked for the abolition of poor relief in the 1820's,[32] asked why removing magisterial interference from select vestries would not solve the problem.[33] He was answered by Robert Cuttar Fergusson, a Scottish Liberal M.P. who became judge advocate-general in 1835:

> It had already been seen, that both Magistrates and Overseers of the poor were frightened and intimidated to the concession of all the paupers required, not because the concession was just or in any degree called for, but because they had no power to resist the demand. Hence was it essentially necessary to erect a body distinct and separate from the local authorities to remedy these evils and to establish a uniformity of practice.[34]

On the twenty-third, the metropolitan opponents tried to pitch their appeal to the majority of the house which represented rural constituencies. Sir Samuel Whalley of Marylebone declared that the central board would have autocratic powers and once the bill passed "there would not be a county gentleman who would not become a mere cipher in the district where he reside."[35] Edward Cayley, Liberal M.P. for the North Riding of Yorkshire, replied that "this claim . . . was principally raised by those who were themselves anxious to establish autocracies in parish vestries."[36] Only one influential voice from among the landed interest was raised in opposition: T. L. Hodges, whom Villiers had recommended as a royal commissioner,[37] declared that one effect of the bill "would be

---

31. On the seventeenth of May, the *Guardian* rejoiced in the large majority for the second reading and declared that the poor law commission's powers "have been greatly magnified and misrepresented." On the same day, favorable leading articles appeared in the *Newcastle Chronicle* and the *Hull Rockingham*.

32. See Poynter, op. cit., pp. 296-97.

33. *Hansard*, 3rd ser., 23(1834):998 (May 14.)

34. Ibid., c. 1001 (May 14).

35. Ibid., c. 1277 (May 23).

36. Ibid.

37. See p. 19.

to wean the people of the country of that feeling which they at present entertained of looking up to their neighbours for protection."[38] Apparently, this appeal to paternalism was the strongest card for opponents to play, and where opposition to the bill was voiced by landed leaders, it was most often couched in these terms.

On May 26, Poulett Scrope, whose articles in the *Quarterly Review* opposing parts of the reforms are described in Chapter 2,[39] delivered the best speech against the bill during its passage. Beginning with the paternalist theme, he argued that

> in the rural districts, where Vestries consisted of flinty-hearted and bargain-driving farmers, insolvent struggling men, perhaps, whose first and only object was to save their pence, and grind down the labouring poor in order to hire their labour at the cheapest rate—to allow such vestries to refuse relief altogether to any pauper, without appeal, was to annul the Poor-laws altogether.

Then with a nod toward the Cobbettite sentiment that was to be found among some rural M.P.s as well as in the ranks of the urban radicals, he continued:

> At a time when the vested interest of worthless pensioners of high rank on the public purse was recognized by Parliament as a sacred title—was the same Parliament prepared to abrogate, at a word, the legal and ancient title of the poor to existence—a title 300 years old, as old, as legal, as fully recognized in Acts of Parliament, as the title of the wealthiest noble to his estate, and founded on still more evident principles of justice and truth![40]

Together with this impassioned plea for the rights of the poor went an incisive analysis and criticism of the royal commission's report and the bill. Scrope approved of a central board and the doctrine of less eligibility but opposed the workhouse test. On the basis of the evidence published by the commission, he claimed that only four cases of the successful application of the workhouse test were shown—at Bingham, Southwell, Uley, and Llangaddoch—and even in these instances the result was simply to drive many paupers into neighboring parishes, where the rates rose accordingly. But the report also revealed numerous examples of the success of

38. *Hansard*, 3rd ser., 23(1834):1300(May 23).
39. See pp. 43-44.
40. *Hansard*, 3rd ser., 23(1834):1320-34 (May 26).

the less eligibility principle, in the form of what later came to be called the "outdoor labor test"—at Cookham, Swallowfield, Hatfield, Welwyn, Lechhampstead, Turton, Pultney, Carlisle, Burghfield, and Ilfracombe. Most of the parishes enumerated by Scrope owed their successful reforms to the diligence of individual squires and magistrates, such as Chadwick's friend Henry Russell at Swallowfield, or the Reverend Thomas Whately, the "depauperizer" of Cookham whom Villiers had recommended as a royal commissioner.[41] The influence of such men was substantial, both in their localities and in Parliament. Scrope's mention of these examples of "improved management" was not only a good debating point but also a foreshadowing of the New Poor Law in action—the less eligibility principle was to be almost universally applied to the able-bodied, while the offer of the workhouse was treated by most boards of guardians as one of several policies open to them—hardly the "self-acting" test imagined by some Benthamites. The same day that Scrope offered his analysis, William Cobbett finally opened fire. The aging radical had been silent during the second reading, but he rose now to support Scrope and reiterate the charge of centralized despotism and the threat to a paternal social order: "By the present Bill three extraordinary gentlemen, perhaps from Scotland—perhaps, for all he knew, from Hanover—were to take the management of the poor from the hands of the gentry, and to destroy the powers of the local magistracy."[42] Scrope had given notice of an amendment to limit the commission's power and would obviously have the support of Cobbett, other radicals, and perhaps a number of rural members as well.

Before Scrope's attempt to preserve outdoor relief came before the house, another fight commenced over the issue of plural voting.[43] On the ninth of June, the thirty-third clause (fortieth in the final enactment) came up for debate. Colonel Robert Torrens, a radical M.P. for Bolton, moved to eliminate plural voting, declaring: "The more the Poor-laws were left in the hands of the lower classes of rate-payers, the better would they be administered."[44] This issue was of concern to most of those who had struggled to extend the

41. See p. 19.

42. *Hansard*, 3rd ser., 23(1834):1337 (May 26).

43 On the fight against the undemocratic poor law franchise and the attempts to reform it during the next sixty years, see Brundage, "Reform of the Poor Law Electoral System, 1834-94."

44. *Hansard*, 3rd ser., 24(1834):330 (June 9).

parliamentary franchise, since plural voting seemed to be a retrograde step. Francis Place, an active supporter of the principles of the reform, held equally strong views against plural voting,[45] and this attitude was reflected by other radical leaders. An example is Joseph Hume, who had spoken so powerfully in favor of the bill on its second reading but now seconded Torrens' motion. Althorp responded by appealing to the majority who were either major landowners themselves, or represented their interests:

> Owing to a variety of causes, the occupier of the soil was not so much concerned in an increase of the Poor-rates as the landlord was. . . . the landlord was ultimately the suffering party, while at present he had not the power of influencing the management of the poor, or of voting at the vestry. . . . he would just put the case of a landlord who had in his possession the greatest portion of a parish, and who would not have more power, though he had infinitely more interest in the administration of its parochial concerns, than any of the occupiers of property in it, unless this cumulative right of voting should be granted to him.[46]

George Grote, who like Hume had spoken for the bill on its second reading, asked Althorp to exempt populous urban parishes and the reply was that the great number of urban occupiers made it impossible for them to be overborne by landowners. Lord Howick, the prime minister's son, pointed to the efficient administration of poor relief in Scotland, where "the heritors [landowners] having votes had been productive of the most beneficial effects in the administration of the Poor-laws."[47] Cobbett confined his support of the motion to observing the connection between the plural voting clause and the Select Vestries Act: "Great as had been the innovation upon the rights of the parishioners by the operation of this Act, yet it was now contemplated to take away the remaining rights of the tenants and give them to the landlords."[48] Torrens' motion was defeated 128 to 35, and the division list reveals the isolation of the urban radicals. The only two county members voting for the motion were

45. See p. 53.
46. *Hansard*, 3rd ser., 24(1834):331–32 (June 9).
47. Ibid., c. 334. This was very close to the statement made by Castlereagh in 1817. See p. 9.
48. Ibid., c. 335. Cobbett claimed that the operation of Sturges-Bourne's Act had been responsible for riots near Winchester and in Sussex.

Joseph Hume (Middlesex) and Major Beauclerk (East Surrey)—representatives of areas where London radicalism was an important force. The government could be well pleased at the steadiness of rural M.P.s and at the fact that only four of the metropolitan M.P.s voted in the minority. The bulk of the opposition came from M.P.s representing northern and midlands industrial towns.[49]

The next day's debate represented a more serious challenge. Poulett Scrope moved the amendment of which he had given notice earlier—"that no rule or order of the Commissioners shall prohibit the guardians of unions from giving relief out of the workhouse to such of their sick or impotent poor, and to such widows, orphans, and illegitimate children, as they may think fit so to relieve."[50] This was an alteration much more likely to capture the support of county members. The vote against Scrope's motion was 148 to 40, but this time the solid support of the bill by rural members was broken. Ten English county M.P.s were in the minority, and a number of the burgesses voting with them represented rural constituencies.[51] Scrope tried again three days later, this time offering an amendment preserving the power of justices at petty sessions to order relief, but it was defeated 107 to 25.[52] The difficulty of mounting an effective opposition to the bill is demonstrated by the makeup of the minorities for Scrope's two amendments and Torrens' amendment. Except for some of the M.P.s from northern and midlands industrial towns, there was little in the way of a solid core of opposition. Metropolitan M.P.s who opposed plural voting did not oppose the powers of the commissioners, while the rural members who voted with Scrope considered plural voting to be highly beneficial. Cobbett, who might have served to bridge some of these differences, was too eccentric in his analysis of the bill and in his tactics to function as anything more than a colorful maverick. Picking up on the praise of the Scottish system voiced earlier by Howick, he declared: "The hope was to make the landlords what the heritors were in Scotland by means of three commissioners, who were to be stuck up here in London to bear all the blame."[53] This was a

49. Ibid., c. 337. Besides Hume and Beauclerk, London M.P.s voting for the motion were William Clay (Tower Hamlets) and Charles Tennyson (Lambeth).
50. Ibid., c. 346 (June 10).
51. Ibid., c. 351.
52. Ibid., c. 433 (June 13).
53. Ibid., c. 347 (June 10).

perceptive observation, but it failed to link up the various concerns of other opponents. On another occasion Cobbett attacked Lord Althorp, charging that "he had not the honesty, the sincerity, the manliness, to deny relief directly. But he put the power of denying it into the hands of his three red herrings stuck up in London."[54] The attack on Althorp was impolitic, as the chancellor of the Exchequer was widely respected for his honesty, manliness, and geniality. Finally, Cobbett made himself appear foolish when he insisted on putting to a vote a motion for appointing a select committee "to inquire whether it be just to assess one-fourth of the value of tithes and abbey-lands for poor relief before any of the other land is rated." It was defeated 111 to 3.[55] Indicative of the gulf between the Cobbettites and others who opposed the bill was the statement of Colonel Torrens when Cobbett dissented from Torrens' suggestion for public financing of emigration. Cobbett, he said, "was the advocate of barbarism—he belonged to another age, to an age that was past, and he (Colonel Torrens) was happy to find him amongst his opponents."[56]

Following these illustrations of the divisiveness of the opposition, two other notable provisions of the bill were taken up by the House of Commons—settlement and bastardy. Nassau Senior was in frequent consultation with the cabinet committee between the second and third readings, and revealed in his diary "one of the most material deviations from the Report and from the original bill, namely the alteration in the settlement clause, an alteration for which I am responsible."[57] The report and bill called for abolishing all heads of settlement except birth, a change that would burden towns with children born to resident but nonsettled laborers who had previously been removable (or chargeable) to the parishes of their parents' settlements.[58] It was probably this consideration

54. Ibid., c. 386 (June 13).
55. Ibid., cc. 446-47 (June 16).
56. *The Times*, June 17, 1834. Torrens was supporting an amendment to the emigration clause (clause 62 of the final enactment) that would have financed emigration by the sale of colonial lands rather than by a charge on the rates. *Hansard*, 3rd ser., 24(1834):455-56 (June 16). Cobbett did, however, support another amendment to the clause made the same evening—T. L. Hodges' motion that no money be expended on emigration "until some provision for the relief of the poor of Ireland be by law established." It was defeated 139 to 20. Ibid., cc. 471-74.
57. MS Diary 173, p. 117.
58. See J. S. Taylor, "The Impact of Pauper Settlement 1691-1834."

that prompted Senior to convince Althorp to change the bill. The latter was already receiving intimations of discontent from the towns. J. C. Gotch, a wealthy and influential Liberal banker from Kettering had written to Lord Milton asking him to bring the subject to Althorp's attention. Althorp told Milton he was aware of the objection, uncertain what to do about it, and that "his ultimate object was to do away with settlement altogether; but that this could not be done without preparation."[59] Abolition of the law of settlement raised a whole host of problems, of which the specter of a national poor rate was the most prominent. Althorp realized that his view was unlikely to find favor in Parliament, although the idea was not without proponents among leaders of the landed interest.[60] Accordingly, he fell back on the suggestions put forward by Senior—in place of settlement by birth, to keep the existing law but abolish settlement by hiring and service, apprenticeship in the sea service, and occupancy of a tenement (except for those who paid poor rates for a year). Rather than presenting these alterations as a government measure, Althorp got George Pryme, Liberal M.P. for the borough of Cambridge, to move them in committee.[61] *The Times* complained that these important changes were made "without notice and without consideration," a procedure typical of the entire measure, for Althorp had brought in a bill "which was essentially a different bill from that which he had described [on April 17]."[62]

If the settlement clauses slipped through with little comment, those dealing with bastardy aroused considerable interest. The report had attacked the abuses of compelling marriage or maintenance of bastard children through the unsupported evidence of the

59. Lord Milton to J. C. Gotch, June 8, 1834, Northamptonshire Record Office. The date on the letter—May 8—is clearly a mistake, for the envelope is dated June 8 and postmarked June 9.
60. In December 1833, John Cooper, steward of the duke of Grafton's Northamptonshire estates, advocated abolishing the law of settlement in a pamphlet entitled *A few Hints on the Present Working of the Corn and Poor Laws*. Upon abolition, according to Cooper, "a servant's continuance with his master would depend upon his usefulness, and the master's retaining a good servant would depend upon his kindness to him, which would produce obligatory feelings, in place of the now compulsory ones; and without such feelings existing between masters and servants the system will never work well." There is a copy of this pamphlet in the first volume of correspondence between the guardians of the Potterspury union and the poor law commissioners. MH 12/16727.
61. Pryme to Althorp, June 11, 1834, Shaw Lefevre MSS, HLRO.
62. *The Times*, June 18, 1834.

mother—a system, it was charged, that served as an incentive to lewdness, blackmail, and population growth.[63] The report and the bill called for the complete abolition of the various laws establishing liability and punishment of putative fathers. Each illegitimate child was henceforth to be the sole responsibility of the mother and have her parish of settlement until the age of sixteen. Like the original provision to abolish settlement, this was viewed with misgivings by some urban M.P.s. Mark Philips, Liberal M.P. for Manchester, charged that if the father's liability were removed, "the charges on the parishes in large manufacturing towns and villages would be much increased." This was countered by Lord Howick, who declared that the existing system was responsible for "those early and improvident marriages, which tended greatly to increase the burthen of parochial rates."[64] But financial concerns were secondary—most members were concerned about the moral implications of the change. However convincing the government's case that the new law would restore female virtue, there seemed something wrong in allowing the seducing male to get off scot-free. The telling epithet "philanderer's charter" was applied, and the government had to accept an alteration restoring affiliation proceedings—but to be held before two magistrates instead of one. A more indignant response and a more protracted and interesting debate was to occur in the House of Lords over the bastardy clauses.

The bill was reported out of committee on June 27, and the third reading took place on the first of July. In reiterating his opposition, John Walter again pointed out the discrepancy between the remedial measures and the bill: "The professed principle of the Report, was that the poor should not be brought into contact with the local authorities, whilst the act and operation of the Bill was positively to put them into contact, and perhaps into collision with each other."[65] Two Liberal M.P.s from northern towns called for restricting the act to rural areas. One of them, Edward Baines of Leeds, declared that "at Manchester and other places, there was no necessity for the exercise of that power, the parishes being well adminis-

63. See Ursula Henriques, "Bastardy and the New Poor Law," hereafter cited as "Bastardy."
64. *Hansard*, 3rd ser., 24(1834):535 and 538, (June 18).
65. Ibid., c. 915 (June 27).

tered. Instead of 5 s. and 15 s. in the pound, in most of the manufacturing parishes, the rates were scarcely over one-eighth of the annual rental."[66] This argument was to be raised many times in the next few years, but Althorp replied that "however low might be the rates in many places, the situation of the poor was not what it ought to be." Furthermore, he said, if parishes with low rates were exempted, "it would make the Bill what they had been accused to wishing to make it, a plan to save the pockets of the ratepayers only."[67]

The third reading took place in a thin house, which to T. L. Hodges indicated "something like a compact had been entered into relative to the passing of this Bill." In moving for the rejection of the bill, Hodges drew the house's attention to the connection with the Select Vestries Acts:

> The present Bill was . . . the sequel of that passed in the year 1819, and perhaps a necessary consequence of that. However, he was sure that many hon. Gentlemen would not have voted for the former measure if they had anticipated what would have been the effect of it.[68]

Some of Hodges' supporters expressed their apprehension that the bill would destroy paternalism at the local level.[69] Cobbett returned to his charge that the bill was devised by and for major landowners, who "would not trust the farmers with their own affairs, and the disposal of their own money, lest they might be tempted to pay the labourers out of rent."[70] The vote on the third reading was 187 to 50, and whatever the truth about Hodges' charge of a "compact" on the bill, few Tories voted in opposition. Of the fifty-three opponents (including the tellers and one M.P. who was paired), only fifteen were Conservatives. Of the remainder, thirty-one were Liberals and seven were Irish.[71] Most of the opposition came from boroughs—only twelve knights of the shire voted negatively. The

66. Ibid., c. 929 (June 27). The other northern M.P. was G. F. Young (Tynemouth and South Shields).
67. Ibid.
68. Ibid., c. 1029 (July 1).
69. G. R. Robinson (Worcester) asked: "Would not the affections of the lower classes be alienated from the higher?" Ibid., c. 1044.
70. Ibid., c. 1051.
71. Ibid., c. 1061.

north and industrial west midlands provided the largest number of opponents of any region—twenty-one—while only three metropolitan M.P.s voted with the opposition.

The government could affort to feel pleased with their victory in the House of Commons, even though the number of opponents had increased between the second and third readings. But they now had to turn their attention to the upper house. Their task was complicated by the eruption of a ministerial crisis more severe than the conflict over the Irish Church in May, which had resulted in the resignations of Stanley, Graham, Richmond, and Ripon. The July crisis, growing out of the renewal of the Irish coercion bill, ended with the resignation of Earl Grey on the eighth of July and the reconstitution of the ministry under Melbourne;[72] but this crisis scarcely interrupted the course of the New Poor Law. The day before Grey's resignation, his son wrote to Chadwick: "My Father says that it would be of much use to him if he could have a copy of the P.L. Bill interleaved and all the material alterations from the original bill noted on the blank lines."[73] The day after he resigned, Grey received a letter from Lansdowne urging that the bill be pressed forward in the House of Lords:

> However disagreeable it may be, it will I am sure give you satisfaction hereafter to have done. It has not been treated as a party question—it is sure to pass, and will remain a lasting credit to you and to your government, and the labours of the session will not be lost to the country.[74]

Chadwick was no doubt pleased to be asked to prepare an annotated copy of the bill for Grey, as he was anxious to have a hand in securing the bill's passage and his own appointment as a paid commissioner. He even wrote to Le Marchant telling him of some verse and "caricature illustrations of the poor law" worked up by Alfred Power and others which "would help in getting the laugh on our side."[75] Nothing apparently came of this scheme, but Chadwick soon had a more sober assignment—convincing the marquis of Salisbury to give his wholehearted support to the measure. Salis-

---

72. Elie Halévy, *The Triumph of Reform 1830-1841*, pp. 169-77.
73. Lord Howick to Chadwick, July 7, 1834, Chadwick Papers, UCL.
74. Lansdowne to Grey, July 9, 1834, Grey MSS, Department of Palaeography and Diplomatic, UD.
75. Chadwick to Le Marchant [July 1834], Brougham Papers, 10,837, UCL.

bury was recognized as an influential voice among the Tory peers, and Chadwick had solicited his opinions at the end of 1833.[76] He communicated with Salisbury again at the beginning of July, and Salisbury replied with a lengthy letter setting forth his views on the bill. He expressed his distaste for the central board and offered such amendments of its powers "as I thought would leave it sufficiently despotic for all good purposes and diminish its capability of doing evil." Salisbury accepted most of the powers enumerated in the bill, but on the power to group parishes into unions, he wished to reserve the right of parishes to refuse to be incorporated "upon shewing before Magistrates that they have sufficient means within themselves of carrying into effect the rules and regulations of the Commissioners."[77] He also wished to retain the pauper's right to appeal to magistrates. The clause he found most objectionable was that calling for all outdoor relief to the able-bodied to cease on July first, 1835, a provision which had gotten through the House of Commons unscathed. Chadwick and Senior conferred with Salisbury on the eighth. Senior found the insistence on keeping an appeal to magistrates highly objectionable, but nonetheless wrote to Grey that "if the adoption of all these amendments is to be the price of passing the bill, perhaps I may be allowed to state that I do not think it an extravagant or even a great price."[78]

Three days before the second reading in the House of Lords, Brougham asked Senior to prepare a statement on the role of magistrates under the new system. Senior responded with a memorandum in which he described how the boards of guardians would

exercise the powers now divided between the Vestry and the Magistrates. In fact as the Magistrates will necessarily be members, and the most influential members of the boards of guardians, the bill does not take away their power, but enables them to exercise it in a more beneficial manner. It converts the Magistrate from a functionary without jurisdiction till an appeal has been made to him, into an administration [sic]. It enables him to form and carry into execution his own plans of improvement, instead of being a passive spectator or a mischievous opposer of the improvements of others.[79]

76. Chadwick to Le Marchant, November 1833, Brougham Papers, 19,798, UCL.
77. Salisbury to Chadwick, July 6, 1834, Chadwick Papers, UCL.
78. Senior to Grey, July 1834, Brougham Papers, 10,171, UCL. Senior and Chadwick were successful in convincing Salisbury not to press his amendment for exempting parishes. MS Diary 173, pp. 156-57.
79. MS Diary 173, pp. 173-74. The official published text of the act sent to parishes

In moving for the second reading on July twenty-first, Brougham did not employ this argument. Instead he launched into a gratuitous attack on compulsory provision for the poor, despite Melbourne's and Althorp's attempts to prevent it.[80] The poor laws, he charged, had been a blight on the country ever since the time of Elizabeth: "Every permanent fund set apart for their support, from whomsoever proceeding, and by whomsoever administered, must needs multiply the evils it is destined to remedy."[81] This blatantly abolitionist stance contrasted sharply with "keeping windward of the humanity-mongers," which Chadwick had achieved in the opening paragraphs of the remedial measures,[82] and provided *The Times* and other critics with an excellent target. Brougham compounded this tactical error with a glowing tribute to Malthus.[83] He then went on to the work of the royal commission. Chadwick was warmly praised, but the kindest words were bestowed on Sturges-Bourne:

> His knowledge . . . is practical—not theoretical; he had applied his well-informed mind to the consideration of the whole question—was the author of the only legislative measures which ever professed to find a remedy for the evil—while, besides his talents and learning, for calmness of temper, and for sagacity, and soundness of judgment, he was, perhaps, better adapted than almost any other person to join this Commission.[84]

Brougham mentioned the excellence of the Scottish system several times—on one occasion explicitly stating that the purpose of the measure was to approximate English practice to that of Scotland.[85] Answering the charge that the central board would be an engine of tyranny, the lord chancellor declared that the commissioners' pow-

---

and boards of guardians contained a lengthy introduction by Nassau Senior which uses language nearly identical to that in his memo ("administration" was changed to "administrator") and adds: "evidence of improvements made by magistrates have been made by them as members of boards or vestries, the situation in which the Act places them; not as a court of appeal, the situation from which the Act removes them." John Tidd Pratt, *The Act for the Amendment and better administration of the law relating to the Poor, in England and Wales*, pp. viii–ix.

80. Webb and Webb, *The Last 100 Years*, 1:97–98n.
81. *Hansard*, 3rd ser., 25(1834):215 (July 21).
82. See p. 37.
83. *Hansard*, 3rd ser., 25(1834):224 (July 21).
84. Ibid., c. 225.
85. Ibid., c. 235.

ers would be far less than those of the tyrannical small fry who dominated parish vestries whom he characterized as

> men of all others the most likely to abuse them—men self elected, unknown, of no weight, and of narrow mind; those powers . . . excercised in a corner—in the dark—not in the face of the country—with no one to watch, to revise, to control— . . . wielded beyond the reach of the Legislature, by persons not removable by the Crown, accountable to no Secretary of State, overlooked and checked by no king in Council, as this Central Board will be—and exercised by men far too small to be perceptible by the public eye, therefore far removed from any influence of public opinion.[86]

Finally, Brougham returned to his own longstanding interest in reforming the poor laws, suggesting that he would have offered his own reform but for the appointment of the royal commission, which "necessarily rendered it impossible to bring the question under the view of Parliament at any earlier period."[87] In the brief debate that followed, the duke of Wellington expressed general support of the measure but brought up one of the objections raised by Lord Salisbury to Chadwick—the abolition of the allowance system the following summer. This provision was consequently dropped from the bill. Earl Radnor also spoke in favor of the bill, but qualified his support of the central board to a limited period only.[88] Despite the lukewarm support of some of its proponents, the bill passed its second reading by a vote of seventy-six to thirteen.[89]

A much more lively session took place in the committee stage when the bastardy clauses were taken under discussion. The chief opponent of changing the law was Henry Philpotts, bishop of Exeter, who delivered himself of an emotional denunciation of the clauses.[90] Philpotts was answered, then and on subsequent occasions, by Bishop Blomfield—an exchange that was quickly dubbed the "battle of the bishops." The changes in the bastardy clauses tended to restore some of the rigors of the original bill, and were proposed by the duke of Wellington. Affiliation proceedings, which the lower house had inserted, were kept, but they had to be brought

86. Ibid., cc. 241-42.
87. Ibid., c. 251.
88. Ibid., cc. 268-69.
89. Ibid., c. 275. Those voting Not Content were the dukes of Beaufort, Cumberland, and Newcastle; the marquis of Londonderry; Lords Abingdon, Alvanley, Boston, Colchester, Combermere, Kenyon, Redesdale, Rolle, and Wynford.
90. Ibid., cc. 586-94 (July 28).

before quarter sessions instead of any two magistrates. Maintenance payments were to cease when the child attained the age of
seven, and the father could not be sent to prison for nonpayment.[91]
Though beaten in committee, the opponents of the bastardy clauses
tried again during the third reading on August eighth.[92] The government chose not to accept a compromise suggested privately by
Thomas Whately,[93] and nearly lost the clauses altogether: They
were approved by a vote of ninety-three to eighty-two.[94]

One further change made by the House of Lords deserves
attention—the alteration of the plural voting clause. The original
bill had put occupiers on the same scale as landowners, but Senior
had convinced Althorp to restrict all occupiers to a single vote,
partly to appease the metropolitan vestries:[95] The Lords restored
some of the plural voting rights for occupiers. Those rated between
£200 and £400 were given two votes and those rated over £400 were
given three, a change Senior described as a "middle course" between the original bill and the amended version. He was invited to
dine with Althorp on August tenth to discuss the changes and
expressed his opinion that there were "few country parishes which
it will affect at all, and still fewer where it would produce a difference of more than one or two votes."[96] It is doubtful whether such a
feeble concession to the larger occupiers really met the complaints
of those like the tenant farmer who wrote to *The Times*:

> I certainly had too high an opinion of an English aristocracy ever to
> think that they could ever stoop so low as to rob me and others of the
> respectable tenantry of the country of the little influence we possess
> in our parish meetings and at the same time take to themselves such
> extraordinary powers—powers of passing laws in the Senate, and

91. See Henriques, "Bastardy," pp. 113-14.
92. Philpott's speech is in *Hansard* 3rd ser., 25(1834): 1061-78 (Aug 8). Blomfield's
reply is in ibid., cc. 1078-88.
93. Two days before the third reading, Whately suggested to Brougham that
affiliation proceedings remain as they were under the old law with all money paid by
fathers going toward the county rate. This would have removed the financial
incentives for illegitimate births but at the same time punished "philanderers."
Whately to Brougham, August 6, 1834, Brougham Papers, 43,366,UCL.
94. *Hansard*, 3rd ser., 25(1834):1096-97 (August 8). Eight of the staunchest foes of
the bill in the upper house drew up a formal portest which was printed in *Hansard*
immediately following the division list. It was also sent in the form of an open letter
to *The Times*, which published it on August 14, the day the king signed the bill into
law.
95. See p. 54.
96. MS Diary 173, pp. 256-57.

then retiring into the country to preside as judges in our parochial
meetings to enforce them; for thus the landlord will be enabled to act,
by being possessed of six times the power of any one of his tenantry,
and in most cases, and particularly in rural parishes, a preponderance over the whole.[97]

The perceptiveness of this observation is revealed by the contents
of a pamphlet by John Meadows White explaining the purpose of
the bill, which he described as "an extension of the system of
parochial guardians or select vestries." He declared that the key to
sound administration lay in giving power to property owners "on
whom the burthen of the poor rate ultimately falls," and making
magistrates ex officio guardians, thereby securing "the benefits of
their habits of business and intelligence," and their direct participation in the system.[98]

The Lords' amendments were accepted by the Commons after a
short debate, and the bill was signed by King William IV on August
fourteenth. In proroguing Parliament in person the next day, the
king praised the new law and called for its "prudent and judicious
application," which he fondly hoped would "increase the comforts
and improve the conditions of my people."[99] Such royal optimism
did not strike a responsive chord amongst the lower orders. A few of
the poor were already aware of the magnitude of the reform; others
could be expected to develop a similar awareness as the law began
to be implemented. The task of the three newly appointed poor law
commissioners was going to be hazardous and difficult. Nor would
the response of the poor be their only worry—the affluent and
articulate opponents of the bill, both within and outside Parliament, were determined to maintain a steady pressure against the
commissioners' proceedings. At a dinner in St. Martin-in-the-Fields
a few days after the bill received the royal assent, Colonel Evans
expressed the hope that enough public outcry would ensue so that
in five years the commissioners would not be reappointed "unless
their powers should be curtailed."[100]

97. *The Times*, August 11, 1834.
98. John Meadows White, *Remarks on the Poor Law Amendment Act as it affects
Unions, or Parishes under the Government of Guardians or Select Vestries*, pp. 42,
44, 48.
99. *Hansard*, 3rd ser., 25(1834):1267-68 (August 15).
100. *The Times*, August 19, 1834.

Chapter IV

The "Tyrants of Somerset House"

Even before the introduction of the bill in Parliament, canvassing for the three commissionerships had begun. Men with any hope of preferment from the government began exerting themselves through various channels of influence. One of the earliest to make representations was William Day, who wrote to Brougham in June 1833 setting forth his claims:

> It is essential in the formation of such a Board not only that those who compose it should agree in their opinions amongst themselves, but also that those opinions should be in accordance with the general views of the Government on the subject. That mine may not be mistaken or misrepresented, I take the liberty to enclose the accompanying pamphlet.[1]

Day's pamphlet, described in Chapter 2,[2] which provided a means of applying the power of landlords directly on local administrative boards, was influential in causing Chadwick to alter the electoral system in his bill to a plural voting system. Day's letter to Brougham shows not only that his advice to Chadwick was not disinterested but also that he clearly assumed the government's "general views on the subject of the poor laws" approximated his own.

1. Day to Brougham, June 8, 1833, Brougham Papers, 1211, UCL.
2. See pp. 30-31.

Two other early and unsuccessful applicants were Zachary Macaulay and the Reverend Thomas Whately. Macaulay, the slavery abolitionist and father of the historian, wrote a long letter to Earl Grey in May 1834, declaring the coincidence of his views with those of Malthus, Chalmers, and Senior and stressing his need for income because his post on the charity commission, and its annual salary of £800, had just terminated. With Grey's resignation and the cabinet reshuffle in July, Macaulay pressed his claim to Brougham, expressing a "secret hope" that the latter would emerge as the new prime minister.[3] Whately was the reformer of the parish of Cookham, whom Thomas Hyde Villiers had earlier recommended as a royal commissioner.[4] He wrote to Brougham after receiving his copy of the royal commission's report in March 1834, that the men appointed to the new central board required "great firmness of mind, unwearied application to the business they undertake, and clear views of the subject proposed to them." Modestly disclaiming the possession of all of these qualities, Whately nonetheless stressed the need to support his family.[5] By August, when it was obvious that Whately would not be chosen, he wrote somewhat rancorously to Brougham:

> I find it reported that the Commissioners are to be chosen from Persons of *Rank* and *Station*. I am *quite sure* this will give *great offence*. From my own experience, I would say that *one* such man as Mr. Chadwick, would be worth an *hundred* of those, I allude to, and that, to conciliate local magistrates, the appointment ought to fall upon Persons in whose experience and judgment, on the particular questions, likely to come before them, they could feel confidence. A *man* of *Rank* and *Station*, would *not* command this confidence but rather *excite jealousy*.[6]

Another potential commissioner eclipsed by men of rank and station was Francis Place. As an able and effective propagandist in behalf of the reform, Place was considered an excellent candidate in radical circles. Writing to Harriet Martineau at the end of March, Place professed his belief that he was well qualified for the task,

    3. Z. Macaulay to Grey, May 2, 1834; Grey to Macaulay, June 8, 1834; Macaulay to Brougham, July 12, 1834, Brougham Papers, 43,027, UCL.
    4. See p. 19.
    5. Whately to Brougham, March 2, 1834, Brougham Papers, 47,198, UCL.
    6. Whately to Brougham, August 3, 1834, Brougham Papers, 27,557, UCL.

even though it required someone "precise diligent and resolute, and above all caring nothing for obloquy and imputation, one who will not be put aside from his purposes by the fears of his friends, or indeed by anybody." Place was too realistic in his political perceptions, however, to expect an offer from the government:

> even to think of putting into office—the Radical Tailor,—Pooh!—I doubt that any man has the courage to venture even such a suggestion at the Council Board. No—no—it is an office for a man who has a *name* and connections.[7]

Of all the candidates, Chadwick had the strongest hope and expectation, despite his lack of rank and station. He stood in the public estimation as perhaps the most knowledgeable man in the kingdom on the subject of the poor laws and the principal framer of the reform. Even those who believed that the appointments would be a "job" (i.e., patronage dispensed to the well connected but not necessarily well qualified) considered Chadwick indispensable and assumed that a place would be found for him on the board. Chadwick, aware both of these public expectations and of his own private services to the cabinet in drawing up the bill, was sanguine. In April, Charles Mott wrote to Chadwick unnecessarily urging him to accept an appointment, as "indeed it is expected and has already been named in the House of Commons."[8] At the end of June, Nassau Senior sent a memo to Melbourne on the appointments, in which Chadwick's name headed a list of five. Chadwick's appointment, he declared, was imperative, because his "merits are peculiar and do not resemble those of the other four."[9] When this recommendation was ignored by the government, Senior's dismay was almost as great as Chadwick's.[10]

Although minsters bypassed Chadwick, they did pay heed to the other names on Senior's list. Senior had bracketed the names of James Stephen and Thomas Frankland Lewis, and those of George Nicholls and Thomas Whately, indicating that the men bracketed

---

7. Place to Martineau, March 31, 1834, Place Papers, B.M. Add. MSS 35,149, fo. 279. On March fourth, Place wrote to Albany Fonblanque in a similar vein. Graham Wallas, *The Life of Francis Place*, pp. 332-33.

8. Mott to Chadwick, April 24, 1834, Chadwick Papers, UCL.

9. Senior to Melbourne, June 30, 1834, Chadwick Papers. Part of the memo is reprinted in Finer, op. cit., pp. 106-107.

10. Finer, op. cit., pp. 105-11.

together had much in common and the cabinet should select one from each pair. Senior did express a preference in each case— Stephen over Lewis and Nicholls over Whately. Stephen, the colonial undersecretary who had prepared the bill for the abolition of slavery in 1833, was a figure of proven administrative competence,[11] but the government decided on Lewis. The reasons for this choice are probably those given by Senior in his memo:

> He has . . . the advantage of having long turned his attention to Poor Law Amendment (having been one of the celebrated committee of 1817), and of being a county member [Radnorshire] and a privy councillor, circumstances which must give him great weight with the public and particularly with the country gentlemen.

Thus, as with Sturges-Bourne on the royal commission, Frankland Lewis' connection with the select committee of 1817-18 and the Select Vestries Acts, was a potent qualification. The fact that he was a Tory also helped forestall criticism about a "Whig job."[12] The selection of Nicholls brought onto the board a man whose poor law reforms at Southwell had become widely publicized even before the report of the royal commission. He was, moreover, the manager of the Birmingham branch of the Bank of England. Whately, whose reforms at Cookham were as well known, was perhaps rejected because he was a clergyman.[13] Given the government's concern to avoid a confrontation with the Dissenters (they had eliminated Chadwick's provision for making resident clergy ex officio guardians), it was prudent not to confront the country with a commissioner in holy orders.

Only one of the three appointments might be described as an out-and-out job: that of J. G. Shaw-Lefevre, a young Whig who had

11. Commenting to his father on Senior's memo, Lord Howick praised Stephen's merits at great length, and described the important assistance he had received from Stephen in the colonial office. It is perhaps significant that Howick said nothing about Chadwick. Howick to Earl Grey, June 8, 1834, Grey MSS, Department of Palaeography and Diplomatic, UD.
12. But Henry Goulburn, a cabinet minister under Peel and a man closely involved with the leadership of the Conservative party, warned Lewis that the poor law commissioners might be made "scapegoats" if the act failed. Goulburn to Lewis, August 12, 1834, Harpton Court MSS, c/409, NLW.
13. Senior argued that this would actually be an advantage because it would "conciliate a body whom it is very important to influence, the country Clergy." Senior to Melbourne, June 30, 1834, Chadwick Papers, UCL.

distinguished himself as a student at Cambridge and was a friend, protegé, and bailiff of Lord Althorp. The latter had secured Lefevre his post as colonial undersecretary in 1833, and was of course delighted when on August 4 the cabinet named Lefevre to the poor law commission, a post which paid £2000 a year.[14]

Chadwick could not but feel bitter about being displaced by someone with few relevant qualifications, but in the end he grudgingly accepted the post of secretary to the commission at £1,200 per year. Althorp gave Chadwick to understand that he would be a virtual "fourth Commissioner" and the next in line for board position, but this was neither put in writing nor communicated to the three appointees—a source of infinite vexation and wrangling for the next twelve years. In subsequent years, when Chadwick pressed Althorp to use his influence to secure him a commissionership, Althorp (by then Earl Spencer) declared that Chadwick's "station in society" did not warrant it.[15] This was only part of the story: Althorp regarded Chadwick, despite his adroit politicking and helpful posture while on the royal commission, as a doctrinaire Benthamite whose abrasive personality was likely to incite resentment and mistrust in the country. The government had its own ideas of how the poor law should be administered. Even though Chadwick had provided them with the full elaboration of a system which strengthened the hands of landowners in poor law administration, as a commissioner he would be all too likely to push for greater uniformity and centralization. These concerns are brought out in a letter from Spencer to Lord John Russell in 1838 advising against naming Chadwick to the board:

> He is clearly in ability and knowledge quite fit to be a Commissioner but in such an appointment you have many other things to take into consideration. I only hope and trust that you will not appoint any one who is likely to make any alteration in or to impede in any way the present working of the Law.[16]

---

14. Lord Althorp to Earl Spencer, March 31, 1833, August 4, 1834, Papers of the second Earl Spencer, Box 3, Althorp. The commissioners' salaries had been raised from £1,000 to £2,000 shortly before this.

15. Finer, op. cit., p. 109.

16. Earl Spencer to Lord John Russell, April 28, 1838, Russell Papers, P.R.O. 30/22/3A, ff. 395-96. S. E. Finer (op. cit., p. 144) maintains that Spencer's letter "put Chadwick's case very strongly." But the last sentence of the quotation, which Finer omits, shows Spencer's intent to have been just the opposite.

On Saturday, August twenty-third, the three commissioners took the oath of office and held their first board meeting in the former offices of the factory commissioners in Whitehall Yard. Chadwick's appointment as secretary was confirmed, and the post of assistant secretary conferred on George Coode who, like Chadwick, was a barrister of the Inner Temple. Three clerks were also appointed, one of them authorized to frank letters. The only other business transacted was to approve a design for the commission's seal and send notice of the appointments to the *Gazette*.[17] The next several weeks were spent in answering preliminary queries from parish overseers and magistrates, sending out circular letters and copies of the statute, appointing additional office personnel, and begging the treasury for larger quarters. The volume of business quickly swelled to the point that Chadwick delcared it would be impossible to dispatch material to some seven hundred parishes a day, and secured approval for a nightshift of clerks. Two weeks later, the commissioners moved into Somerset House.[18] Despite the hectic pace of these first weeks, Chadwick enjoyed his duties immensely. The commissioners were still feeling their way into the complexities of poor law administration, and Chadwick took the initiative in drafting circular letters, replying to inquiries, and sending out questionnaires—demanding labors exactly suited to his temperament that produced a heady optimism which he communicated to Lord Howick. The latter replied:

> I am very gald to hear that you have so far reason to be satisfied with the working of the bill. I trust it will continue to answer our expectations but I fear the real difficulties which will have to be encountered have hardly yet begun to be felt.[19]

A cautionary tone was clearly needed, for the winter season, with its high unemployment, would offer a crucial test of the act's effectiveness; and as the assistant commissioners were appointed and the boards of guardians began to be created, Chadwick would find himself systematically excluded from policy formation and important correspondence.

17. PLC Minutes, August 23, 1834, MH1/1.
18. Ibid., September 9 and 24, 1834.
19. Howick to Chadwick, November 7, 1834, Chadwick Papers, UCL.

One of the major tasks occupying the board during this initial period was considering and interviewing candidates for assistant commissioners. There was some concern that the awarding of these posts, at annual salaries of £700, might involve wholesale jobbery. Charles Mott, who wanted an appointment himself, had written to Chadwick in August warning of the necessity to secure experienced and capable men, for the assistants were "the hinge upon which the good or bad results of the measure will turn." Gentility, he felt, would be a decided disadvantage:

> How would a young scion of nobility, for instance, who has nothing to guide him but the useless (in this instance) experience of gay life and Drawing room habits, do to suggest alterations in the food and clothing of Paupers, or encounter the artful lies and deceptions of the wholesaled Trade of imposter?[20]

Such fears were exaggerated—although traditional channels of patronage were employed, none of the appointees were dissolute fops or men lacking in some kind of practical administrative experience. It was clear that the labors would be arduous and the hours long, and among other things considerable physical stamina was essential. The practical criteria for the position were well summed up in a letter from commissioner Lefevre to Lord Lansdowne concerning the latter's recommendation of a former artillery officer:

> I am aware that Major Light can have no experience as to Poor Law matters, but where we find a person possessed of good sense, diligence, and conciliatory manners combined with an aptitude for business proved either in professional or public employment or in any other useful pursuit, it is more than probable that after a short training he would render valuable service to our Commission.[21]

Although these criteria were certainly utilized, they strike a sharp contrast to what one candidate was told on being turned down. Frederic Hill, younger brother of both the radical lawyer Mathew Hill and the postal reformer Rowland Hill, had devoted

20. Mott to Chadwick, August 11, 1834, Chadwick Papers, UCL.
21. Lefevre to Lord Lansdowne, November 27, 1835, Shaw-Lefevre MSS, HLRO. In the event, Light's name was withdrawn because of a "scruple" on the part of Lord Glenelg, who had originally recommended him. Glenelg to Lefevre, n.d., Shaw-Lefevre MSS, HLRO.

many years to the study of poor law reform and published a number of works exposing the abuses of the Old Poor Law. On the strength of Mathew's acquaintance with Lefevre, Frederic secured an interview with Nicholls and Lewis, but Nicholls told him that despite his "character and knowledge of the subject," priority would be given to "those who under the old system had taken part in reforming the management of the poor in their districts."[22] The actual reason in this case was probably the Hills' close involvement in radical causes—Frederic was active in Birmingham politics and had served as defense counsel for Major Cartwright and later for the Nottingham rioters. For a position that would involve working closely with the traditional leaders of landed society, a radical background was a liability, but Frederic Hill ultimately secured a post as inspector of prisons.

A military background was considered an excellent qualification, and four of the assistants appointed during the first eighteen months were former officers. The most impressive and colorful of them was Major Francis Bond Head, who was among the first four men appointed on October 28, 1834. Born in 1793, Head had served thirteen years in the Royal Engineers (1811-25), fought at Waterloo, and traveled throughout South America as manager of the Rio Plata Mining Association in 1825-26. His lively narrative style made his books about his travels and adventures very popular (he was known as "Galloping Head"). In August 1834, Head approached Denis Le Marchant about a position, and Le Marchant passed this on to Brougham with the observation that Head's writing talent would make him useful and also that "he evidently is a very superior man (he is in comfortable circumstances)." Since Lefevre had already committed himself to Head, Le Marchant got Brougham to urge Frankland Lewis to support him, thus ensuring the appointment.[23] An extremely energetic and forceful figure was thus secured in the service of the poor law commission, but Head was to prove too flamboyant, independent, and eccentric to make an ideal assistant commissioner, and he resigned a little over a year later.

The other three initial appointments proved more enduring. Col-

22. F. Hill to M. Hill, October 15, 1834, Shaw-Lefevre MSS, HLRO.
23. Le Marchant to Brougham, August 1834, Brougham Papers, 10,318 and 22,795, UCL.

onel Charles Ashe A'Court, younger brother of Lord Heytesbury, was eight years older than Head and had served as a magistrate and deputy lieutenant of Wiltshire. Temperamentally, he was a sharp contrast to his military colleague, exhibiting a pessimism and anxiety that made his tenure as an assistant commissioner one of protracted agony. Many of his letters are filled with the sort of complaint he made to Lefevre after only three months on the job: "I am heartily sick of my employment and will most gladly retire whenever I can do so without inconvenience to the Board. I am in truth but ill calculated for the constant drudgery I am subject to." And in a classic case of psychological projection, he once described a chairman of one of his boards of guardians: "He is evidently a nervous man and imagines difficulties which *may* occur, but which have not yet presented themselves."[24] Despite repeated threats of resignation, A'Court held his post until 1842. Daniel Goodson Adey, magistrate and deputy lieutenant of Hertfordshire, owed his appointment to the influence of Lord Salisbury.[25] Adey proved a competent official, but after resigning in 1840 he tried unsuccessfully to secure reappointment in 1841.[26] The last of the original appointees was Edward Gulson, who served until 1868. Gulson, a Quaker fellmonger, had served as an unpaid director of the poor in Coventry since 1830, where he had achieved great savings by instituting a labor test in the house of industry and home inspection of those on outdoor relief. While holding his post in Coventry, Gulson had been in frequent communication with Lord Althorp, which may account for the prompt and favorable attention given to his application at Somerset House.[27]

Five more assistant commissioners were named at the beginning of November, bringing their number up to nine, the maximum the commissioners were allowed to appoint without treasury sanction.[28] The most able of these were Chadwick's acquaintances, Alfred Power and Charles Mott, whose advice on his draft bill is described in Chapter 2.[29] For Mott, his appointment involved giving up an annual income of £1,500 as contractor to the Lambeth

24. A'Court to Lefevre, February 8 and June 12, 1834, MH32/2.
25. *The Times,* November 13, 1834.
26. Adey to Lefevre, December 7, 1841, Shaw-Lefevre MSS, HLRO.
27. Gulson to PLC, September 1, 1834, MH 32/28.
28. PLC Minutes, November 4 and 5, 1834, MH 1/1.
29. See p. 32.

workhouse.[30] Henry Pilkington, a former assistant commissioner of inquiry, was also appointed. W. H. T. Hawley, a Hampshire country gentleman, was to prove the most durable of the entire corps, serving until 1874. W. J. Gilbert, the last of the original nine, is one of the few about whom no background information is extant.[31] All nine were quickly put into the field in the south and midlands to begin forming poor law unions, but the size of the task and the clamor of many magistrates and parish officials for prompt attention necessitated the appointment of more assistants. On January first, the commissioners requested sanction for an additional nine from the treasury, which replied several weeks later expressing surprise at the number and asking the commissioners to state the number "urgently and indispensably necessary," whereupon they retreated to a request for three, which was granted.[32] This reluctance on the part of the treasury does not seem attributable to the fact that the Tories briefly held office, for Peel and his cabinet were favorable to the New Poor Law. Whig and Tory governments alike were eager not only to economize but also to preclude any public outcry about patronage that suddenly doubling the number of assistants would create. This concern with public opinion is shown in Lord Melbourne's refusal of an assistant commissionership to George Cornewall Lewis, the commissioner's son. Although Melbourne was urged by Lefevre and Nicholls, who supported their case with a letter from Nassau Senior, the prime minister refused, "considering the jealousy and hostility, with which every proceeding of the Commissioners is viewed and scrutinised."[33]

By the beginning of 1836, there were twenty-one assistant commissioners, but the commissioners had received treasury approval piecemeal, no more than three appointments being sanctioned at a time. Among the fifteen men appointed after the original nine up to 1838 (three being replacements for assistants who resigned), it is

30. Mott to PLC, November 3, 1834, MH 32/56.
31. For the backgrounds of most of the assistant commissioners, I am indebted to David Roberts, *Victorian Origins of the British Welfare State,* which provides a wealth of biographical detail on the inspectorate in all the major departments.
32. PLC Minutes, January 1 and 24, February 5, and 18, 1835, MH 1/2.
33. Melbourne to Lefevre and Nicholls, June 16, 1835, Shaw-Lefevre MSS, HLRO. By 1839, Melbourne's government felt secure enough on this issue to name G. C. Lewis to the commission upon his father's retirement.

possible to discern some clear or likely sources of influence in their appointments. Edward Carleton Tufnell, a barrister, was the brother of the Whig M.P., Henry Tufnell, and son-in-law of the earl of Radnor.[34] Captain Sir Edward Parry, R.N., was recommended by Thomas Garnier, dean of Winchester.[35] An ardent Whig and a friend and adviser of Lord Palmerston, Garnier was Parry's brother-in-law. Richard Earle, a landowner and barrister, had been a friend of Lefevre at Cambridge, and following his term as an assistant commissioner became an estate agent for the earl of Derby.[36] The appointment of Robert Weale, a solicitor, was due in part to the representations of the duke of Richmond.[37] Richard Digby Neave was recommended by E. Penhryn (later first Baron Penhryn), an important Whig country gentleman and lord lieutenant of Caernarvonshire.[38] William James Voules owed his appointment to the recommendation of the first lord of the admiralty, Admiral Pechell, and to his acquaintance with Lord Sefton and the Whig M.P., Robert Vernon Smith.[39] Among the remaining officers, landed gentry, and professional men named as assistants during the first three years, several deserve notice. John Revans, appointed in February 1836, had served as secretary to the royal commission of inquiry and sought to make use of his connection with Chadwick (when it appeared he would be a commissioner) to secure a position under the new board. But Chadwick refused his assistance, and relations between the two men consequently remained strained.[40] William Day also secured a post, after failing in his early bid to become a commissioner. He busied himself for the first year or so of the act's operation as a highly efficient and diligent vice chairman of the Uckfield union, of which his friend and patron, Lord Liverpool, was chairman. Hawley, the assistant

34. Roberts, op. cit., p. 162.
35. Garnier to Lefevre, January 21, 1835, Shaw-Lefevre MSS, HLRO. Garnier penned a rather unctuous pamphlet to the laborers, asking them to recognize the wisdom of the new law. *Plain Remarks upon the New Poor Law Amendment Act, More Particularly Addressed to the Labouring Classes.*
36. Earle to Lefevre, August 31, 1835, MH 32/21; Earle to Lord Fitzwilliam, December 31, 1841, Fitzwilliam MSS, Bundle DF, Northants Record Office.
37. Henry Pilkington to the duke of Richmond, March 14, 1835, Goodwood MSS, 1571, fo. 96, West Sussex Record Office.
38. E. Penhryn to Lefevre, March 1, 1836, Shaw-Lefevre MSS, HLRO.
39. Pechell to Thomas Frankland Lewis, August 21, 1834, MH 32/73.
40. Finer, op. cit., pp. 105, 109.

in Sussex, expressed delight at hearing of Day's appointment, but regretted his loss to local administration: "He will be a sad loss to me—I seldom visited the Uckfield Union—now I suspect I must constantly be there."[41] Sir Edmund Walker Head, Bart., who was to have a distinguished career as a colonial governor, was appointed an assistant commissioner in 1836 and succeeded to the commissionership vacated by Lefevre in 1841.

The appointment of assistant commissioners was essential to carry the law into operation, but for Chadwick it meant an abrupt end to his domination of the business of the commission. As the assistants were sent into the countryside, they took over the task of communicating with local officials. Their reports to the commissioners at Somerset House were prepared by the secretaries each was authorized to engage, an arrangement which inspired a mocking reference to Chadwick's position by *The Times*:

> The Assistant Commissioners are the comets, the traveling prodigies, whose function is to feed the central sun with light, but who can conceive any occasion for a secretary to such eccentric bodies? Surely the Secretary of the Board might have undertaken the correspondence of the nine; or does he find his nothing to do so oppressive that he cannot bear any addition to it?[42]

The method of procedure adopted by the commissioners effectively excluded Chadwick. Each of the three board members was given primary responsibility for overseeing and corresponding with a certain number of assistant commissioners; the same division of labor applied to correspondence with major landowners and magistrates within each commissioner's district. They met as a board at 2 P.M. each day to dispose of items on the agenda and approve of the letters drafted by each, but the latter process quickly became a formality.[43]

It was clear from the outset that the assistant commissioners would have to work hard for their £700 salaries. Separation from families, endless travel on appalling roads, indifferent food and

---

41. Hawley to Chadwick, January 16, 1836, Chadwick Papers, UCL. For Day's impressive poor law career, see R. A. Lewis, "William Day and the Poor Law Commissioners." Day is described as an official "of little distinction" in Roberts, op. cit., p. 162.
42. *The Times*, November 13, 1834.
43. PLC Minutes, November 15, 1834, MH 1/1. Finer, op. cit., p. 119.

lodging at wayside inns, encounters with hostile laborers and farmers—these were the daily realities of their employment. Isolated in their districts, they desperately needed sustenance from Somerset House and eagerly fed on the occasional praise given by their superiors. They also welcomed the friendly receptions given by many landed magnates. Nonetheless, the rigors of the job undermined the health and morale of several of the assistants and compelled them to resign. Colonel A'Court was the chronic complainer of the corps. After taking up his first assignment in Hampshire, he wrote to Chadwick: "I have worked like a slave to complete my inspection of this district."[44] To Lefevre, he complained:

> I am really shocked to reflect on the length of time it requires to inspect even one very insignificant district. All I can assure you is that I am not idle. I commence my work very shortly after seven in the morning and seldom leave my desk till after 10 at night.[45]

Six months later he lamented: "I really never had such hard work in my life. One more such district and I really think it would quite kill me."[46]

The duties were indeed onerous. To begin with, each assistant had to make a detailed inspection of his district, sending back full reports on the poor relief picture in the various parishes. This involved not only a great deal of wearisome travel but also lengthy discussions with magistrates, overseers, farmers, and other locals, not all of whom were eager to cooperate. Before deciding on which parishes should make up a poor law union, he had to confer with local landowners and magistrates and convene a public meeting. He had to inspect parish books and draw up tables of average poor rates (for the past three years), which were used to determine each parish's contribution to the poor law union's establishment charges. After the commissioners declared the poor law union, a board of guardians was elected, union officials appointed, and the size, plan, and cost of a workhouse decided upon. The assistant had to be present at the first several guardians' meetings, at which

44. A'Court to Chadwick, November 15, 1834, Chadwick Papers, UCL.
45. A'Court to Lefevre, November 30, 1834, MH 32/1.
46. A'Court to Lefevre, May 11, 1835. MH 32/2. A'Court was making similar complaints to his fellow assistants, prompting Gulson to ask Chadwick whether he intended to "cut and run." Gulson to Chawick, February 11, 1835, Chadwick Papers, UCL.

these crucial items were decided, in order to encourage the guardians to build a workhouse (or sometimes to discourage an overly extravagant design) and prevent, if possible, wholesale jobbery in the appointment of union clerks, workhouse masters, relieving officers, schoolmasters, and others who constituted the poor law "civil service" at the local level.

Once this was accomplished, he had to keep in communication with his new unions and return periodically for inspections. If the district included a populous town with a strong anti-poor law movement, the burden of the assistant's "routine" duties was compounded by intense anxiety for his own personal safety. Making travel arrangements was itself an irksome and time-consuming process. Assistants occasionally traveled by public coach, but generally had to hire horses, gigs, and post chaises to penetrate most parts of the countryside. The one-guinea per diem for traveling expenses was seldom sufficient. A'Court's account for the fifty-five days between November 5 and December 29, 1834 shows a total of £103-12-6. He added: "Innkeepers seem to think a Poor Law Commissioner fair game."[47] At the end of 1836, A'Court estimated that during the past year he had traveled 6,193 miles, visited 147 poor law unions (as well as various other public and private meetings), and written 4,000 letters. It is important to realize that in the 1830's, when a national rail network was yet to be established, traveling conditions in many counties were little better than they had been in the seventeenth century. W. J. Gilbert, whose first assigned district was Buckinghamshire, wrote that

of all Counties perhaps this affords to the traveller the fewest conveniences—there are no public roads as in Hampshire and Kent running from one town to another—no one horse close carriages, and the gigs and saddle horses are more remarkable the one for the scars upon the knees, and the other the rattle of the wheels, then either speed or commodiousness.[48]

From the far north, W. J. Voules sent a harrowing account of crossing the Pennines on Christmas eve:

47. A'Court to Lefevre, December 29, 1834, MH 32/1.
48. Gilbert to Lefevre, August 7, 1835, MH 32/26.

You will scarcely believe that in one of the most terrific snow storms that I ever witnessed I was last night left on the top of one of our highest range of Mountains (a drunken Post Boy having refused to go on, and sat down by the road side, and having no servant with me) with no alternative but that of riding Post myself fifteen miles through the storm, surrounded by precipices and the road nearly obliterated by the snow.

This adventure occurred on Voules' return from a violent demonstration of workers at Alston.[49]

Stress and overwork took their toll. Sir Edward Parry, the assistant in Norfolk, had to resign after less than a year, fearing another "determination of blood to the head." Even though offered a leave of absence, Parry declined because of the crushing burden of work: "The affairs of *Norwich alone* require all the energy and decision which can be brought to bear on that seat of corruption and misrule."[50] Richard Hall, a vigorous young assistant, had expressed impatience and eagerness for action while serving his apprenticeship under the experienced Gulson at the end of 1835. Within eighteen months, however, fatigue and chest pains brought a warning of consumption from his doctor, and required a leave of absence for several months to restore him to health.[51] Taking time off was not always possible, and some stricken assistants had to soldier on. Early in June 1836, Robert Weale complained of being exhausted and unwell, but concluded stoically: "I must however still bear up, for I may literally say I have not one hour not already appropriated until the 24th Instant."[52] Sir John Walsham was laid up with "rheumatism in the eyes" and threatened by his doctor with "all manner of calamities if I leave my room, or put the said eyes to any of the use for which nature intended them."[53] The influenza outbreak of the winter of 1836–37 hit the assistants hard. W. H. T. Hawley wrote of being "so completely floored" as to be "hardly able to hold my pen."[54] Similarly stricken, Richard Earle

49. Voules to Lefevre, December 24, 1836, MH 32/73.
50. Parry to T. F. Lewis, January 21, 1836, MH 32/60.
51. Hall to Nicholls, December 15, 1835, June 21, 1836, and August 31, 1836, MH 32/34.
52. Weale to Nicholls, June 4, 1836, MH 32/85.
53. Walsham to Lefevre, n.d., Shaw-Lefevre MSS, HLRO.
54. Hawley to Lefevre, January 23, 1837, MH 32/39.

was fortunate that his wife was able to take over many of his duties, including correspondence.[55]

An important element in keeping up the morale of the assistant commissioners was the sense of camaraderie with the officials at Somerset House and with their fellow assistants. All were eager to know about the success of the venture in other districts, and they learned through communication with Somerset House and direct contacts among themselves. Shortly after taking up his first assignment in Berkshire, Gulson wrote anxiously to Nicholls: "Can you find time to write me a note? What are the other Assistants about—and how do they get on—do they prosper? have any of them broken heads yet?"[56] Some bolstered their flagging spirits with displays of bravado in dispatches to London. Sir John John Walsham, learning the ropes from Charles Mott in Surrey, informed the commissioners regarding a successful attempt to dissolve an incorporation that

> their forces under the distinguished command of General Mott, this morning checked the enemy in their strongly fortified position at Hambledon. The action commenced at 12—and ended after a very severe contest in the complete discomfiture of the enemy, and in the surrender of their *United States* to the *orders* of the Triumvirate.[57]

Such aggressive imagery no doubt served as a psychologically useful reinforcement of their sense of mission. Gulson, with five years of service in England and Ireland, having completed the last poor law union in his Irish district, described with only partial satire his dismay at having no more worlds to conquer: "I asked myself where and in what part of the world I should form my next Union . . . —in Scotland? or the West Indies?"[58]

Another factor that helped build morale was the sense of participation in an administrative transformation of the country—not only the centralized machinery but also the new poor law unions. Because they incorporated the power and influence of local elites, the new unions were potential local authorities for other major govern-

---

55. Margaret Earle to Lefevre, January 19, 1837, MH 32/21.
56. Gulson to Nicholls, December 26, 1834, MH 32/28.
57. Walsham to Lefevre, December 3, 1835, Shaw-Lefevre MSS, HLRO.
58. Gulson to Lefevre, November 30, 1839, Shaw-Lefevre MSS, HLRO.

mental services. Gulson favored large districts on the grounds that "we are forming the Unions with a view to other and more extended purposes than our own."[59] A full appreciation of the possibilities of the poor law unions underlies many of the reports of James Kay, possibly the most skilled, articulate, and intelligent of the assistant commissioners. Shortly after taking over Norfolk, on Parry's resignation, Kay reflected that the union machinery "might be extended to other matters of great importance to the social weal," including police, road repair, regulation of charities, and the collection of statistics:

> Thus in one convenient centre would be united the whole of the executive authority of the District, and the new Unions would usurp the place of the ancient Hundreds, the form and extent of which have ceased to bear a proper relation to the altered circumstances of society.[60]

There was a similar awareness at Somerset House. When George Nicholls was sent to direct the implementation of the Irish Poor Law in 1838, he stressed to his assistants the necessity of care in drawing union boundaries,

> for when the country shall have been worked up into unions, each having an organized machinery and a principle of self-government, and with the market town as a centre or little capital, it can scarcely be doubted that they will be made available for other purposes as well as for the administration of the Poor Law.[61]

Such statements display a concept of the local machinery much different from that held by modern historians. Rather than simply a local administrative convenience under the thumb of a central agency, a board of guardians was regarded as an "executive authority," situated in the "capital" of a district, operating on a principle of "self-government." It is not true that the commissioners and their assistants took pride in their work only to the extent that they were able to impose centralized control. For many of them, the most deeply felt satisfaction lay in helping to create

59. Gulson to Nicholls, June 19, 1836, MH 32/28.
60. Kay to PLC, February 26, 1836, MH 32/48.
61. *Sess. Papers* (Commons), "Fifth Annual Report of the Poor Law Commissioners," p. 25. (1839, 20:29).

powerful, respectable, and efficient new organs of local government.

The determination of which parishes were to make up the unions was, for the most part, left to the local leaders who would dominate the boards of guardians. An early statement of commission policy appeared in a directive to Colonel A'Court that "it can rarely happen that it would be desirable for the Board to create a union unless the parishes of which it was to be formed were to be desirous of joining it."[62] This did not prevent the central officials from trying to obtain more coercive powers vis-à-vis obstreperous London parish vestries or local act and Gilbert Act unions that refused to dissolve. They also regretted being unable to coerce boards of guardians that resisted building a workhouse or balked on some other vital policy.[63] A few of the assistant commissioners also believed in the necessity of imposing stronger controls, even on the most cooperative local boards. William Day, for example, wrote to Lefevre in the summer of 1836: "The Country Gentlemen *never will* work out the Bill beyond a year or two, and it *must* ultimately fall into government machinery."[64] Inasmuch as this prediction turned out to be wrong, the necessity for such a centralized takeover never arose.

Despite the factors working toward a strong espirit de corps, some sharp disagreements and clashes of personality erupted among the commissioners and assistant commissioners. Territorial arrangements of unions and conflicting relief policies provided fertile sources of dispute. Francis Bond Head, after completing the unionization of east Kent, was incensed to find that the western part of the county had been assigned to Mott. Head had worked hard to establish contacts in west Kent, creating an influence far more useful than what he called the "tinsel power" of an assistant new to the county;[65] but at that time the relationship between the two assistants was probably already strained. Mott had previously

---

62. PLC to A'Court, November 26, 1834, MH 32/1.

63. Daniel Adey wrote from Sharnbrook of the "absolute necessity of a controlling power," regretting that any option had been permitted in the building of workhouses. Adey to PLC, December 19, 1834, MH 32/5.

64. Quoted in R. A. Lewis, "William Day and the Poor Law Commissioners," p. 171.

65. Head to Lefevre, October 12, 1835, Shaw-Lefevre MSS, HLRO.

written to Lewis complaining that the workhouse dietaries Head suggested to his Kentish unions "are quite as good as the agricultural Labourers get throughout England."[66] Mott had as powerful a personality as Head, and neither this collision nor Mott's sharp disagreement with the strong-willed James Kay over the disposition of an incorporated hundred in Suffolk is surprising.[67] Indeed, Mott appears to have been a difficult character in his public dealings as well as in his relations with his colleagues, for a pro-poor law squire near Farnham had occasion to complain to Lefevre of "an absence of conciliation which is certainly very desirable in setting the new machine to work."[68]

When Edward Gulson undertook to join some Berkshire parishes into unions he was frustrated to find that Gilbert had already appropriated them for some of his unions in Bucks. In most instances, the assistants working in adjacent counties met together to work out the assignment of border parishes, but Gulson complained to Nicholls of Gilbert's determination to "pursue his own course" and to Chadwick of "a slight taint in the atmosphere" regarding Gilbert's arrangements.[69] Gulson also found fault with Thomas Stevens, a Berkshire squire and vice chairman of the Bradfield union who became an assistant commissioner in 1836. Asked for his opinion prior to Stevens' appointment, Gulson told Nicholls "he will not do." He described Stevens as "theoretical in the extreme—and gladly advocates anything which will bring him into notice." Not only was Stevens an advocate of the discredited allotment system and the labor rate, but in his private affairs was "equally theoretical and speculative—draining land—irrigating meadows—erecting a saw mill worked by an aqueduct from the adjoining hills." Finally, Stevens was "not the man to conciliate those who do not agree with him." After such an unqualified denunciation, it must have been difficult for Gulson, on hearing of the pending appointment, to assert that he had discovered evidence of a newly acquired "staid and cautious temperament" on Stevens'

66. Mott to Lewis, July 16, 1835, MH 32/56.
67. Kay to Lewis, August 4, 1835, MH 32/48.
68. G. T. Nicholson to Lefevre, April 4, 1836, Shaw-Lefevre MSS, HLRO.
69. Gulson to Nicholls, April 24, 1835, MH 32/28. Gulson to Chadwick, n.d., "Private and Confidential," Chadwick Papers, UCL.

part.[70] A similar antipathy characterized the relations between A'Court in Hampshire and Henry Pilkington, operating in adjacent Sussex. E. C. Tufnell reported to Lefevre that the last letter he received from A'Court

> fell by a most unfortunate blunder of the clerks in our office into Pilkington's hands, the only person in the world that should not have seen it, as it contained an insinuation that Pilkington was an "ass." He however took it calmly enough, though a more choleric personage might have taken serious offense at it.[71]

The hapless Pilkington was soon to find himself forced into resigning as a result of a number of blunders committed in Lincolnshire and Nottinghamshire.[72]

Differences in relief policies among the assistants were often a problem because the commissioners did not always provide them with a clear policy. The size of workhouses is a good example. Although the royal commission's report had favored separate houses for the various categories of indoor paupers, a split developed in the corps of assistant commissioners. Major Head became the champion of a single large workhouse for each union, while William Day plumped for the system of smaller separate establishments. Somerset House at first favored Day's proposal. While Day was still the vice chairman of the Uckfield union, the commissioners sent out copies of Day's letter advocating his plan as an instructional letter to the assistants. Not only was the separate house system said to be much cheaper (existing parish workhouses often being suitable) but it also avoided giving rebellious laborers a single tempting target.[73] The new boards of guardians, however, showed a clear preference for large union workhouses, viewing them not as vulnerable targets but as proud and powerful symbols

---

70. Gulson to Nicholls, January 11 and November 21, 1835, MH 32/28. Only six weeks after Stevens' appointment, Gulson returned to the charge that "the most idle and dissolute people in his own parish are relieved profusely." Gulson to Nicholls, February 29, 1836.

71. Tufnell to Lefevre, September 1, 1835, MH 32/69.

72. See p. 133. He sent a pitiful letter to Lefevre shortly afterward, begging for some kind of employment. Pilkington to Lefevre, February 23, 1836, Shaw-Lefevre MSS, HLRO.

73. PLC Minutes, November 3, 1835, MH 1/3.

of the new order. In his annual report in 1836, Richard Earle declared that "the assistant Commissioners generally have found more difficulty in inducing guardians to be moderate in the designs for their new Houses than in encouraging them to incur the necessary expence."[74] Confronted with this rejection of commission guidelines on workhouses, Somerset House backed down. Frankland Lewis wrote to Earl Fitzwilliam that there was "no doubt that a Central workhouse is if it can be obtained at a Moderate Cost a Better thing than a Collection of Houses." After enumerating the relative cheapness of supervising a single large house, Lewis admitted that "we have never been able to lay down any general Rule which we could abide by."[75]

This vacillation and uncertainty on the part of the commissioners left many of the assistants perplexed. When they attempted to impose their regulations rigidly in the face of concerted opposition, they often found themselves unsupported by their superiors. A notable example is the issue of separation of sexes in the workhouses. Commission directives enjoined absolute separation in all cases, but a strong sentiment in Parliament and throughout the country opposed it for members of the same families, especially aged couples. In march 1835, Lord Brougham dismayed poor law officials by declaring in the House of Lords that such separation was never contemplated. A'Court was aghast:

> Does he mean that separation of the sexes is not intended! Why our instructions say that such separation must be *entire* and *absolute!—I* have invariably held that language. At my public meeting tomorrow which I hear is to be most numerously attended, and at which a short hand writer is expected to be present, I must take special care to avoid the subject—tho' that it will be forced upon me I have no doubt.

Lefevre feebly replied that although separation was still official policy,

> after all whatever may be our notions the pressure of public opinion or the will of Parliament may oblige us to modify our plans in this

74. Earle to PLC, June 25, 1836, MH 32/21.
75. Lewis to Fitzwilliam, March 22, 1836, Fitzwilliam MSS, Bundle AF, Northants Record Office.

respect, so that it is necessary that this subject should be dealt with very cautiously.[76]

Alfred Power wrote despairingly to Chadwick that "Ld. Brougham's defences will be the death of us." Countering Brougham's assertion that separation of family numbers had "never entered the head of any person, even in a dream," Power declared acidly: "I have often dreamed, and even talked in my sleep, about separating husband from wife and parent from child. How is it he [Brougham] has suddenly got so ultra-humane?"[77]

Considering the commissioners' extreme caution in dealing with workhouse regulations, where their statutory powers were greatest, it is not surprising that their attempts to restrict outdoor relief were even more equivocal. In 1835, they began to issue outdoor relief prohibitory orders to various unions, and by 1836 a total of sixty-four unions were under such order.[78] Numerous exceptions, however, gave boards of guardians wide discretionary powers, and this lax posture was weakened further in subsequent years through the issuance of a separate stream of orders to other unions permitting an outdoor labor test for the able-bodied.[79] The most frequently used exceptions were those permitting the guardians discretion in cases of "sudden and urgent necessity." But the statute itself had provided an even wider exception that was proof against the most peremptory order Somerset House could devise. The fifty-second clause, which gave the commissioners the right to regulate outdoor relief to the able-bodied and their families, permitted guardians to delay the operation of the order for thirty days, pending an appeal to the commissioners. In cases where such relief took the form of food, temporary lodging, or medicine, the guardians were only required to report the case and could not be overruled by the commissioners. When a member of a board of guardians which had received a prohibitory order complained that the exceptions did not seem to cover cases of protracted unemployment, Lefevre pointed out that "the legislature had provided a loophole . . . so that any

76. A'Court to Lefevre, March 19, 1835, Lefevre to A'Court, March 20, 1835, MH 32/2.
77. Power to Chadwick, March 19 and 21, 1835, MH 32/63.
78. *Sess. Papers* (Commons), "Second Annual Report of the Poor Law Commissioners," p. 7 (1836, 29:8). These were eventually consolidated into an outdoor relief prohibitory order in 1844.
79. Webb and Webb, *The Last Hundred Years,* 1:149.

special exception for such cases in our Rules became unnecessary."[80]

Despite their lack of power to coerce the local authorities on
many vital questions of relief policy, the commissioners were able
to effect changes by employing to the full their powers of publicizing the benefits of strict regulations. The goodwill that prevailed
between most assistant commissioners and their boards of guardians was vital to this. Once an assistant gained a measure of
acceptance in a district, he could begin the task of educating his
guardians on such matters as medical relief, workhouse dietaries,
or efficient relieving officers. While very few boards were willing to
apply any policy in a doctrinaire manner, it was possible to create a
shift in attitudes that was partly responsible for the tightening of
relief policies and the concomitant financial savings which quickly
appeared. Of course, in many districts, the grandees who dominated the boards needed no such cajoling: They had long been
eager to adopt a stricter posture but hampered by the absence of
effective local machinery and the interference of individual magistrates. Even in these cases, however, expert advice was often necessary. The will to act had to be combined with a knowledge of
successful techniques, something the commissioners were able to
provide because of their extensive network of communications. In
the same letter in which he pointed out the loophole preserving the
guardians' freedom of action, Lefevre went on to claim that "one of
the great advantages of the system under which we act is that we,
the Central Board, serve as reservoirs of the information which
comes in from all quarters."

Besides this form of publicity directed at those closely involved,
the commissioners directed their efforts more broadly to win over
"public opinion." A significant number of persons in all ranks of
society viewed the new law with anxiety or dismay, and even in the
most receptive districts, the assistant commissioners usually encountered an intractable minority of opponents among squires and
farmers. Regional and local resistance to the system, in London,
Wales, and the north, had to be countered. As to the laborers,
outbreaks of violence in several districts upon the implementation
of the act indicated widespread opposition. Some attempt to con-

80. Lefevre to William Heathcote, November 21, 1835, Shaw-Lefevre MSS, HLRO.

vince the doubters and mollify the opponents was clearly needed, especially since *The Times* and other hostile newspapers, as well as parliamentary opponents of the law, had not moderated their attacks. The need was well expressed by one of Lefevre's correspondents:

> If you could get a popular writer, a 2nd Cobbett with sounder principles—or even a 2nd Hannah More—or a Times or a penny magazine to handle the question in a lively manner either didactically or perhaps better still in the form of dialogues or anecdotes, it would be of immense advantage in disabusing the public mind.[81]

Actually, a writer capable of defending the law in a "lively manner" was in the corps of assistant commissioners—Major Head. He had already written an effective and highly readable defense of the commissioners' proceedings that appeared in April 1835 in the *Quarterly Review*.[82] That Head's article was accepted by an influential Tory journal which had previously published Poulett Scrope's criticisms was an unanticipated bonus.[83] Moreover, the *Quarterly* had initiated the project: Murray and Lockhart approached Head in January and asked him for an article on the act's implementation. After securing their agreement to let him "go to the whole truth and to the whole extent of the truth," Head requested Lefevre's sanction:

> You know the influence of the Q. Review, and it does seem to me, that leaving my own leisure and disinclination out of the question, it is really *our duty* to attend to such an offer from the first literary journal in the country.[84]

Permission was granted but with some trepidation, Lefevre commenting warily: "I can only hope that there is nothing in it which would make it appear that the board furnished the materials, for this would be a breach of our duty." There was certainly no reluctance on the parts of the author or the *Quarterly Review's* editors. Murray told Head that an additional quantity of the journal would

81. J. Hodgkin to Lefevre, July 11, 1835, Shaw-Lefevre MSS, HLRO.
82. [Francis Bond Head], "English Charity."
83. See p. 43.
84. Head to Lefevre, January 28, 1835, Shaw-Lefevre MSS, HLRO.

be printed because of his article and begged him to accept 100
guineas—twice the usual payment.[85]

Head's 66-page article described the implementation of the law in
East Kent and, though unsigned, left no doubt as to the author's
identity. He criticized the large and sumptuous Kentish workhouses built before 1834, which provided fare and lodgings superior
to those enjoyed by independent laborers. His account is spiced
with vivid anecdotes of workhouse life and quotations such as one
from a workhouse master that "we gives 'em as much victuals as
ever they can eat."[86] Regarding the Canterbury court of guardians,
Head observed: "The fitting pride of this court is to stuff the pauper
at the expense of the lean rate payer."[87] Most of the article de-
scribes the process of union formation and offers a flattering account of the valuable assistance given by peers and gentry. Head
concludes by absolving the magistrates from blame for the maladministration of the Old Poor Law, for "it was utterly impossible for
them to govern a vessel which had neither rudder, compass, nor
pilot."[88] Head's article was a considerable publicity coup. Even the
timid Colonel A'Court, while wishing that Head "had treated his
subject with more seriuosness," conceded: "His paper is however
both clever and amusing, and will induce many to read up to this
subject, which in its more sober part is anything but inviting."[89]

Sobriety was the keynote of the official publicity channel of the
poor law commissioners—the annual reports. Although these were
required by the statute to be submitted to the home secretary, they
functioned, like the royal commission's report, as a means of influ-
encing public opinion. The first annual report, signed on August
eighth 1835, established the basic format followed in subsequent
years—a 35-page report with another 100 pages or so of appendices.
The latter included the assistant commissioners' reports, circular
letters sent to magistrates and overseers, workhouse plans and
rules, election orders, forms for keeping accounts, lists of unions
formed, and miscellaneous correspondence. Initially, Chadwick,
who had the task of preparing the report, sought to maintain the

85. Lefevre to Head, April 1, 1835; Head to Lefevre, April 9, 1835, Shaw-Lefevre
MSS, HLRO.
86. Head, "English Charity," p. 479.
87. Ibid., p. 485.
88. Ibid., p. 538.
89. A'Court to Lefevre, May 20, 1835, MH 32/2.

dignified, dull style of the royal commission's report. There was probably a touch of envy in A'Court's criticism of Head's light-hearted approach in the *Quarterly Review*, for some of the assistants found their reports returned to them for a more sober revision. Richard Hall returned his revised draft to Chadwick with the acid observation: "I have availed myself of your suggestions and *rewritten* my report, carefully abstracting all that was *learned* and *poetical*. I am sure it will now be *stupid* enough, and *prosy* enough too."[90] In subsequent years, the commissioners themselves seem to have taken over the job of editing the reports of the assistants. In his original draft for the fourth annual report, Hawley lashed out at the perpetrators of abuses in his district, but Nicholls compelled him to alter it and "recognize the necessity of applying a subdued and cautious Phraseology to official documents."[91] Not only the tone of the assistants' reports but even the contents were sometimes altered. In summarizing Alfred Power's report from Berkshire for the first annual report, Chadwick stated there was no redundant laboring population—part of the official orthodoxy. On reading the report, Power reacted angrily: "The Report is a good dish of fritters ala Chadwick—but what made you suppose there were no surplus labourers in any of the parishes in my district, or at least that I thought so?"[92]

Because of such editing, the annual reports do not always reflect the actual conditions in the country during the implementation of the act. The assertion that no surplus agricultural labor existed is a good example, but it was belied by the commissioners' early and active efforts to provide emigration from the countryside to the manufacturing districts or the colonies. The first annual report contains an account of Somerset House's successful initiatives with certain manufacturers and the trial made at Bledlow, Bucks, which ultimately resulted in resettling eighty-three persons in Lancashire.[93] These efforts were extended, and by the end of the year the services of an emigration agent (at £400 per year) had been se-

90. Hall to Chadwick, July 10, 1835, Chadwick Papers, UCL.
91. Hawley to Nicholls, February 1, 1838, MH 32/39. In the following year, Edward Senior was rebuked for the "improper language" in his report. Senior to Lefevre, January 1, 1839, MH 32/66.
92. Power to Chadwick, September 12, 1835, Chadwick Papers, UCL.
93. *Sess. Papers* (Commons), "First Annual Report of the Poor Law Commissioners," p. 21 ff. (1835, 35:131).

cured.[94] Another important aspect of the operation of the New Poor
Law obscured by the annual reports is the formation of poor law
unions. The first report delcared that the most convenient union
area was "that of a circle, taking a market town as a centre, and
comprehending those surrounding parishes whose inhabitants are
accustomed to resort to the same market."[95] This statement was
accepted at face value by the Webbs and by more recent historians,
who have consequently strengthened the notion that the poor law
commission was "acting by its own volition, without request from,
or consent of any local inhabitants."[96] The brief discussion of
union formation earlier in the chapter shows this statement is wide
of the mark,[97] and the full degree of involvement and initiative on
the part of landed magnates in drawing boundaries will become
evident when we examine the detailed implementation of the act in
subsequent chapters. Although they masked the true nature of the
process, the commissioners were able to report that at the end of the
first two years they had combined 7,915 parishes with a total
population of 6,221,940 into 365 unions. This represented 43 percent
of the population of England and Wales and 65 percent of the total
poor rates expended.[98] Most of these unions were in the south, east,
and rural midlands. The unionizing of the west and the north
required another two years and was to prove much more difficult. It
would no longer be possible to maintain the easy assurances of the
first report that where violence had broken out, it had been quickly
contained by bringing in detachments of metropolitan police, who
"invariably acted with perfect coolness, and under the best discipline, and left impressions highly favourable to them."[99]

On being presented with the first annual report, Lord John Russell told the commissioners that it was "exactly what he wished to
receive."[100] Copies were sent to the chairman, clerk, and auditor of

94. PLC Minutes, December 16, 1835, MH 1/4.
95. *Sess. Papers* (Commons), "First Annual Report of the Poor Law Commissioners," p. 12 (1835, 35:122).
96. Webb and Webb, *The Last Hundred Years,* 2:81, 113. See also E. C. Midwinter,
Social Administration in Lancashire 1830-1860, p. 16.
97. See p. 92.
98. *Sess. Papers* (Commons), "Second Annual Report of the Poor Law Commissioners," p. 4 (1836, 29:5).
99. *Sess. Papers* (Commons), "First Annual Report of the Poor Law Commissioners," p. 36 (1835, 35:146).
100. PLC Minutes, October 9, 1835, MH 1/3.

each poor law union and also to those persons in each district named by the assistant commissioners.[101] Others were sent on request to influential proponents of the new system, like Lord Howick, who asked for half a dozen copies: "I find there is still to my surprise and regret a prejudice against the bill in minds of some well disposed persons which I should be glad to remove."[102]

One of the most effective proselytizers of the New Poor Law was King William IV, who maintained and even strengthened his initial favorable attitude. When assistant commissioner Gilbert was granted an audience to discuss the proposed Windsor union, he reported the king's exact words:

> I am much interested in this measure and shall be glad to know how it proceeds, and beg that you will, now that I have seen you, call here from time to time to let me know how it proceeds. Some of the details of the Bill might possibly be amended, but call and let me see you from time to time, situated as I am I necessarily take great interest in a measure that so strongly affects the welfare of the Country. It is one of the greatest measures that has ever passed the legislature.[103]

Before leaving, Gilbert offered to present his majesty with a copy of the first annual report, but the punctilious Frankland Lewis replied that such a presentation must be made by the prime minister, the home secretary, or the commissioners.[104] When Gulson was given an audience three months later, a number of important visitors were kept waiting for hours while the king held forth on the virtues of the new system and denounced the Sussex riots, offering his opinion that beerhouse keepers and small shopkeepers were to blame, and remarking that "all such persons must be put down."[105] Two "appropriately bound" copies of the first report were presented to the king by Lord John Russell in December.[106] The home secretary also asked the commissioners for a list of all unions formed

---

101. PLC Minutes, November 27, 1835, MH 1/4.
102. Howick to Chadwick, December 14, 1835, Chadwick Papers, UCL.
103. Gilbert to Lefevre, July 18, 1835, MH 32/26. Gilbert told Chadwick: "The King is much pleased with any little attention and the Commission appears to be in great favour with him." Gilbert to Chadwick, July 22, 1835, Chadwick Papers, UCL.
104. Lewis to Gilbert, July 28, 1835, MH 32/26.
105. Gulson to Nicholls, October 18, 1835, MH 32/28.
106. PLC Minutes, December 15, and 19, 1835, MH 1/4.

and two sets of colored maps, one of which was given to the king.[107] Upon perusing these, the king expressed his great interest in the union plans and his complete approval of all those submitted.[108] The king's approval was largely a response to the fact that the new system was being shaped to suit the wishes of the traditional leaders of society. This is revealed by a detailed examination of the act's implementation in Chapter V.

107. PLC Minutes, January 7, 1836, MH 1/5.
108. Sir Herbert Taylor to Lewis, May 2, 1836, Harpton Court MSS, C/3027, NLW.

Chapter V

Implementation at the Local Level: A Regional Example

This chapter is concerned with the implementation of the act in the rural midlands and East Anglia—the counties of Bedford, Huntingdon, Northampton, Cambridge, Suffolk, Norfolk, Rutland, Leicester, Nottingham, and Lincoln. The amount of detail necessary to convey the nature of the process precludes an examination of the entire country. These ten counties have been selected to show the interaction of local interests and central government in a rural district which had experienced many of the problems of the Old Poor Law and was thus politically amenable to the reform. Wherever these conditions were duplicated in other parts of the kingdom—notably in the south but also here and there in the west and north—similar patterns of implementation are evident.

As in the south, the dispatch of assistant commissioners into this region was often prompted by requests from certain key landed magnates. One of the earliest calls came on November 12, 1834, when the commissioners received letters from Lord John Russell, his brother the marquis of Tavistock, and Thomas Bennett of Woburn, steward of the duke of Bedford's estates, expressing apprehension over incendiarism and other possible disturbances.[1] Two

1. PLC Minutes, November 12 and 14, 1834, MH 1/1.

days later, assistant commissioner Adey had a lengthy interview with Lord Charles Russell, Colonel Seymour, and Bennett, and the meeting concluded with a discussion of a possible poor law union around Woburn.[2] Ten weeks prior to this meeting, Bennett had begun working to incorporate the parishes making up the estate into a union. In a letter to W. G. Adam, the duke's London agent, Bennett wrote that they "must endeavour to keep the parishes which the Duke possesses the large share of them as much together as possible. . . . a classification like this on all large Estates would ensure a strict attention both on the part of the proprietor and his agents, than if conducted in larger unions—and from past experiences the working of the poor laws must never be again left entirely to the occupiers alone."[3] In mid-October, when Bennett received a request from the poor law commissioners for his views on a union, he assured Adam: "I have no doubt they will be anxious to consult the feelings of proprietors as to the Unions, in so far as it does not interfere with the proper execution of the Law."[4] The public meeting convened by Adey the day after his arrival made him fully aware of the strength of local feeling regarding the size of unions. When he mentioned a union of thirty or forty parishes, the magistrates clerk and Bennet told him flatly that it was out of the question. He secured agreement only by suggesting the petty sessions divisions as the basis for the Woburn and Luton unions, and wrote apologetically to Chadwick that it was impossible to use "any divisions but what the people are accustomed to."[5]

In reality, it was less a question of using existing administrative areas (there were substantial departures from the petty sessional divisions) than of bending to the wishes of the owners and agents of great estates. The Russells had been propitiated by the Woburn Union, while at Luton, Adey reported that the principal proprietor, the marquis of Bute, was not only favorable to the union but was about to donate a piece of land for the workhouse.[6] Indeed, Lord

2. Adey to PLC, November 14, 1834, MH 32/5.
3. Thomas Bennett to W. G. Adam, September 7, 1834, Russell Estate Correspondence, R 3/3813, Bedfordshire Record Office.
4. Ibid., October 16, 1834, R 3/3818.
5. Adey to Chadwick, November 15, 1834, Chadwick Papers, UCL. Just before the introduction of the New Poor Law into Parliament, Adey himself had a hand (as a magistrate) in redrawing the Bedfordshire petty sessions divisions. Adey to Chadwick, May 18, 1836, Chadwick Papers, UCL.
6. Adey to PLC, November 22, 1834, MH 32/5.

Bute pressed Adey for an early declaration of the Luton union, and took the chair at the newly formed board of guardians.[7]

Despite his setback in the southern part of the county, Adey was still convinced of the superiority of large unions and determined to incorporate the remainder of the parishes around the county town of Bedford. He assured the commissioners that any resistance of rural parishes to the idea of one large union around Bedford would be negated by the great savings possible from using the large and efficient Bedford workhouse.[8] But a proposed union of 101 parishes, whatever its financial advantages, would clearly swamp the interests of many squires, and Adey had to retreat again. He suggested a compromise by which the four remaining sessional divisions would become separate unions for outdoor relief and combine for workhouse purposes at Bedford. This too was received coldly by the local gentry, whose resistance was backed by Frankland Lewis, and four separate unions were created: Bedford, Ampthill, Biggleswade, and Leighton Buzzard. The result of this transaction, as Adey later complained to Chadwick, was the unnecessary expenditure of £20,000 on three additional union workhouses.[9]

Bedfordshire might have appeared more likely than most counties to receive the new law docilely. In a "Speenhamland" county with all the classic symptoms of parochial mismanagement, high rates, and the breakdown of labor discipline, the poor law commissioners probably expected an eager reception, especially considering the great influence of a Whig grandee like the duke of Bedford. But in fact, as shown by their victory on the size of the poor law unions, the locals (including the Russells) were determined to imprint their stamp on the new system—both on relief policies and on union boundaries. At a New-Year's-Eve meeting with a number of gentry near Biggleswade, Adey found them all "friendly to the Bill," but with independent ideas on the workhouse test, "many expressing great doubts of its propriety with respect to the aged and Infirm." Indeed, Adey received many offers of assistance, but he was becoming wary enough to comment to Frankland Lewis that "we shall see by and bye what they understand by the word."[10]

7. Ibid., February 12, 1835.
8. Ibid., November 17, 1834.
9. Adey to Chadwick, May 18, 1836, Chadwick Papers, UCL.
10. Adey to Lewis, January 4, 1835, MH 32/5.

On the delicate question of surplus population, Adey held to the orthodox belief that surpluses were illusory and solely the result of mismanagement. But the duke's steward, who was anxious to have official assistance for emigration of surplus laborers from the district, simply went over Adey's head to John Lefevre. Bennett asked W. G. Adam to pay a visit to Somerset House, and expressed his satisfaction when informed that Lefevre "is willing to allow we have a surplus population" and eager to facilitate emigration.[11]

The unions in Bedfordshire were declared in March 1835, and the first elections held. Bennett, ever the efficient steward, ensured the return of tractable guardians in all the duke's parishes, at one point organizing an effective canvass to head off the threat of independent candidates from two parishes.[12] With a solid body of faithful Russell tenants and supporters returned as guardians, the Woburn union held its first meeting on April 14. Adey was in attendance and managed to provoke the duke's steward by his treatment of the board. Bennett complained that Adey

> assumed a much more dictatorial manner than was at all relished by many present, however I think that he has found by this time that he has to deal with men of intelligence and that he will not again attempt a like tone.—he certainly did not shew-to advantage, he is a quick off hand man, but I doubt much if he is a real man of business.

The main dispute between Bennett and Adey lay in the guardians' preference for a larger, better paid union staff than Adey thought desirable. Bennett's description of the assistant commissioner's policy as "penny wise and pound foolish" may have partly covered the guardians' desire to exercise maximum patronage, but there was good sense in his contention that the first labors were the hardest, and it was best to be "well-manned at the beginning, and as the duties are lightened, an active and careful Board of Guardians will reduce or consolidate their officers."[13] As with most appointments of union officers, the Woburn guardians got their way— the commissioners were loathe to exercise their power of refusing to sanction them.

As far as the laborers were concerned, Bedfordshire had been

11. Bennett to W. G. Adam, November 30, 1834, Russell Estate Correspondence, R 3/3830, Beds. R.O.
12. Ibid. March 29, 1835, R 3/3858.
13. Ibid., April 15, 1835, R 3/3863.

restive for some time—the desire of the county magnates to have their unions in operation at the earliest date was largely prompted by the desire to confront disorder with effective organization. As in many other parts of the country, the paupers were unhappy at the anticipated change from payment in money to payment in kind. Even before the change was made, news of it produced a riot at Ampthill, where the union chairman was Earl de Grey, who was also the lord lieutenant. Although the disturbance was quickly contained, it produced consternation in some quarters. The auditor of the Luton union wrote to Lord de Grey just after the riot: "The feeling against the New Poor Law is stronger than I was aware of—and in quarters where I did not expect it—still I consider Luton quite able to take care of itself."[14] The vigor of the new boards of guardians, backed by the military and London police, proved sufficient to prevent further outbreaks, and by the end of 1836, major financial savings coupled with a more docile peasantry were producing satisfaction. Bennett, for example, exulted to the duke of Bedford:

> Your Grace will be pleased to know that our surplus labour has under the operation of the Poor Laws as now administered, nearly vanished, and we may justly consider the market for labour in a sound and healthy state—I know of no Farmer, who employed a man more than is absolutely necessary, and I have had no few applications from men wanting work during the period I have been here.[15]

In a similar mood of self-congratulation, the duke's heir, the marquis of Tavistock, wrote to his brother, Lord John Russell:

> Mr. Adey says that our Bedford Board is the best he is acquainted with. I could tell you of more than one parish in this county where the rates have been reduced from ten to three and 3½—labourers greatly improved both in their habits and their condition—and the farmers better served.[16]

14. Charles Austin to Lord de Grey, May 15, 1835, Lieutenancy Correspondence, L.C.G. 12, Beds. R.O. This box of correspondence contains many letters on the Ampthill riot. Several months later, Austin had to call on the poor law commissioners to send London police to protect the unfinished Luton workhouse. PLC Minutes, September 24, 1835, MH 1/3.

15. Bennett to the duke of Bedford, December 4, 1836, Russell Estate Correspondence, R 3/3974, Beds. R.O.

16. Lord Tavistock to Lord John Russell, December 26, 1836, Russell Papers, P.R.O. 30/22/2D, fo. 255.

In the small neighboring county of Huntingdon, Adey's problem was to prevent his proposed poor law unions from severing any estate boundaries. One of the centers initially selected was Kimbolton, an area under the influence of the duke of Manchester; but such an arrangement would have required ten Bedfordshire parishes, as yet unincorporated, to go to Kimbolton, which would have severed Lord St. John's estate.[17] After delaying the declaration of unions several months, during which he conferred with the duke of Manchester and Lord St. John, Adey finally abandoned the Kimbolton union. Both peers approved of a plan whereby the county was divided into three unions (Huntingdon, St. Ives, and St. Neot's), with all of Lord St. John's parishes going into the Bedford union.[18] By this time, Adey had come to recognize the necessity of working closely with local magnates and maintaining cordial relations with them after the formation of the unions. In Huntingdonshire, and even in Bedfordshire, the political complexion of most boards was Tory, and Adey fought any tendency to depict the New Poor Law as a Liberal triumph. He flatly refused to ask the union clerks in his district to send information on the advantages of the new system to *The Reformer*, a Liberal paper in Huntingdonshire. This had been suggested by Sir Cullen Smith, a friend of Chadwick, and in turning down the request Adey wrote to Frankland Lewis:

> I have always stated that I considered the P.L. Act as no party Act— as it was passed with the approbation of the leaders of all parties and the introduction of party into the question is most unjust and injurious. Let us take care we do not lay ourselves open to the charge by supporting party Newspapers.[19]

To the west lay Northamptonshire, the county of "squires and spires," and the first moves were made there in September 1834. The duke of Grafton's steward, John Cooper, requested that the commissioners make a poor law union of four adjoining parishes belonging to the duke near Potterspury. Cooper pointed out that a "Central Poor House," built at the duke's expense, was nearly complete. He ended by observing that the parishes "are all Agricul-

---

17. Adey to Lewis, February 22 and 27, 1835, MH 32/5.
18. Ibid., October 3, 1835.
19. Adey to Lewis, December 7, 1836, Chadwick Papers, UCL.

tural and there is a superabundant Poor Population."[20] In November, Cooper wrote again, reiterating his plea for a union and asking "directions for the Management of the Poor House, which now stands ready, occupied to commence under your directions."[21] Already fully deploying their assistants further to the south, the commissioners had to wait till the following March to make a start on the county. After a brief orientation in Bucks from assistant commissioner Gilbert, Richard Earle's first assignment in Northants was to confer with Cooper. He availed himself of Cooper's offers of assistance but was concerned over the latter's notions of a poor law union: "You may depend upon my utmost to meet the Duke's wishes, but I fear that his Agent's idea of an Union are rather too limited. I must try to expand them by persuasion."[22] Earle was partially successful, for the Potterspury union finally formed had eleven parishes—the four Cooper originally mentioned, four others partially owned by the duke of Grafton, and three unconnected to the estate. Even this expanded version had an unusually small population—fewer than six thousand—and Earle felt compelled to apologize to his superiors for "paying more attention to his Grace's wishes than I should have done, had the property and convenience of others been equally concerned."[23] The addition of four adjoining parishes in Bucks the next year did not significantly dilute the domination of this union by the Grafton interest.

The other eleven poor law unions in Northants were not all drawn so obviously along estate lines as at Potterspury. But, as I indicate elsewhere, most contained some dominant landholding interest, such as the Cartwrights at Brackley, the Knightleys at Fawsley, Earl Spencer at Brixworth, and Earl Fitzwilliam at Peterborough, while the other unions represented at least politically harmonious incorporations.[24] The other point of interest in the boundaries of the Northants poor law unions lies in the isolation of the county town from contiguous magnate-dominated parishes.

20. Cooper to PLC, September 23, 1834, MH 12/16727.
21. Ibid., November 17, 1834.
22. Earle to Lewis, March 29, MH 32/21.
23. Earle to PLC, April 8, 1835, MH 12/16727.
24. Anthony Brundage, "The Landed Interest and the New Poor Law," hereafter cited as "The Landed Interest."

The creation of separate unions around Brixworth and Harding-stone was dictated chiefly by the reluctance of the peers and squires in these parishes to be incorporated with an unruly urban area in which radicalism and Dissent were prominent.[25]

That most squires in the county were Tories had no bearing on their attitude to the law: From "Cartwright's Corner," a district in the extreme southwest under the influence of the Tory Cartwright family,[26] Earle wrote:

> Political bias, which as you know exists in a strong degree and in one direction throughout this district, appears to have been suspended on this question, and I think I am not too sanguine in calculating on the active and useful cooperation of many and the good will of the re-mainder.[27]

Indeed, shortly after the bill had been signed into law, the high Tory *Northampton Herald* promised to "do all in our power to assist in the administration of this new law."[28]

With such a favorable consensus operating in Northampton-shire, the twelve new boards set to work with a will, encountering almost no overt opposition from the laborers. But Earle found that this ardent spirit did not imply an uncritical acceptance of poor law commission guidance. As elsewhere, the boards used their discre-tionary powers fully, coupling a generally strict posture with some-times generous policies, especially to the aged and infirm.[29] Two years later, with all the unions boasting solid new workhouses, Earle still found some of the boards adverse to "offering the house" in the manner envisaged in the 1834 report. The Northampton board, for example, showed a distressing tendency to act upon "false humanity" and "character and merits," the Daventry guard-ians "enquire more about the character of applicants than their means of support," while at Kettering, the "principal Members do not believe at present in the possibility of annihilating out-relief."[30]

25. Ibid., pp. 37-40.
26. W. R. Cartwright of Aynho was the Tory M.P. for South Northants. His brother, Major Cartwright, became the very active chairman of the Brackley board of guardians.
27. Earle to Lefevre, April 28, 1835, MH 32/21.
28. *Northampton Herald*, August 23, 1834.
29. Anthony Brundage, "The English Poor Law of 1834 and the Cohesion of Agricultural Society."
30. Earle to Chadwick, February 11, 1837, MH 32/21.

The strongest boards often tended to be the least amenable to the direction or influence of the assistant commissioner. A prime example was Peterborough, where Earl Fitzwilliam's vigorous leadership led Earle to describe him as "quite the first chairman I have ever yet seen."[31] But there was also a spirit of self-confidence that resisted official instruction, and Earle, with some exasperation, expressed a wish that Peterborough might be publicly compared with the less boastful but more "correct" neighboring board at Stamford, "to show my friends at Peterboro' that they are not perfect, a fact which Ld. Fitzwilliam's eulogies in the House of Lds. has perhaps concealed from their view."[32] Despite his frustration at being unable to cajole his boards into a full application of the "principles of 1834," Earle was notably successful in maintaining cordial relations with the Northamptonshire guardians. When he was transferred to Ireland in 1838, local feeling was well expressed by John Beasley, Earl Spencer's steward and guardian for one of his parishes in the Brixworth union: "I am very sorry we are going to lose Mr. Earle. I hope his removal may be for his good, but I greatly doubt whether you have it in your power to send us his equal."[33]

To the east, in the Isle of Ely, the way in which the commission and the local grandees disposed of the parish of Whittlesey exemplifies the continuance of powerful forces operating against large, troubled parishes that lacked major landowners. Whittlesey and the neighboring parish of Thorney, both of which adjoined the Peterborough union, displayed a considerable mutual antipathy. The populous (over 6,000) open parish of Whittlesey was plagued by high rates and a turbulent host of paupers, while Thorney, entirely in the possession of the duke of Bedford, was considerably better managed and more lightly rated, despite a population of more than 2,000. After the Peterborough union had already been formed, Tchyo Wing, the duke's steward and an Isle of Ely magistrate, requested that Thorney be annexed to Peterborough on the grounds of its proximity and the fact that many of Thorney's nonresident paupers lived within the Peterborough union.[34] Earle set to work on it at once, but found that Wing wanted not only the inclusion of

31. Earle to Lefevre, May 31, 1837, MH 32/21.
32. Ibid., August 3, 1838.
33. Beasley to Lefevre, September 10, 1838, Shaw-Lefevre MSS, HLRO.
34. Wing to PLC, December 5, 1835, MH 12/8828.

Thorney, but the exclusion of Whittlesey, a desire that was put formally in a petition signed by Wing and ninety-four other Thorney parishioners.[35]

The commissioners gave the case top priority, involving not only Earle but the assistant commissioners working up other parts of Cambridgeshire into unions, Colonel Wade and Alfred Power. In his first report on the case, the latter well summarized the problems involved. To take Thorney alone to Peterborough, he said, would leave Whittlesey cut off from any other union center and forced to rely on its own resources, deprived of all the advantages of a wider administrative district:

> I feel it to be very improbable that the necessary changes can be effected in this pauperised and lawless parish, through a Board composed entirely of resident occupiers and other gentlemen without exposing their persons and property to the imminent risk of outrage. The Peterborough Board composed of Guardians chiefly resident elsewhere, would as we know by experience be enabled to do anything in such a parish with perfect ease and safety.[36]

The wisdom of this observation prompted Somerset House to press hard for Whittlesey's inclusion. Frankland Lewis appealed to Earl Fitzwilliam to use his great influence over the Peterborough guardians. But Fitzwilliam, who felt the same revulsion at the prospect of receiving a massively pauperised parish as his colleagues at Peterborough, replied:

> Whenever the subject is mentioned at the Board, there is a sort of murmur that runs from one end of the table to the other, and I must confess that, with respect to myself, nothing but a sense of duty and a desire to relieve you from a difficulty would induce me to accede to it.[37]

Lewis's efforts were followed by equally futile appeals by Earle and Wade, the latter putting in an appearance at Milton, Lord Fitzwilliam's home, to argue his case.[38] Although Fitzwilliam agreed

35. Ibid., March 10, 1836.
36. Power to Lefevre, January 13, 1836, Shaw-Lefevre MSS, HLRO.
37. Fitzwilliam to Lewis, March 28, 1836, MH 12/8828.
38. Earle to Fitzwilliam, July 13, 1836, Fitzwilliam MSS, Bundle BX, N.R.O.; Wade to Lewis, July 16, 1836, MH 32/74.

to have the matter put to a vote, the approval of two-thirds of the guardians was required for annexing any parish, and the matter was quite hopeless. The Peterborough board, after voting thirty-one to seven against Whittlesey, approved the inclusion of Thorney by twenty-eight to fourteen.[39]

After this failure, the commissioners had no choice but to form a Whittlesey parish board of guardians, a virtual continuation of the select vestry which had already demonstrated its inability to stem pauperism. Wade reported that the "members of the Select Vestry will almost all be elected Guardians and are quite determined to set their shoulders to the task,"[40] but clearly they would face nearly the same pressures as under the Old Poor Law and be subject to all the disadvantages outlined in Power's report. The whole episode demonstrates how the commissioners' limited powers and obvious deference to landed magnates could result in the continuing isolation and deprivation of unruly open parishes under the New Poor Law.[41]

Elsewhere in Cambridgeshire, the creation of poor law unions was proceeding smoothly. Of the eight unions formed in the county, the earliest move resulted from a request from the earl of Hardwick to Frankland Lewis to form a union in the vicinity of his estates. This request was passed on to Power, at that time working in Essex, who wrote to Lord Hardwick that as soon as he had finished his present operations, "I would visit that part of the county of Cambridge in which his Lordship is so extensively interested."[42] The resulting Caxton and Arrington union, with Lord Hardwick as its chairman, became a model of strict administration and a target for anti-poor law agitators. The Reverend W. H. Maberly, a fiery Cambridgeshire parson, singled out the Caxton union for particular vituperation. At an outdoor meeting in Cambridge on April 29, 1837, Maberly related approvingly to the crowd a plan hatched by some Caxton laborers to seize Lord Hardwick and "stamp his g—s out," upon which revelation (according to a local newspaper), "the air resounded with such a yell of delight that plainly shews the

39. Peterborough Union Minute Book, July 16, 1836, N.R.O.
40. Wade to Lewis, August 11, 1836, MH 32/74.
41. See B. A. Holderness, "'Open' and 'Close' Parishes."
42. Power to Lewis, March 26, 1835, MH 32/63.

diabolical disposition of his auditory."[43] Despite such colorful demonstrations, there were no serious acts of resistance in Cambridgeshire.

Stronger opposition broke out in Suffolk, not only among the
laborers but also among a number of the gentry. This area had seen
successful local initiatives in devising somewhat more effective
poor law administration, particularly the incorporated hundreds
established during the eighteenth and early nineteenth centuries, a
number of which were still flourishing.[44] The incorporated hundreds had some of the advantages of poor law unions—lessened
vulnerability to the paupers of any one parish, professional staff,
and larger workhouses than any single parish could afford—but
the poor law commissioners considered them generally ineffective
because of their sometimes inconvenient boundaries, lack of a
plural voting system for guardians, and numerous abuses that had
crept into their administration, despite the attentions of the local
gentry. The latter were bound to resent this criticism of their ma-
nagerial talents, which accounts for much of the upper-class resistance.

Before the end of 1834, the commissioners dispatched assistant
commissioner Charles Mott into Suffolk to examine the incorporated hundreds. Reporting on four of them, Mott called attention to
some gross abuses in the workhouses—lack of classification and a
profuse diet. But he concluded that Suffolk, although "as heavily
pauperised as any part of England, presents in its incorporated
Hundreds every facility for carrying into immediate operation the
full measures of the new Poor Law." The only major change he
suggested was to reconstitute the boards according to the provisions of the new law—that is, plural voting and ex officio membership for magistrates.[45] For the most part, this policy was adopted,
several of the unions formed by Mott being territorially the same as
the incorporated hundreds.

When James Kay relieved Mott of Suffolk in August 1835, he
threw himself into his new labors with characteristic zeal. Arriving

---

43. Clipping from the *Huntington, Bedford, and Peterborough Gazette, and Cambridge Independent Press*, May 6, 1837, included in Wade's reports, MH 32/74. For
other of Maberley's activities, see Edsall, op.cit., pp. 41-43.

44. See p. 6.

45. "Mott's Report on Hundreds of Mutford & Lothingland, Blything, Wangford,
and Bosmere & Claydon," December 1834, MH 32/56.

in Ipswich from London at 3 A.M., he set off with Mott at 8 A.M. and spent the full day touring the workhouses of the incorporated hundreds and the evening drawing up summonses to the church-wardens and overseers of the Ipswich parishes.[46] During the next few months, Kay was engaged in declaring more unions, attending the first meetings of those recently formed, and trying to win over public opinion. In the last endeavor he was partially successful: At the first meeting of the Woodbridge Union, he received the enthusiastic cooperation of Sir Philip Benton, "who *was* a most violent opponent of the measure," while the first meeting at Sudbury saw the conversions of the chairman and vice chairman, likewise former "violent opponents" of the law. In the same communication, Kay claimed a brilliant success for his two-hour address to a meeting of magistrates at Haverhill, at which he received their unanimous approval for a proposed union there.[47] Not all the Suffolk magistrates active in administering the New Poor Law were to Kay's liking. He was particularly critical of W. A. Shaldam, chairman of the Plomesgate union, in part because he was a "popularity hunter," but mostly because of his ardent belief in paper currency. In an outburst that perhaps tells more about his own obsessions than Shaldam's, Kay declared: "Fanatics of that class are always unstable people—without exception wrongheaded if not worse." But the bleak prospect at Plomesgate was relieved by the vice chairman, a young lawyer from Wickham Market, whom Kay found "strongly in favor" of the new law.[48]

In this atmosphere of mixed emotions on the part of the leaders of Suffolk's rural society toward the New Poor Law, the laborers demonstrated their hostility in the most unequivocal manner. The beginning of the East Suffolk disturbances came in the village of Stradbroke in the Hoxne union, where, even before Kay's arrival in August, a powerful current of resistance by the laborers was being encouraged by certain anti-poor law Anglican parsons.[49] The Hoxne union relieving officers were harrassed, and Kay himself was pelted with stones on a visit in late November. More serious

---

46. Kay to Lewis, August 4, 1835, MH 32/48.
47. Ibid., October 10, 1835.
48. Ibid.
49. This account of the East Suffolk outburst is based chiefly on Edsall, *The Anti-Poor Law Movement 1834-44*, pp. 34-37.

disturbances occurred in Ipswich, where the impolitic decision of an enthusiastic board of guardians to apply the full rigor of the workhouse test at the beginning of winter led to the near destruction of the workhouse by an enraged mob. Discontent spread to other villages and was particularly intense during the week before Christmas. As elsewhere, London police, special constables (of whom Kay was one), and military units managed to restore order, though these were not supplied in sufficient force to make anyone immediately confident of the outcome. A few magistrates who had been part of the large "wait and see" group were stung by the train of events into a wholehearted defense of the new law, and Kay at one point exulted to Lewis that the paupers "have ensured our victory by their premature movements." But this was followed by a more sober analysis the next day: "The Magistrates are some of them opposed to the law—others are lukewarm and unwilling to act—others are naturally stupid and supine." Furthermore, some were disinclined to act "on account of the severity (as they term it) of the new workhouse regulations."[50]

Despite his misgivings at the end of the year, Kay was able to tell Frankland Lewis a month later of "the most remarkable change" in the attitudes of the Suffolk magistracy, especially in the Plomesgate, Hoxne, and Boswell and Claydon unions, where most magistrates had been "undisguised opponents" of the law: "They have suddenly chaffed round to the wind, and they now sail before the gale of the popular voice, which is everywhere becoming more decidedly in favor of the new measures." He suggested that a likely reason for this change was the evidence of a 30 to 50 percent financial savings under the new system.[51]

In saying the "popular voice" was becoming favorable to the law, Kay could hardly have been referring to the laborers, for there is plenty of evidence to show a continuing spirit of resistance, likely to break forth into occasional acts of rebellion. This was clearly evident in Bury St. Edmunds in the summer of 1836 when Kay appeared before the court of guardians (formed under a local act) to persuade them to adopt the commissioners' regulations. On his arrival at the guildhall, Kay found large numbers of workers in the

50. Kay to Lewis, December 26 and 27, 1835, MH 32/48.
51. Ibid., January 24, 1836.

audience, who "gave sufficient evidence that they were ready for an uproar." After addressing the crowd for twenty minutes "in a conciliatory tone," Kay turned to discuss details with the court of guardians, but was prevented by the angry and menacing shouts of the laborers. The guardians managed to clear the room and carried on the discussion with Kay for an hour and a half, "notwithstanding the clamour" outside. The guardians proved receptive to the new regulations, and "cordially agreed to an adoption of all the provisions of the law, and particularly to proceed forthwith with an alteration of the workhouse." Having proved their mettle behind locked doors, Kay and the guardians had to face the hostile crowd outside. They made their way in a compact body to the inn "amidst the hootings of the lowest rabble you can conceive, headed by a few of the desperate radicals, and the beershop keepers." Kay's hat was struck from his head, and his coat was torn, but despite some rough jostling and hurling of missiles, no one sustained any serious injuries. As a final indignity, as Kay rode out of town a half hour later, "the old women screamed loudly out of the windows, in all the streets through which I passed."[52]

The affray in Bury St. Edmunds demonstrates how often the outbreak of resistance by the laborers was one factor in winning waverers among the upper classes over to the New Poor Law. This was certainly the case in the Hoxne union, which had seen the first of the East Suffolk outbreaks. By the spring of 1836, several of the magistrates who opposed the law had come around, and the Reverend Sir Henry Owen, who was ardently pro-poor law, was elected chairman of the union.[53] A few months later, the board passed a resolution against outdoor relief and requested Somerset House to issue a prohibitory order.[54] Indeed, throughout Suffolk, a certain set of attitudes toward the poor by the leaders of society was beginning to harden. The latter's control over the poor law machinery gave them a potent measure of social control and helped to accentuate that division between flinty hearted gentry and farmers on the one side, and a cowed and disspirited peasantry on the other—a picture so vividly painted in Ronald Blythe's *Akenfield*. A contemporary opponent of the New Poor Law in Suffolk described the spirit that

52. Ibid., July 16, 1836.
53. Owen to Lefevre, March 28, 1836, Shaw-Lefevre MSS, HLRO.
54. Ibid., May 31, 1836.

motivated the new boards of guardians and prompted the adoption of severe workhouse regulations and stringent outdoor relief:

> The spirit of domination strongly manifested by some of our country gentlemen was at the bottom of these extreme regulations. The independence of their positions places them beyond the pale of contradiction in their own sphere, and they will not brook the violation of authority. With them, system is everything—their horses are accustomed to go so many miles, their labourers to perform so much work: and why should not these rascals of paupers be placed in solitary confinement, and be shortened of their diet, for disobedience, and thus bring their tempers as well as their stomachs into subjection, and make them feel the power of the village squire.[55]

In Norfolk, the New Poor Law received a similarly mixed reception from the gentry, though the laborers appear to have been less active in their opposition. Sir Edmund Parry, who was directed to begin the unionization of Norfolk in the spring of 1835, experienced some difficulty in convincing the leaders of Norfolk society of the advantages of the new system. One of the most important of the landed magnates to need convincing was Thomas Coke of Holkham. Most notable for his agricultural improvements in the eighteenth century, Coke was an active and vigorous octogenarian at the time the New Poor Law was passed. Born in 1752, he had entered the House of Commons in 1776 and sat continuously for Norfolk from 1807 to 1832. Though a zealous Whig in politics, Coke was, according to what Parry had heard, "furious about the Poor Laws still."[56] So, deferring the creation of a union in the Holkham district, Parry concentrated on other parts of the county, and ultimately formed ten unions before his resignation in February 1836. In most of these, he had to deal with considerable skepticism on the part of local squires. One such figure was Sir Thomas Beevor of Hargham, who described himself to Parry as a "Cobbettite." Mollified by Parry's approach and by a conciliatory answer from the commissioners to his memorial, Beevor agreed to Hargham being taken into a union and, indeed, was elected chairman of the Wayland board of guardians. Beevor's "conversion" opened the door for others, and Parry ascribed such successes to the tactful handling of Beevor:

55. John Glyde, Junior, *Suffolk in the Nineteenth Century*, p. 185.
56. Parry to Lewis, May 11, 1835, MH 32/60.

Where Parishes belong to single Proprietors, the latter have often expressed to me a wish to remain as they are; but I have never had any difficulty in getting them to asquiesce, on pointing out to them the principles laid down in your reply to Sir Thos. Beevor's Memorial.[57]

As the new unions began their operations, there was some apprehension of overt resistance by the laborers. Parry reported that the chairmen of quarter sessions, "both staunch friends of mine," had written to Lord John Russell, stressing the need to create an efficient rural constabulary: "What they expect is that the building of the Workhouses will be the signal for tumult among the lower orders."[58] In the event, no such rebellion materialized; but there were other sources of resistance—particularly corrupt vested interests in some of the boroughs. Regarding King's Lynn, of which Parry himself was a freeman, he reported that a system "of the most abominable villainy" was in operation: "The greater part [of the poor rates] goes to the Brewers, who are influential people, and, in most instances, paupers receiving relief in the morning have been at the *Theatre* in the evening!!"[59] It was perhaps the necessity of dealing with such unregenerate local authorities, along with the hard work of convincing recalcitrant squires and the fear of pauper rebellion, that ultimately resulted in Parry's nervous breakdown and resignation.[60] In relieving Parry of his district in February 1836, Kay wrote that "Sir Edw. is much exhausted, and appears very nervous, and anxious."[61]

Kay's arrival in Norfolk injected a much needed spirit of determination, and within a few months the rest of the county was safely unionized. The key to further progress turned out to be Parry's bugbear, Thomas Coke. Whereas Parry had been frightened away from the vicinity of Holkham by the mere rumor of Coke's displeasure, Kay opted for a frontal assault, which payed off handsomely. One of his first steps was to invite himself to Holkham to confer with Coke and hold a public meeting on the subject of two or three proposed unions. The result of this maneuver surpassed Kay's expectations, and he was able to exult to Lewis that Coke had

57. Ibid., August 5, 1835.
58. Ibid., June 17, 1835.
59. Ibid., May 11, 1835.
60. See p. 89.
61. Kay to Lewis, February 20, 1836, MH 32/48.

welcomed him to Holkham in a most cordial manner. He conferred privately with Coke for an entire day on the extent of proposed union around Coke's estate, and the two men proceeded the next day to the public meeting at Walsingham, over which Coke presided. Kay addressed the gathering for three hours and received unanimous approval for the two proposed unions. After the meeting, Coke insisted on placing his coach and four at Kay's disposal to carry him the further fourteen miles to Norwich, and offered his assistance in preparing the way for Kay in the still unincorporated parts of the county.[62] The venerable patriarch of Norfolk was as good as his word, and a fortnight later Kay was able to report: "Mr. Coke's influence has I find already procured for my operations in these hundreds great advantages."[63]

But if the gentry seemed to be falling into line, the boroughs still proved obstreperous. The most exasperating of them was Norwich; and even before appearing there, the usually confident Kay wrote apprehensively to Lewis that "though the Orders [of the commissioners] have not yet been burned by the common hangman, I have no confidence that my eloquence will prevail above the voice of faction."[64] Like Bury St. Edmunds, Norwich had a court of guardians under a local act, but where Bury had proved receptive to the commission's regulations, Norwich defiantly refused to accept them. The city's poor law administration was, according to Kay, dominated by a strident and corrupt Tory faction. Norwich, indeed, was something of an obsession with Kay, and as he warmed to his subject he lapsed into medical metaphors:

> Norwich is the Norfolk St. Pancras and I hope I shall now soon have time to lay siege to this city. Norfolk and Cornwall are the *two feet* of England, in which extremities the circulation languishes, and life manifests itself less vigorously than in parts near the social heart. Norwich is a gouty importune on the great toe of England into which all the humours of the body politic have run together to form an angry boil, busily generating corruption. The correct practice is to open the tumour freely with the lancet and let out the pus.[65]

62. Ibid., February 23, 1836.
63. Ibid., March 6, 1836.
64. Ibid., March 22, 1836.
65. Ibid., May 1, 1836.

Because the commissioners lacked the power to perform such surgery, Kay suspended operations in Norwich in the vain hope that a bill presented to the cabinet giving much greater powers over local incorporations would be enacted.[66] The city continued to revel in a picturesque defiance of the central authority, as Kay reported that "every market day about a dozen blind men are now employed to recite ballads to the poor people on the market hill, the substance of which is the horrors of the Poor Law Commissioners' proceedings."[67]

Even among the leaders of Norfolk's rural society, where Kay had made such a promising start, signs of discontent soon appeared. Although the gentry took an active part on the new boards of guardians, they tended to resent any attempt at interference by the commissioners. In part, Kay ascribed this attitude to the desire of Tory squires to work the act "as an antiministerial engine," hoping for an early dissolution of Parliament so that they could use the anti-poor law cry for party purposes. He thought others were influenced by the "baneful effect" of the resistance of the London parishes.[68] But mostly, the resistance to central control was a measure of the concern of talented and dedicated local administrators at seeing their authority eroded. "I do not think," Kay wrote, "that any part of England could produce more able, subtle, and active magistrates than the eastern division of Norfolk. I am sure the magistracy are not anywhere more fastidiously jealous of any encroachment upon their authority." Having found that at "one fell swoop two thirds of the business of the petty and quarter sessions was annihilated," the magistrates turned their attentions to controlling the boards of guardians, which they proceeded to shape into proudly independent local authorities. They were able to accomplish this, Kay went on, by using their local influence and the deferential feelings of the yeomen, who "naturally feel proud of this new position [as elected guardians], but unconsciously yield themselves to the seductive influence of those by whom they have so long been led in every public proceeding."[69]

66. Ibid, July 9, 1836. On the refusal of the cabinet to push such legislation, see p. 171.
67. Ibid., October 13, 1836.
68. Ibid., September 28, 1836.
69. Ibid., October 13, 1836.

By the beginning of 1837, the suspicion of central control felt by the boards of guardians, in Suffolk as well as Norfolk, prompted Kay to adopt a very cautious line with regard to issuing prohibitory orders. In responding to an enquiry from Somerset House as to the state of his unions and the expediency of prohibiting outdoor relief except in cases of emergency, Kay replied by describing the response of two "respectable" chairmen, "both of whom expressed their conviction that the Unions were totally unprepared for such an order, and their own *personal repugnance to be parties in its execution*." Kay concurred in this opinion, fearing that a peremptory order on outdoor relief, besides being unenforceable, would destroy such authority as he enjoyed over his boards:

> I cannot too emphatically express my opinion that such an order is, at the present moment, only calculated to occasion open, and almost universal resistance to the Commissioners' authority in Norfolk and Suffolk, and to prevent the continuance of that cordial concurrence between the Boards of Guardians and the Assistant Commissioner which happily now exists.

He concluded by recommending a much more qualified prohibitory order, so riddled with exceptions as to ensure the continuance of local discretion.[70] This politic recognition of the impossibility of going beyond what local feeling would countenance, coming from one of the most vigorous "centralizers" in the corps of assistant commissioners, is a good illustration of how the nature and essence of the New Poor Law was shaped in its initial encounters with local interests.

While Kay was making his way through East Anglia, other assistant commissioners were active in the east midlands and Lincolnshire. Except for the industrial portions of Leicestershire and Nottinghamshire, this area was extensively agricultural, but there was wide variation in the degree of involvement by landed magnates. The tiny county of Rutland was one of the most heavily dominated in the country, a very powerful influence being exerted from Belvoir Castle by the Tory duke of Rutland. Indeed, his influence spread into the surrounding counties, and it was most fortunate for the poor law commissioners that the duke was one of their most active partisans.

70. Kay to PLC, February 7, 1837, MH 32/49.

The first assistant commissioner to establish direct contact with the duke of Rutland was Richard Hall, who began unionizing southern Leicestershire in the summer of 1835. In planning his moves further east, Hall at first toyed with the notion of making Rutland a single poor law union, but he considered it necessary to consult the duke before making any "definitive arrangement respecting his Territory."[71] The death of Lord Robert Manners, the duke's son, caused a delay of several months, but when Hall was ultimately invited to Belvoir, he could report to Nicholls: "The Duke of Rutland is very zealous in the cause, and there is a party now at the Castle of persons likely to catch the tone of our noble Host."[72] Another assistant commissioner who found the duke an opening wedge with the aristocracy and gentry was Edward Gulson, who was operating in Nottinghamshire and Lincolnshire. Gulson, like Hall, was invited to the castle along with scores of local notables, and wrote to Nicholls that "of course I cannot do better—as it will open my way through the counties."[73] The duke insisted that Gulson make Belvoir Castle his headquarters whenever he visited the area, and on such visits there were invariably numerous important guests present—clearly an ideal means for fostering and maintaining a favorable attitude toward the New Poor Law. The spirit of these assemblies is conveyed in Gulson's description of his first attendance at Belvoir:

> To describe the splendour and magnificence would be impossible but what is more to my present purpose is the telling you of the *extreme anxiety* evinced by the Duke that all parties should be convinced of the benefits accruing from your proceedings. The party was composed of very many friends among the Nobility—and of some waverers—but I think the latter were mostly won over by the facts adduced and the arguments used by his Grace.[74]

One such gathering included, among others, the duke of Wellington and Prince Esterhazy, and the prospect of an assistant commissioner being on terms of intimacy with such European luminaries caused Nicholls to minute the report excitedly: "Mr. Lefevre!!"[75]

71. Hall to Nicholls, September 18 and November 14, 1835, MH 32/34.
72. Ibid., February 18, 1836.
73. Gulson to Nicholls, February 10, 1836, MH 12/9228.
74. Gulson to Nicholls, February 29, 1836, MH 32/28.
75. Ibid., January 1837.

As regards the territorial arrangements, Hall's plan for a "county union" had to be scrapped. Instead, two union centers for Rutland were established (Oakham and Uppingham) and some Rutland parishes were connected with unions in other counties. The duke of Rutland's parishes were taken to Grantham, just over the border in Lincolnshire. This union was formed by Henry Pilkington, whose mode of proceeding was described to a select committee many years later by Sir John Trollope, a Lincolnshire squire who became president of the poor law board during Lord Derby's brief government in 1852:

> When the assistant commissioner formed those unions, he consulted the convenience of the public as much as he could and the persons locally connected. Those gentlemen who are so locally connected wished their respective parishes to go to those unions with which they were more habitually connected. The Duke of Rutland carried the whole of his Leicestershire parishes to the Grantham Union. Many of those parishes are certainly nearer to Melton Mowbray than to Grantham.[76]

Like most leading members of the nobility, the duke of Rutland owned parishes lying literally all over the map. The heart of his estate was a cluster of contiguous parishes around Belvoir Castle which were consolidated into a powerful new local authority under his control. Parishes lying elsewhere were absorbed into other unions, but since these were likewise under the influence of men of property and station, similar beneficial effects followed, as can be seen by the duke's telling Gulson that "his steward in Cambridgeshire had written that he had *readily relet* a farm at an advanced rent solely from the effect of the P.L.A. Act."[77]

Although it is impossible to determine precisely the effectiveness of the duke of Rutland's labors for the New Poor Law, it is undeniable that the attitude of the aristocracy and gentry in this district was markedly cordial. More than slightly dazzled by his reception in Leicestershire, Richard Hall exclaimed to Nicholls, after telling of his invitation to Belvoir Castle:

76. *Sess. Papers* (Commons), "Minutes of Evidence from the Select Committee on Boundaries of Parishes, Unions, and Counties," 1873, vol. 8, Q. 2505.
77. Gulson to Nicholls, April 2, 1836, MH 12/9228.

My reception everywhere has been most satisfactory; . . . I passed three days with Mr. Halford [Tory] M.P. for the southern division, and with him visited the parishes round his residence; I am to be his guest during the [quarter] Sessions, and shall by him be introduced to all the Gentry then assembled at Leicester. I am going Today to dine with Lord Denbigh, who owns a large portion of the property near Lutterworth, and in short I have more invitations than I could, were I so disposed, accept, and as many houses placed at my disposal as would quarter a Field Marshal and all his staff.[78]

In the northern part of the county, he was welcomed by Charles March Phillipps, Liberal M.P. for the northern division, who was "anxious that the Law should be systematically enforced as soon as possible in the vicinity of his Estates, and offers his House as my headquarters whenever I can commence operations there."[79] At an agricultural association dinner at Leicester, packed with gentry and farmers, "Immediately after the health of the Royal Family and Lord Lieutenant, that of the stranger guest [Hall] was proposed, and drunk with all due rattling of glasses and thumping of tables."[80]

As if all of this were not heady enough for Hall, he also received the enthusiastic assistance of the most "ultra" of the county's important Tory leaders—Earl Howe, whose outspoken resistance to Whig principles during his tenure as lord chamberlain had caused Grey to insist that the king dismiss him from court.[81] Of course, King William's own enthusiastic and oft repeated praise of the New Poor Law may have accounted in part for Lord Howe's attitude, for during their first meeting Howe told Hall "that the King takes the greatest interest in the measure." On the same occasion, the subject of a poor law union was discussed, Lord Howe expressing complete satisfaction at the prospect of having all eight of his parishes in the Market Bosworth union. To express his approval, Howe provided Hall with introductions to all his "friends and partisans."[82] At the first meeting of the Market Bosworth board of guardians, Earl Howe was elected chairman, and as one of his initial undertakings

78. Hall to Nicholls, October 3, 1835, MH 32/34.
79. Hall to Nicholls, November 30, 1835, MH 12/6581.
80. Hall to Nicholls, December 5, 1835, MH 32/34.
81. Michael Brock, *The Great Reform Act*, p. 244.
82. Hall to Nicholls, November 23, 1835, MH 32/34.

persuaded Lady Byron to sell a parcel of land for the new union workhouse. He told Hall "that in *his* Union the rates are reduced £900 this quarter." Even the Countess Howe took a keen interest in the affairs of the union, and "acquired amongst her friends the soubriquet of 'the Assistant Commissioner.'"[83]

Despite the immensely helpful posture of the Leicestershire peers and gentry, there were some obstacles to a smooth implementation of the act. One was the existence of several Gilbert Act incorporations in the county. As elsewhere, the configuration of these interfered with the planned new unions. In a 24-page report written at the beginning of 1836, Hall explained the procedures he had developed for convincing Gilbert union guardians to agree to a dissolution. After ensuring that the incorporation was in fact legally constituted under the 1782 act, he would pay a surprise visit to the house of industry. Then he would confer with the visitor, usually a man "of superior station," whom he tried to use as an intermediary to obtain the required two-thirds of the guardians signatures. He would then appear before one of the guardians' monthly meetings and explain in a most conciliatory manner the advantages of the new system. He would also point out that sections 32 and 35 of Gilbert's Act required them to find work outside the workhouse for any pauper who demanded it, a provision that magistrates had not enforced and paupers appeared ignorant of, but which the commissioners could both enforce and publicize. Some guardians by this time being won over by the combination of tact and subtle threat, Hall would rather bluntly point out that the commissioners had the power to order the appointment and fix the salaries of paid officers, regulate relief, make all furnishing of provisions by open contract, and direct each parish to expend one-tenth of a year's rate, or £50, on the workhouse. After the meeting, more signatures could be gathered privately. If subsequent meetings were still necessary, Hall escalated his pressure by questioning such items as the legality of guardians' salaries (on which Gilbert's Act was silent) and threatening them with having to meet weekly instead of monthly. These tactics proved successful for Hall in eight incorporations, comprising 115 parishes, for the dissolution of which the signatures of eighty-three guardians were required.[84]

---

83. Ibid., February 13, 1836.
84. Hall to PLC, January 9, 1836, MH 32/34.

Somerset House thought so highly of this technique that Hall's report was copied and sent to all the assistant commissioners as a guideline for dealing with local incorporations, but even for Hall it did not prove completely effective. The obduracy of the Barrow incorporation forced Hall to abandon his efforts, despite the assistance he received from the gentry: "I gained the consent [for dissolution] of every Parish in which any *Gentleman* had influence; but the Majority are in the hands of small proprietors who cannot or will not hear reason." The twenty-five guardians received a combined annual salary of £365, which Hall believed partly explained their resistance, as well as their willingness to stir up the "lower orders" against the new law.[85] Hall believed that another reason for the intransigence of some Gilbert Act guardians was their sheer ignorance. Because of the lack of property qualifications and the lack of plural voting, they were generally socially and intellectually inferior to guardians under the New Poor Law. According to Hall, they were "usually very uncultivated and prejudiced persons, many of them unable to write their own names," and that "arguments of a *general* nature failed with them, because totally unintelligible; something purely local, or directly personal, must be urged."[86] Hall may indeed have exaggerated the differences in the level of political sophistication between guardians of the 1782 and 1834 acts. This is strongly suggested by his report to Nicholls that of the hundreds of guardians in Leicestershire under the new law, no more than fifteen were duly elected. In many parishes, he continued,

when they learned that they were to choose what they call and write 'a garjent,' recourse was had to the ancient and intelligible method of tossing up. I have found it absolutely necessary to forbear from all inquiry into the Elections, and to satisfy myself with a simple affirmation that the party appearing is entitled to act.[87]

Partly from his arduous and sometimes fruitless labors to dissolve Gilbert incorporations, Hall's health began to break down. In the summer of 1836, the commissioners gave him a three-month leave of absence, upon the expiration of which he was ordered to exchange districts with Thomas Stevens.[88] This gave Hall the

85. Hall to Nicholls, March 12, 1836, MH 12/9806.
86. Hall to Nicholls, January 28, 1836, MH 32/34.
87. Ibid., February 13, 1836.
88. PLC Minutes, July 11 and October 24, 1836, MH 1/7. Gulson described to

already unionized counties of Berkshire and Oxfordshire (the areas to which he had originally been assigned), sparing him the strain of further public addresses and confrontations. It also brought a relatively fresh and vigorous official into Leicestershire to complete the process of unionization. The Barrow incorporation held out until the middle of 1837, and Stevens had to gather the necessary signatures one by one in protracted private negotiations. All of this would have been unnecessary if the government had agreed to push the bill drawn up by the commissioners giving them power to dissolve any existing union.[89] On one occasion, the Barrow guardians taunted Stevens with Hall's empty threat: "He [Hall] told us that we should be dissolved by act of parliament in three months, but the act has not passed yet, and never will."[90]

Besides destroying the remaining incorporations, Stevens had to contend with two particularly troublesome boards of guardians, Leicester and Hinckley, where party politics and commercial distress combined to thwart the advancement of "sound" principles. The inhabitants of Leicester resembled those of many other nineteenth-century towns in their love of the sound and fury of politics (although, of course, many were genuinely motivated by substantive issues). The introduction of a board of guardians provided them with a further opportunity to enjoy the eminently satisfying spectacle of processions, placards, oratory, and sensational stories and letters in the press. Hall had reported that the very first election of guardians was "made entirely a Party Question," with the Tories enjoying a preponderance,[91] while Stevens complained:

> At Leicester the reporters are now admitted, to the great hindrance of business. . . . The Union cannot work well whilst the reporters are admitted, and party spirit runs so high that the Guardians will never be able to exclude them without a positive order on that account from the Commissioners.[92]

Nicholls how on one occasion Hall had been "*mobbed* in a very disagreeable manner and degree—on attending a *manufacturing* vestry to induce the Guardians to dissolve an incorporation." Gulson to Nicholls, March, 7, 1836, MH 32/28.

89. See p. 171.
90. Stevens to Lefevre, February 3, 1837, MH 32/68.
91. Hall to Nicholls, June 23, 1836, MH 32/34.
92. Stevens to Nicholls, March 15, 1837, MH 32/68.

The newspapers avidly publicized any tales of distress on the part of the paupers or seeming inhumanity on the part of the guardians, at Hinckley as well as at Leicester. The massive unemployment in the stocking trade that struck both towns in 1837 brought Stevens to the verge of despair:

> The distress among the hosiers is very great indeed and Hinckley and Leicester are greatly embarrassed and the Guardians are *frightened* and have swerved from the right course. I do what I can but nothing will keep them up to the mark now. The press makes the difficulty much greater.[93]

Stevens' attempts to stiffen the spines of these two boards by strongly worded letters and exhortations at board meetings proved unavailing. At this juncture, the commissioners decided temporarily to reassign Hall to the district, and in his first report in this mission he declared: "A more evil-minded population than that of Hinckley and its neighbourhood cannot, I think, be found." Nonetheless, he criticized Stevens for insufficient tact, recommending a more judicious blend of caution and firmness: "I could have wished that Stevens had communicated his sound doctrine in a tone somewhat less peremptory, convincing the parties to whom his letter was addressed."[94] Hall found the same fault with Stevens' communications to the Leicester board, and suggested to him that he write fewer letters and couch them in a more conciliatory tone: "Politics are doing us much mischief at Leicester, and his letters almost always find their way into some newspaper, where they are commented on with all the unfairness of faction."[95]

Taking a closer look at the problems that beset these unions, Hall believed that one reason for the weakness of the Hinckley board was the absence of ex officio guardians. There was only one county magistrate ("an old timid clergyman") resident within the union—consequently the board was "destitute of vigour and intelligence." The guardians were intimidated by a dense population of "discontented and demoralised" workers, many of whom surrounded the town hall in a menacing fashion on board days, thus preventing the guardians from building a new workhouse or abolishing out-

93. Ibid., May 8, 1837.
94. Hall to Nicholls, May 16, 1837, MH 32/35.
95. Ibid., May 29, 1837.

door relief. By bringing in troops temporarily and having the vigorous chairman of the Lutterworth board attend at Hinckley, Hall managed to get the guardians to adopt stricter policies. These included procuring twenty tons of stone for the stoneyard, to be used as an outdoor labor test, and abolishing nonresident relief to the able-bodied, many of whom lived at Leicester.[96] The latter measure had to be rescinded a few weeks later, on Hall's own recommendation, because of a threatened march on Hinckley by nonresident paupers. Hall took this occasion to press upon the commissioners his view that, because of the widespread belief in the manufacturing villages of the inapplicability of the workhouse test, it had to be applied "with an elasticity whereby it can be accomodated to every variety of circumstance."[97] Two weeks later, he pointed out that the extreme precariousness of the commissioners' position prevailed not only at Hinckley and Leicester but in such hitherto safe rural unions as Market Bosworth and Market Harborough: "I am constantly fearful that the extreme pressure upon the Guardians upon the one side will, if accompanied by any strictness on the other (that is on *your* part) drive them altogether from the field, or lead to open resistance to your authority."[98] Like Kay in East Anglia, Hall attained an involvement in the day-to-day political and social realities of Leicestershire that made him fully aware of the practical limitations of central control.

In Lincolnshire, operations were commenced early in the autumn of 1835 by Henry Pilkington, who had been transferred north from Sussex. His initial public meetings in the county (at Stamford, Bourn, and Grantham) went well, although the chairman of the Bourn meeting, General W. A. Johnson, spoke in opposition to the new system.[99] At an agricultural association meeting in December, the New Poor Law was denounced by the influential Tory M.P. for Lincoln, Colonel Sibthorp, and by several other speakers. One opponent added, however: "Some good might come out of the evil;

---

96. Ibid., May 16, 1837.
97. Hall to PLC, June 5, 1837, MH 32/35.
98. Hall to Nicholls, June 17, 1837, MH 32/35.
99. *Lincoln, Rutland, and Stamford Mercury*, October 2, 1835, General Johnson offered more detailed charges against the new system in a letter to the editor published on the twenty-third of October. These included the allegedly unconstitutional powers and vast patronage of the commissioners, the oppressive costs of workhouses and union officers, and the unfairness of the bastardy clauses. Johnson was elected as an anti-poor law M.P. for Oldham in the 1837 general election.

the machinery might help Agriculturalists to unite, and might be applied to Dissenters' Registration and some other useful purposes."[100] A few parishes tried to resist being absorbed into the new unions: The overseer of Deeping St. James wrote defiantly to Somerset House that the parishioners "are determined thay will not come into any Union thay will manage their own Poor as thay think Proper and not be under the Comershers [*sic*] controul." Although the parish officers had heard Pilkington's address at Stamford, "thay pay very little Regard to what he says."[101] As was usual when resistance was offered by parochial small fry, these objections were brushed aside and Deeping St. James was brought into the Bourn union with thirty-six other parishes. Good effects began to show themselves even before the opening of the union, as evidenced by the overseer of Swinstead telling Pilkington of a thatcher who had recently obtained regular employment after being on the parish for years. When asked why, the overseer replied: "O, he heard of this new Law and supposed if he applied for Relief he should get clap'd into a Workhouse."[102] The first meeting of the Bourn board of guardians was auspicious, the four ex officio guardians, including Lord Willoughby de Eresby, evincing a determination to take an active hand in running the union.[103] In general, the attitude of most of the Lincolnshire magistrates was similar, no doubt partly influenced by the duke of Rutland's advocacy of the New Poor Law and his interest in the affairs of the Grantham union.

With such powerful local assistance, Pilkington probably expected the implementation of the act in the rest of the district to be relatively free of trouble, but he allowed himself to be drawn into the tangled affairs of a Gilbert Act incorporation, and to procure its dissolution he committed a number of blunders that both ruined his career and caused a temporary setback to the progress of the new law. Claypole, near the Nottinghamshire border, was the center of an incorporation of twenty parishes. Its visitor—Sir Robert Heron, Bart., a Whig M.P. for Notts—was not so fearful of having the Claypole incorporation dissolved as he was of having its compo-

100. Ibid., December 11, 1835.
101. John Twell to PLC, October 25, 1835, MH 12/6657.
102. Pilkington to PLC, October 31, 1835, MH 12/6657.
103. Ibid., November 27, 1835.

nent parishes united with the larger town of Newark, which, he pointed out to Frankland Lewis, "has a very turbulent population particularly the Quarter called Botany Bay which is a beehive of Thieves and Poachers."[104] Receiving little satisfaction from either Lewis or Nicholls, Heron urged Pilkington to assume the burden, even though this would involve him in the affairs of Nottinghamshire, a county that lay outside his assigned district. Nicholls was astounded to hear that Pilkington had conferred with Heron and was about to propose a Newark union which would, however, be centered at Claypole. On receiving a severe reprimand for this act of independence, Pilkington pleaded that his Newark proposal was really just a preliminary sketch and that he would gladly drop the whole thing. Furthermore, he explained, since he had been obliged to form the Grantham union at the duke of Rutland's urging, this necessarily involved planning the adjacent Newark and Claypole districts.[105]

Simply ordering Pilkington to avoid the area did not close the matter, for he had already reached an understanding with Heron on the terms for dissolving the Claypole incorporation and forming the Newark union. These included a generous remuneration to the Claypole parishes for giving up their recently built workhouse to the new union and retention of Claypole as the actual administrative center of the union. On the basis of this, Heron had immediately set about obtaining the required signatures for disolution. Pilkington was reluctant to admit to the commissioners the extent of his concessions and was forbidden by their orders from following up his initial efforts. His failure to do so perplexed Heron and created suspicion in the minds of other local magnates on the introduction of the new system.

To break this impasse, Somerset House assigned another assistant commissioner to the district, Edward Gulson, who was transferred from Berkshire to Lincolnshire and Nottinghamshire. Gulson asked Nicholls to explain the nature of Pilkington's troubles: "I have heard that my Colleague has come to a stand still—and I want to avoid so bad a road as he has traveled." Evidently Nicholls was still unaware of Pilkington's concessions, for he replied by

104. Heron to Lewis, November 11, 1835, MH 12/9411.
105. Pilkington to Nicholls, December 14 and 15, 1835, MH 12/9411.

simply repeating the order to meet with Pilkington, and mentioned that the latter was being assigned to Westmorland and Cumberland. When Gulson arrived at the end of January 1836 and conferred separately with Pilkington and Heron, he was surprised to learn of the agreement to repay the Claypole parishes all the money they had invested in their workhouse in return for signatures on the dissolution order. He reported that Heron was "so implicated (evidently through Mr. Pilkington) that he will almost feel bound to pay the money himself—rather than break his word to them."[106]

When they learned of this, the commissioners demanded to know all "conditions entered into" for the Claypole dissolution, to which Pilkington responded with the rather feeble assertion that there were no conditions "expressed or understood . . . but those which honourable feelings naturally suggest."[107] In reply, the commissioners demanded Pilkington's resignation, which was received and accepted on the twenty-second of February.[108] But he did not go quietly—at the beginning of March he wrote to the various boards of guardians requesting testimonials of his efficient and courteous behavior, a request that Gulson claimed was disagreeable to the duke of Rutland and injurious to Pilkington himself.[109] The matter was finally patched up, but the former Claypole parishes were quite upset when the valuation placed on their workhouse a few months later came to only half the original cost of building.[110] Heron became the chairman of the Newark union, which remained a house divided against itself, the Claypole and Newark segments retaining their separate identities and interests. According to Gulson, the result was

a feeling of jealousy between the two parties—which requires my vigilant attention to keep down. Sir Robert Heron is on the one side very anxious, energetic, and enthusiastic, and is in great fear that Newark should ever gain a point on his Claypole Parishes or division—and the Newark people are equally alive to him—so that all my efforts are required to soften and allay—but all will go well.[111]

106. Gulson to Nicholls, January 28, 1836, Nicholls to Gulson, January, 29, 1836; Gulson to Nicholls, January 31, 1836, MH 32/28.
107. Pilkington to Lefevre, February 5, 1836, Shaw-Lefevre MSS, HLRO.
108. PLC Minutes, February 22, 1836, MH 1/5.
109. Gulson to Nicholls, March 7, 1836, MH 32/28.
110. G. H. Packe to Lefevre, September 30, 1836, Shaw-Lefevre MSS, HLRO.
111. Gulson to Nicholls, April 2, 1836, MH 12/9228.

Having at least partially resolved the dilemma that Pilkington's rashness created, Gulson was ordered to remain and continue the unionization of the two counties. This meant, at least in Notts, more Gilbert Act incorporations to dissolve. Undoubtedly, the most troublesome of them was the Thurgarton incorporation, bailiwick of the Reverend John T. Becher, whose squabbles with the royal commission of inquiry are described in Chapter 2.[112] After some preliminary inquiries, Gulson reported: "I have already seen enough to shew me that Mr. Becher will not lose his *patronage* if he can help it."[113] Appearing at Becher's house to plead his case directly, Gulson was handed this terse message by a servant: "The Thurgarton House or its Incorporation has nothing whatever to do with the Poor Law Commissioners or they with it." Such a setback required the use of countervailing local influences, the most potent of whom was that Tory grandee, the duke of Newcastle, who had already directed his heir, Lord Lincoln, and his protégé, W. E. Gladstone, to examine the question.[114] The duke invited Gulson to visit him at Clumber, a meeting also attended by Richard Digby Neave, a newly appointed assistant commissioner who was learning the ropes from Gulson before going to Cheshire. Neave's description of the encounter provides a good insight not only into the ideas of the duke of Newcastle, but also into the way favorable attitudes were transmitted within the closely knit confraternity of the English nobility:

Tho'he deems the Commission an infringement on the rights of the Subject, he listened for two hours to Mr. Gulson's explanation of the Principle and illustrations of the working of the Bill with deep interest and seemed influenced by the assistance given to the cause by the Leaders of the Party Lords Ellenborough, Barrington, and Redesdale, and further mentioned a most satisfactory letter from Ld. Stradbroke on the working of the Bill in Suffolk.

The duke was also said to be influenced by the "favorable turn" done for the duke of Rutland at Grantham, evidently a reference to

112. See pp. 39-40.
113. Gulson to Nicholls, February 10, 1836, MH 12/9228. One incriminating piece of evidence Gulson discovered in a surprise visit to the Thurgarton Workhouse was "the *hog tub* . . . stuffed half full of *fine* bread."
114. Gulson to Nicholls, February 12, 1836, MH 32/28.

the drawing of the union boundaries along estate lines there.[115]At the conclusion of the meeting, the duke of Newcastle told Gulson that "he would assist me in overcoming the influence of the Visitor [Becher] which he says he knows to be powerful—but interested." Gulson ended his report by reassuring Nicholls: "You caution me against politics. I will take care that I have nothing to do with them—and that I will not be led away by those who have."[116]

Matters were brought to a head at a public meeting at Newark attended by over two hundred people concerned with the fate of the Thurgarton incorporation. The antidissolution party (followers of Becher) were there in force, determined to thwart Gulson: "No stone was left unturned to damage my cause—even to the disputing my right to call the Meeting or even to enter their Workhouse where the meeting was held." But Gulson had heavier artillery at his disposal—the duke of Newcastle had already spoken to some of the other leading landowners in the incorporation, and all were willing to pressure their tenants to sign the dissolution order:

> His Grace said all he could—and directed his Steward to obtain the signature of all the Guardians in his parishes—Admiral Southern did the same—Sir Robert Bromley the same—and Lord Manvers expressed himself *most warmly* in our favour. His Lordship said he had given up *a day's hunting* and he would *give up another* and *another* to obtain for the Parishes the advantages set forth.[117]

The sporting squires and farmers in the audience must have been particularly impressed with such extensive proof of Lord Manvers' dedication. Gulson reported victory within a week and included his outline of the new Southwell union, in which Nicholls was, of course, keenly interested. The only territorial concessions Gulson had to make were the exclusion of three parishes near Nottingham, "because they partake considerably of Manufacturers," and the inclusion of all Lord Manvers' parishes in the district. The latter became chairman of the Southwell board of guardians, and Becher continued to smart under the sting of his defeat, charging that "the Guardians had used him shamefully after his exertions."[118]

115. Neave to Nicholls, February 14, 1836, MH 32/59.
116. Gulson to Nicholls, February 15, 1836, MH 12/9228.
117. Gulson to Nicholls, February 23, 1836, MH 32/28.
118. Ibid., March 1 and 18, 1836.

Equally indignant was Thomas Nixon, visitor of the nearby Basford incorporation, who had supported Becher's resistance, realizing that his union would be the next to go. The same powerful forces that carried the day at Thurgarton also prevailed at Basford, but Nixon softened more quickly and agreed to take the chair of the new Basford board of guardians. Indeed, the most formidable obstacle for Gulson at Basford had been *Mrs*. Nixon: "I never got such a dressing in my life as I did from that quarter—for 'daring to interfere' with them—and it is proverbial in the vicinity that however you may succeed in soothing and pleasing *Mr*. Nixon—one day—it is little use as to the future."[119] The other famous Nottinghamshire reformer to be affected was the Reverend Robert Lowe of Bingham, whom the 1834 report had credited, along with Nicholls, with developing the workhouse test—an attribution partly responsible for the negative attitudes of Becher and Nixon.[120] Lowe was very favorable to the new system, and Neave described the visit he and Gulson paid to Lowe at Bingham as "most gratifying—he seems the Pattern of Poor Law Magistrates."[121] Lowe became the highly effective chairman of the new Bingham board of guardians, and was an occasional guest of the duke of Rutland at Belvoir Castle, where he proved of valuable assistance in proselytizing on behalf of the New Poor Law.[122] All in all, Gulson had reason to be well pleased with his skillful handling of the Nottinghamshire reformers, particularly where such sensitive egos were involved— but without the powerful assistance of the duke of Newcastle and others this might well have proved impossible. When Chadwick wanted Gulson to report fully on the maladministration of the incorporations and contrast it with the sound principles of the new system, Gulson declined, recognizing that any crowing over the victory might alienate new friends:

If I tell all I have seen in Becher's territory—I shall be taken up for manslaughter. *I am certain*—ill as he is—that *it would kill him*—and

119. Ibid., May 8 and 22, 1836.
120. See p. 40. Despite Nixon's support of Becher on the dissolution issue, he had earlier tried to establish his own claims over Becher's as the first reformer in Notts, informing Chadwick that "the House at Basford was established some years before—and served as a model for that at Southwell under the direction of Mr. Becher." Nixon to Chadwick, October 15, 1834, MH 12/9228.
121. Weale to Nicholls, February 14, 1836, MH 32/59.
122. Gulson to Lefevre, April 14, 1838, MH 32/28.

I am asked by the Gentry who have so manfully assisted me—*to spare him*—and to allow the matter to rest and proceed in quiet—now that we have it all our own way. . . . once shew up the whole truth to the public and my supporters will fall from me—and Becher will assuredly be quite killed.[123]

The rest of Nottinghamshire easily fell into line. Earl Spencer took an active hand in winning over the gentry around East Retford and became chairman of the new board of guardians. In addition to his power as a landowner, Spencer's influence was great because he was, in Gulson's words, "proverbial for sincerity" and, in Earle's "Parliamentary Father of the P.L.A. Act."[124] The duke of Portland was elected chairman in the neighboring Worksop union, and in the Radford union, Mr. Gregory of Hungerton Hall, a friend of Frankland Lewis, donated an acre of land worth £1,000 for the workhouse.[125] Even the towns proved relatively amenable to the new system. Gulson was relieved to find that Nottingham, potentially a trouble spot, got under way smoothly—in marked contrast to Leicester:

The Board is highly respectable—composed of influential individuals of both parties—and if the commencement of the Union proceedings is at all indicative of its future quiet and satisfactory course—nothing can be more auspicious. Everything has gone off *amicably, cordially,* and without one word of dissent either upon principle or detail. Much discussion of course took place and the Meeting was very long—but *exceedingly satisfactory.*[126]

By and large, this nonpartisan approach to the New Poor Law prevailed throughout Nottinghamshire, even during the political excitements of 1837, and the key to maintaining it was the steadiness of the grandees. At a dinner given by the Conservatives of South Notts to Gladstone and Lord Lincoln in February 1837, Sir Robert Bromley attacked the New Poor Law "and tried his best to

123. Gulson to Chadwick, July 10, 1836, Chadwick Papers, UCL. Perhaps Gulson's sense of restraint was partially responsible for Becher living on until 1848. He may have recalled the suicide of the Sutton Courtney overseer (in Berkshire) that resulted from his revelations of the latter's misdeeds. Gulson to Chadwick, February 22, 1835, Chadwick Papers, UCL.
124. Gulson to Nicholls, May 22, 1836, MH 32/28; Earle to Lefevre, June 7, 1835, MH 32/21.
125. Gulson to Nicholls, August 13, 1836, MH 32/28.
126. Gulson to Nicholls, July 8, 1836, MH 12/9228.

make a peg of it upon which to hang political opposition to the party in power." But, as Gulson reported, "his so doing was *coolly* received and was afterwards condemned by almost all of his Conservative friends."[127]

A similar spirit was found in Lincolnshire, though Gulson had to overcome the effects of some of Pilkington's misguided moves and work without the benefit of local magnates in some parts of the county. The poor law unions Pilkington formed in January 1836 in the southern part of the county had started well, partly because of the beneficent influence of the duke of Rutland; but the impending issuance of an outdoor relief prohibitory order by the commissioners a few months later produced considerable consternation. The main reason for this, Gulson reported, was that Pilkington had told his boards of guardians that they had a total discretion to offer relief out of the workhouse. A guardian on the Holbeach board (which had a number of resignations over this issue) had copied down Pilkington's very words: "to the extent of a guinea a week if they chose to do." Consequently, few of the unions had sufficient workhouse capacity, and Gulson recommended an indefinite delay of the order.[128]

This difficulty did not prevent the rest of Lincolnshire from taking readily to the new law. Two vicars from parishes near Boston wrote to Somerset House requesting the immediate formation of a poor law union, one asserting that in the already established Spalding union "the system is found to work so well . . . both in Economy and Discipline, and so calculated to meet the Insubordination and Improvidence of the poor."[129] It was fortunate for Gulson that the local clerical magistrates were favorable, since the uninspiring countryside of the Lincolnshire fens deprived him of the assistance of resident landed magnates:

> Few magistrates and scarcely any Gentry reside in the District, which is altogether flat and fenny; rich and luxuriant indeed for

127. Gulson to Nicholls, February 12, 1837, MH 32/28.
128. Ibid., May 8, 1836.
129. The Reverend John Glover to PLC, May 20, 1836; the Reverend William Bolland to PLC, June 1, 1836, MH 12/6629. Gulson, too, pointed to the alarming breakdown of social discipline in the area. Writing to Chadwick to urge him forward with the rural constabulary inquiry, he exclaimed: "Something must be done and that soon—as regards a police—this country is totally at the mercy of the most disorderly *fen* bipeds I ever beheld." Gulson to Chadwick, September 26, 1836, Chadwick Papers, UCL.

agricultural purposes, but totally devoid of that beauty of aspect which renders a country desirable as the residence of Gentry or landed proprietors.

Though many of the parishes had only been drained and reclaimed in the past thirty-five years, Gulson found that their vestry books revealed some of the earliest examples of the roundsman system. Furthermore, while the labor shortage was such that farmers advertised in the Notts papers, the poor rates were very high.[130] Gulson had grown so accustomed to relying on peers and squires to superintend his unions that he remained uneasy at the prospect of entrusting some of the Lincolnshire boards to parsons and farmers. He need not have worried: Mentioning to Lefevre that in the Boston union "I have no 'big wig' residing," in the same letter he described the opening session of the board as surprisingly cordial and efficient, with good officers chosen and the building of a workhouse resolved upon.[131] Apart from the laborers, the only unhappy element in the new union appears to have been the town of Boston itself. The mayor forwarded a petition drawn up by a town meeting complaining of their underrepresentation on the board. This document pointed out that although Boston had one-third of the total union population, it was to be given only five of the thirty-eight guardians, a disproportion made even worse by the fact that county magistrates could act as ex officio guardians, while those of Boston could not. The commissioners responded by observing that had they attempted to apportion guardians on the basis of the parish with the smallest population (200), then Boston with its 10,000 people would have required fifty guardians.[132]

Another union which got off to a promising start was Sleaford, thanks in part to the active assistance of Earl Winchelsea. That a peer whose ultra-Tory credentials were manifest in a famous duel with the duke of Wellington over Catholic emancipation would cordially cooperate in the implementation of a 'Whig' measure, might come as a surprise to those imbued with the notion that the New Poor Law devastated the local administrative powers of landed magnates. But Gulson, reporting the opening session of the Sleaford board, exulted to Lefevre:

130. Gulson to PLC, August 29, 1836, MH 12/6629.
131. Gulson to Lefevre, September 24, 1836, MH 32/28.
132. John Rawson to PLC, September 9, 1836, PLC to Rawson, September 14,

All the Gentry attended and took a lively interest in the proceedings—Earl Winchelsea is Chairman and Mr. Chaplin (late M.P.) Vice Chairman—a capital Board of Guardians—all as cordial as you can desire—a new workhouse for 200 resolved upon—and I go this day to visit the chairman till Monday.[133]

And to Chadwick, he exclaimed: "We have now the *red hot* Earl Winchelsea as a Chairman—and he is heart and soul with us."[134] The favorable attitude of the vice chairman at Sleaford, the respected Tory M.P. and spokesman for the agricultural interest, Henry Chaplin, was also highly significant in winning over many waverers.[135]

One powerful local Tory leader who remained adamantly opposed to the new system was Colonel Sibthorp, the outspoken M.P. for Lincoln. Quite apart from Sibthorp's intransigence, the county town posed a formidable obstacle because it was the center of an extensive and awkwardly shaped local act incorporation of nineteen parishes. Anticipating great difficulty in securing the dissolution of Lincoln and Grimsby (the other incorporation in the county), Gulson urged Chadwick to do all he could to push the bill giving the commission power to dissolve incorporations without consent: "Pray force this one—or we shall be sadly thrown back and even the Unions near these noxious Incorporations will be incomplete."[136] To Nicholls, Gulson expressed his doubts about procuring the necessary signatures of the Lincoln directors because "Col. Sibthorp and his friends are raising all their forces to prevent the breaking up of their Incorporation."[137] But only a week later he was able to lay before the commissioners the signed dissolution form and the proposal for a "very important Union" centered at

---

1836, MH 12/6629. This episode is an excellent illustration of how well founded were the fears of Nassau Senior about the operation of the clause in the act providing that each parish have at least one guardian. Brundage, "The Landed Interest." p. 33. The problem was particularly acute in Lincolnshire, as Gulson pointed out, because many parishes contained fewer than one hundred inhabitants. Gulson to Lefevre, September 24, 1836, MH 32/28.

133. Gulson to Lefevre, September 24, 1836. MH 32/28.
134. Gulson to Chadwick, September 26, 1836, Chadwick Papers, UCL.
135. An ex officio guardian in the neighboring Newark union described Chaplin as "the best man of business in England . . . tho' he is a tory." G. H. Packe to Lefevre, October 5, 1836, Shaw-Lefevre MSS, HLRO.
136. Gulson to Chadwick, July 10, 1836, Chadwick Papers, UCL.
137. Gulson to Nicholls, August 6, 1836, MH 32/28.

Lincoln, containing sixty-five parishes with a population of 27,000.[138] Whatever the reasons for this sudden and unexpected success, it is clear that Sibthorp's conversion was not among them. While his brother consented (with some misgivings) to become vice chairman of the new union, Colonel Sibthrop remained "so opposed to the whole system" that Gulson had to go personally through every pauper case with the guardians to prevent any inadvertent act of injustice to the poor.[139] Sibthorp's negative posture failed to strike a responsive chord with the other leaders of Lincolnshire society. With the powerful affirmative influence of such peers as the duke of Rutland at Grantham, the marquis of Exeter at Stamford, and Earl Winchelsea at Sleaford, the rest of the squirearchy took an approving or at least neutral stand, and the poor muttered but did not rebel.

Of the various regions of the country, the midlands and East Anglia, as a whole, saw the smoothest implementation of the New Poor Law and the lightest degree of resistance. The reasons for this are not far to seek: The region was overwhelmingly rural, and many parts of it had suffered severely from the maladministration of the old system. Except for the fens, few parts were without local grandees eager to take a leading hand in the establishment of boards of guardians. There were no vast conurbations to mount an effective opposition like that of the London parish vestries. Nor was there that intense regional particularism and jealousy of centralization that prevailed in the north and in Wales. While a northern-style industrial radicalism capable of making noisy resistance was found in Leicester, the other examples of town resistance in the region were closer to the Norwich model—entrenched preindustrial Tory oligarchies fearful of losing their power. At any rate, there were relatively few such trouble spots. More formidable resistance came from the incorporated hundreds and the Gilbert Act and local act unions, but many of the gentry who dominated these local bodies were aware of the advantages of the New Poor Law unions and acquiesced in the dissolution of most of the incorporations. There was a wide variation in the overt reactions of the poor throughout the region, ranging from passiveness in Northampton-

---

138. Ibid., August 13, 1838. The town of Lincoln had 17,000 inhabitants. Grimsby, however, refused to dissolve.
139. Ibid., December 26, 1836 and January 18, 1837.

shire, to limited outbursts in Bedfordshire, to the serious disturbances in East Suffolk. But all such demonstrations were countered
effectively by police and military units summoned by the local
gentry either directly or indirectly through the poor law commissioners.

Perhaps the most significant characteristic of the operation of
the boards of guardians in the midlands and East Anglia was the
determination to administer poor relief with very wide discretion.
Although most ex officio and elected guardians agreed with the
general tenor of the commission's policies on outdoor relief and
workhouse management, they were unwilling to operate on a doctrinaire basis. This posture was apparently independent of the
attitudes toward the act prior to implementation. The ardently
pro-poor law Earl Fitzwilliam was as resolute on having his way at
Peterborough as were the most stubborn Tory guardians of Suffolk.
In general, political affiliation was not an important factor in
determining attitudes. There certainly were tendencies in this direction, especially on the part of lesser Tory squires, but they were
for the most part overcome by the pervasive influence of the leading
Conservative peers. The latter's cooperation was an important key
to the success of the measure, a fact recognized by all the assistant
commissioners as well as by the "tyrants of Somerset House."
Deference to the natural leaders of a still hierarchically structured
society, dependence on a Parliament dominated by the same elements, and the practical necessities of implementing as best they
could a statute deficient in coercive powers, caused the agents of
central government to facilitate the establishment of powerful and
independent new organs of local government.

Chapter VI

Opposition and Consolidation, 1835-1839

The previous two chapters show that the implementation of the New Poor Law was accompanied by a certain amount of resistance by the laborers and a few of their well-to-do sympathizers. But in all the instances described so far, acts of resistance were quickly and decisively countered. By and large, the response of the leaders of society, particularly in the countryside, was positive, and their readiness to exert their considerable local influence in the creation of poor law unions and the operation of boards of guardians was the key to the act's effectiveness in the rural south and midlands. Elsewhere, however, there was somewhat greater opposition, mobilizing hostile sentiments that occasionally bridged social classes and created a crisis for the poor law commissioners and the ministry. This chapter examines the nature and meaning of that resistance and attempts to assess its influence on the pattern of relief policy and the relationship of central government to local government, both of which were clearly established by the time the poor law commission's first five-year term expired in 1839. The violent resistance of certain northern manufacturing towns has drawn the greatest attention from historians, who have depicted the northern agitation as a turning point in the act's implementation—a major setback that blunted the allegedly centralized and Benthamite impetus of the first years of the act.[1] One of the essential tasks in analyzing the impact of the overall pattern of opposition is to put this resistance into perspective. Its importance must be compared, not only with smaller scale outbreaks elsewhere, but with various nonviolent manifestations—in Parliament, the courts, and the press, as well as the silent determination of boards of guardians everywhere to operate with a high degree of flexibility.

The south and west experienced outbreaks of resistance by laborers similar to those already described in Bedfordshire and East Suffolk. In parts of Kent, Buckinghamshire, Devon, and Cornwall, there were spirited if shortlived shows of defiance when the new boards of guardians adopted stricter relief policies.[2] But none of the contagion of the Swing riots materialized, and these incidents actually increased the popularity of the act with most gentry and farmers. As Gilbert reported from Devon:

> If possible it is desirable to avoid the impression the report of a riot against the measure creates—but in other respects a riot is rather desirable—it opens the eyes of the Guardians—and aids the progress of the new system. In the Torrington and other unions there are many men who would never have been induced to carry out the system as they have done but for the riots in those parishes.[3]

A show of military force was sometimes required to quell these riots, but in Kent the eccentric and fearless Major Head was loathe to summon troops. When disturbances spread through the Milton union in May 1835, Head tried to convince the local magistrates and his superiors at Somerset House that to call in soldiers would create adverse publicity. Instead, he summoned a general meeting of laborers at which he planned to face them alone and explain the new system, a technique he had found useful for quelling mutinies in South America. Head was certain he could reason with the rioters, who were "only misguided men, who have risen to oppose they know not what." But the Kent magistracy, led by Lord Camden, brought pressure on the Home Office and Somerset House to

1. See, for example, two articles by Michael E. Rose: "The Anti-Poor Law Movement in the North of England," and "The Poor Law in the North." Nicholas C. Edsall devotes most of *The Anti-Poor Law Movement 1834-44* to the opposition of the north.
2. Edsall, op. cit., pp. 27-40.
3. Gilbert to Lefevre, May 4, 1836, MH 32/26.

cancel the meeting, deal with the riot by force, and administer a rebuke to Head.[4]

In Wales, a somewhat different pattern of opposition emerged. While there was some direct physical resistance by the laborers, many Welsh farmers and gentry also opposed the law and kept up a sullen but dogged opposition on the boards of guardians to commission directives. The Welsh resistance resembled that of the north in that it drew strength from historic regional antipathy to central government and because it claimed exemption from the New Poor Law on the grounds that its economic structure and poor relief system were markedly different from those of the rual south and midlands. When assistant commissioner George Clive began the creation of poor law unions in South Wales in the spring of 1836, he reported the cordial assistance of some of the mining magnates and "enlightened gentry," but noted that the low rates and the alleged absence of able-bodied paupers fostered a widespread opinion "that no advantage would be reaped by the introduction of the new system."[5] Clive described the elected guardians of the Newport union as "either Newport liberty boys or clayheaded farmers," and those from the country parishes in the Clepstow union as "swine," and declared wistfully that "if all the magistrates of the Co. Carmarthen were transported, I should do well."[6]

William Day encountered similar conditions in North Wales and noted "the paucity of country gentlemen to take a lead, and a strong indisposition towards the measure amongst the few who are to be found there."[7] In his initial undertaking, he suffered a severe setback—the attempted dissolution of the Montgomery incorporation. Almost everywhere in England, the necessary two-thirds of the guardians' signatures were garnered through the influence of the landed magnates. But at Montgomery, despite the support of the chairman, Lord Clive (who owned one-fifth of the property in the incorporation), and every magistrate in the room but two, Day was beaten by a vote of eighty-six to forty-three.[8] Though partly

4. Correspondence of Head, the commissioners, Lord Camden, Lord John Russell, and several magistrates from May 5 to 13, 1835, MH 12/5279.
5. Clive to Lewis, March 16, 1836, Clive to PLC, June 1, 1836, MH 32/12.
6. Ibid., May 18 and July 2, 1836, November 24, 1837.
7. Day to PLC, September 1, 1836, quoted in R.A. Lewis, op. cit., p. 177.
8. Day to Sir Edmund Head, December 24, 1836, quoted in R. A. Lewis, op. cit., pp. 177-78.

Welsh himself, Day developed the same prejudice against the inhabitants of the principality as Clive:

> You cannot know the miseries of thirty or forty Welsh Guardians who *won't* build a workhouse, and consequently meet in the parlour of a pot house twelve feet by fourteen and keep all the windows shut and spit tobacco on your shoes—to say nothing of knowing not a word of what they are talking of in an unknown tongue.[9]

After a particularly unfriendly reception at Bala, engineered by the major landowner in the district, Day exclaimed:

> Half Welsh tho' I am myself, yet I confess that if those whom I have lately met, are samples of the ancient Britons, I can but think it a great pity that the Danes did not destroy the whole race. Mrs. Day says they have only so far removed from the savage state as to have lost the only virtue of savages—hospitality.[10]

A more serious incident occurred a few months later at Llanfair in the Llanfyllin union, where the pending termination of paying pauper rents out of rates touched off a violent protest. A menacing crowd of over four hundred laborers surrounded the guardians meeting, pelting the board chairman with mud and rocks when he tried to calm them. A red flag was forced up against the windows, and Day and the guardians were forced to flee the building under a bombardment of eggs and other missiles.[11] Though this demonstration was suppressed, the anger of Welsh laborers continued to smolder until the Rebecca Riots of 1842-43, which were in part a rekindling of overt resistance to the New Poor Law.[12]

To understand the reception accorded the New Poor Law in the north, it is essential to realize that large-scale, well-organized, violent resistance, often considered the "classic" northern response, was confined to a few West Riding and Lancashire textile towns. Elsewhere in the north, even in many towns, the act was either received quietly or with only mild opposition.[13] The violence

---

9. Day to Sir John Walsham, August 9, 1840, quoted in R. A. Lewis, op. cit., p. 180.
10. Day to Lefevre, January 11, 1837, MH 32/14.
11. Day to Lefevre, April 19 and 22, 1837, P.R.O. H.O. 73/52.
12. R. A. Lewis, op. cit., p. 184.
13. See the useful strictures by E. C. Midwinter against making too much of violent northern resistance in op. cit., pp. 24-25.

not only has tended to cloud the vision of some modern historians,[14] it also allowed Chadwick to blame the commissioners for ignoring his advice to begin the implementation of the act in the north. He believed strongly that the most pauperized districts should have been left until last and that the "perfect poor-law weather of 1834-36," attended by good harvests, offered an ideal opportunity for implementing the law in the industrial north.[15] But in arguing thus, Chadwick ignored the fact that the outcry for reform had proceeded from the heavily pauperised south and midlands and that many grandees in that region had begun clamoring for implementing the act near their estates as soon as it passed. For the commissioners to have ignored such requests for two years or more with the excuse that they must begin with the lightly rated and indifferent north would have been politically impossible.

Although northern landed magnates did not have the same financial motives to press for quick implementation as those in the south, they proved a crucially important cutting edge for the new system in many areas. In the spring of 1836, with the rest of the country almost entirely unionized, operations were commenced in Derbyshire and Staffordshire. To prepare his way, assistant commissioner Richard Hall paid visits to several west midlands proprietors staying in London.[16] Lord Hatherton and Earl Talbot proved highly effective in assuring a nonviolent introduction of the act in spite of noisy opposition by the laborers in the Potteries.[17] Much of the support by local peers and gentry was given, like that in the south, in return for major concessions in drawing poor law union boundaries.[18] In the west Riding, the influential Tory Lord Wharncliffe, who was responsible for the harsh bastardy provisions of the law inserted by the upper house, paved the way for the new system. As chairman of quarter sessions, he delivered a favorable address on the act to the magistrates in November 1834.[19] His support was strengthened at one of those pro-poor law country weekends held by the duke of Rutland at Belvoir Castle in 1838, at

14. Finer, for example, claims that the New Poor Law "drove the Northern Counties into a frenzy," op. cit., p. 85.

15. Ibid., p. 115.

16. Hall to Nicholls, May 21, 1836, MH 32/34.

17. *Staffordshire Advertiser,* August 27 and September 3, 1836.

18. Stevens to Lefevre, February 11, 1837, MH 32/68.

19. *Leeds Mercury,* November 1, 1834.

which he found himself seated between Edward Gulson and Robert Lowe of Bingham. Gulson and Lord Wharncliffe worked out the plans for a union of 26,000, two-thirds of it manufacturing, centered on Lord Wharncliffe's parish of Wortley, a few miles north of Sheffield. After the meeting, Gulson wrote excitedly:

> We have agreed upon the Parishes—the centre—the number of guardians—the qualification—and the Rules for Relief. . . . He agrees to become Chairman of the Union—and he also cordially agrees in the building a new workhouse *at once* and of ample dimensions. He has all but fixed upon the situation for the new workhouse and already talks of *"my* Union"—*"my* Board of Guardians"—*"my* Board Room etc."* . . . He said I should "make his house my home." I am confident all will go well in the *Wortley Union* (this seems to sound well I think—the *Wortley* Union).[20]

Another prolaw peer active in the west Riding was Earl Fitzwilliam, who became chairman of the Rotheram union.[21] In Northumberland, the duke of Northumberland extended a lavish welcome to assistant commissioner Sir John Walsham at Alnwick, while Sir James Graham's active exertions in Cumberland were immensely helpful to W. J. Voules.[22] In Westmorland, Voules received a cordial reception from county and borough magistrates in the Kendal town hall, and the local Tory paper reported the meeting sympathetically, noting at the end its report:

> Some silly ridiculous questions were put to the Commissioner by some of the small fry about the mode of electing Guardians, etc., but we pass them by as puerile, unmeaning, and not meriting any notice.[23]

The first union formed in Lancashire, Ulverstone, covered the northernmost part of the county and was launched successfully under the favorable influence of the earl of Derby, the major landowner in the district. The earl of Burlington became chairman of the Ulverstone board of guardians, and Lord Derby donated the land for the workhouse.[24]

20. Gulson to Lefevre, April 14, 1838, MH 32/28.
21. For Fitzwilliam's role as chairman of the Peterborough union, see p. 113.
22. Walsham to Lefevre, July 22, 1836, MH 32/76; Voules to Lefevre, August 22, 1837, MH 32/73.
23. *Westmorland Gazette,* April 23, 1836.
24. Voules to Lefevre, June 16, 1837, MH 32/73. The configuration of the Ulver-

Convening public meetings in northern towns almost always caused apprehension among the assistant commissioners. Until 1837, however, most such assemblies passed off with little more than verbal abuse from the laborers. An exception occurred at Carlisle, where Voules was "most violently assaulted by an organised Mob."[25] On the heels of this incident, Walsham dreaded a meeting he had summoned at Stanhope, because the restiveness of the north combined with "the continuous abuse of the Tory and radical press" led him to anticipate being *"carlisled."*[26] Walsham similarly feared a meeting at Durham composed of fifty Magistrates and gentry and hundreds of ratepayers, but found many parts of his speech cheered while that of an opponent (an eighty-six-year-old former county M.P.) "didn't get a single 'hear'," He nonetheless concluded that it would prove difficult to keep the district quiet.[27]

The greatest apprehension was naturally felt in approaching the center of gravity of the north, the cluster of textile towns in Lancashire and the west Riding. The commissioners realized the combustible nature of the district, with its large, dense population, the well-organized radical agitation for parliamentary and factory reform, recent and bitter trade union agitation, and the presence of skilled leaders and agitators, some of them from the upper classes. The assault had to be planned carefully. In 1835, assistant commissioner James Kay, who had written an influential study of the laborers of Manchester in 1832,[28] was asked for his views on implementing the New Poor Law in the manufacturing districts. He

---

stone union suggests considerable gerrymandering, as do those of several other north Lancashire unions (e.g., Lancaster, Garstang, Clitheroe, and Preston). See the map of the Lancashire unions in Midwinter, op. cit., p. 6. While Midwinter follows the Webbs and others in believing that the criteria for drawing union boundaries were the "rationalising, bureaucratic" ones inherent in Benthamism, he is puzzled that there often "seems to be no rhyme or reason for these artifically built *ad hoc* entities" (pp. 18-19). In Lancashire, as elsewhere, the major factor was probably estate boundaries.

25. Voules to Lefevre, October 1, 1836, MH 32/73.

26. Walsham to Lefevre, November 14, MH 32/76. But the meeting went well, and the ratepayers held a "jollyfication" at the inn for Walsham, where "they drank my health with three times three and one cheer more."

27. Walsham to Lefevre, September 23, 1836, MH 32/76. For Walsham's skillful and smooth establishment of poor law unions in the Newcastle area, see Norman McCord, "The Implementation of the 1834 Poor Law Amendment Act on Tyneside," *International Review of Social History*, 14(1969):90-108.

28. James Kay, *The Moral and Physical Condition of the Working Classes Employed in the Cotton Manufacture in Manchester.*

replied that pauperism in the factory towns was caused by both the "recklessness and improvidence of the native population [and the] barbarism of the Irish Immigrants." Kay held that the New Poor Law could eventually eradicate these evils, but cautioned the commissioners not to "be so sanguine as to expect an immediate result from the application of their orders."[29] In the summer of 1836, Frankland Lewis had Kay confer with Alfred Power about the problems to be encountered when the latter took up the task of establishing the law. Kay reported that he recommended "the Fabian policy" to Power, who appeared "well inclined to a cautious and tentative introduction of the new measures in these difficult manufacturing districts.[30]

When Power commenced operations late in 1836, his methods appeared anything but "Fabian." He recommended the wholesale creation of unions instead of working them up one at a time. This would launch the act "with more dispatch, regularity, and effect" and also provide the machinery for the registration of births, deaths, and marriages required by the 1836 Registration Act.[31] This statute (6 and 7 Will. 4 c. 85) made the poor law unions the registration districts and gave the appointment of the registrars to the boards of guardians, thereby increasing the already significant patronage at the disposal of the guardians.[32] The main impetus for this reform was provided by the grievances of Dissenters, but many northerners thought it a plot concocted by the "Three Bashaws of Somerset House" to lull opposition by creating "registration unions" and adding poor relief functions when it suited them.[33] There appears to be some substance to this charge, because the statute permitted the commissioners to make temporary provision for registration until such time as poor law unions were established. By

29. Kay to Lewis, October 27, 1835, MH 32/48.
30. Ibid., July 3, 1836.
31. Power to PLC, November 25, 1836, MH 32/63.
32. The duties and salary of registrar were bestowed upon the union clerk, the most important figure in the paid local poor law system, who invariably was selected for his services as attorney, election agent, or the like to the dominant figures on the board of guardians. Chadwick complained of the alteration in the bill that gave the appointment of registrars to the local boards, by means of which "a flood of jobs intrigue and Corruption will be let in upon the Guardians, who have hitherto with great difficulty been kept tolerably clear of these vices by the Commissioners." Chadwick to Lord John Russell, July 3, 1836, Chadwick Papers, UCL.
33. A petition from Oldham labeled this approach a piece of "low cunning and deceit," PLC Minutes, May 6, 1837, MH 1/11.

acceding to Power's suggestion for wholesale creation of unions, they fostered the belief that the registration act was a Trojan horse, all the more attractive because of the large Dissenting population in the north.

For the resentment thus engendered to erupt into violence, however, required a concatenation of other circumstances. First of all, the manufacturing areas were hit by a severe trade depression starting at this time. The generally full employment picture in the north gave way abruptly as mills and other businesses had to shut down and tens of thousands were thrown out of work.[34] These conditions persisted over the next several years, resulting in mass misery and desperation that fueled both the militant anti-poor law movement and Chartism. Another factor that encouraged effective militant resistance in the manufacturing areas was the existence of units of organization and agitation—the short time committees dedicated to the passage of the ten hours bill. Finally, the north had talented, vigorous, and outspoken leaders who did not shrink from righteous defiance of the "Poor Man's Robbery Bill"—Richard Oastler, John Fielden, the Reverend G. S. Bull, Joseph Rayner Stephens, and Feargus O'Connor being the most prominent. The tactics employed varied from town to town and according to circumstances, but the movement had its greatest strength outside the large cities, in towns like Huddersfield, Todmorden, Bury, Keighley, Bradford, Preston, Bolton, and Oldham. The tactics ranged from attempting to prevent the elections of guardians to securing the election of opponents of the law, intimidating the new boards from appointing clerks, physically harassing poor law officials, and fighting large-scale pitched battles with police and troops.[35]

Power's response to these outbursts was a growing vindictiveness and determination to force the law on the dissident areas. Throughout the first half of 1837, he insisted that press reports of the resistance were greatly exaggerated, hoping that the commis-

34. In part, the depression arose from a failure of the banks in the United States, where a large amount of British capital was invested. As early as October 1836, Gulson reported that President Jackson's message (the "Specie Circular") which burst the speculative American frontier bubble, ruining many British as well as American creditors, had triggered a severe crisis in Sheffield, Rotheram, and Nottingham. Gulson to Lefevre, October 19, 1836, MH 32/28.
35. The best narratives of this resistance are: Midwinter, op. cit. and the superb biography of Oastler by Cecil Driver, *Tory Radical: The Life of Richard Oastler.*

sioners would continue to support his exertions.[36] By summer, however, the government called for a retreat. Lord John Russell told the commissioners that it was impossible to implement the act in an "excited community" and that they should wait at least a year in towns like Huddersfield. Moreover, he admonished them, a House of Commons select committee had been appointed, and one of its purposes was to determine if the act should be applied to the north at all.[37] It must be realized, however, that the select committee was not appointed solely or even mainly because of northern opposition. It was established in response to the wide and complex array of resistance movements, violent and nonviolent, found in various parts of the country as well as within Parliament. One of the most interesting and important of these was the resistance of several London parishes to the New Poor Law.

During the passage of the bill, the government had been particularly concerned to avoid alienating the metropolis, and Althorp had been dissuaded from exempting London only with the greatest difficulty.[38] As with the north, the commissioners deferred bringing London under the act until the heavily pauperised rural south and midlands were fairly launched. The first union formed near London was Hendon, and Mott was able to report that no strong opposition had been voiced in a four-hour meeting with the magistrates, proprietors, and overseers of the district.[39] There had been apprehension over widespread metropolitan resistance when, barely a month after the formation of the poor law commission, a deputation from Old Tower Without appeared at Somerset House asking that the parish be left alone.[40] But most of the other metropolitan deputations appeared simply to obtain information, while one (St. John's Hackney) requested the commissioners' interference.[41] The unionization of much of the area proceeded with deceptive calm-

36. He claimed, for example, that the *Leeds Mercury* grossly overrepresented the violence of the Huddersfield anti-poor law meeting. Power to Nicholls, January 15, 1837, MH 32/63. In contrast, another assistant commissioner in the north, at the very same time was urging a measured policy because of the economic crisis, the bad harvest, and severe weather. W. J. Voules to Lefevre, January 21, 1837, MH 32/73.
37. Russell to PLC, June 26, 1837, P.R.O. H.O. 73/52.
38. See p. 57.
39. Mott to PLC, March 23, 1835, MH 32/56.
40. PLC Minutes, September 26, 1834, MH 1/1.
41. Ibid., September 30, November 6, December 16, 1834.

ness through the early part of 1836, leading the commissioners to accept Mott's optimistic assessment:

> On the whole I may say the different Boards are proceeding favorably and the New Law has been introduced into the Metropolitan Parishes with much less difficulty than had been anticipated, and with a certainty of complete ultimate success. Instances are now very rare of violent opposition to the introduction of the new system; prejudices yield to the startling facts brought to light, and the extraordinary beneficial effects, produced in all districts where the rules and regulations of the commissioners have been introduced.[42]

Two months later, however, he moderated his views to the extent of admitting that although there was little objection to the rules of relief, there was considerable objection to the electoral system of the New Poor Law.[43]

Plural voting, which had raised the hackles of pro-poor law London radicals like Francis Place and Joseph Hume, caused a setback for the law in the capital in 1836. The trouble began in March, when the commissioners ordered the parish of St. Pancras, organized for poor law purposes under a local act of 1819, to reconstitute itself under the 1834 law and elect a twenty-man board of guardians in place of its forty-man board of directors. Henry Bulwer-Lytton, one of Marylebone's two Liberal M.P.s, appeared at Somerset House to protest the order, but was told nothing could be done.[44] A few weeks later he and his colleague, Sir Samuel Whalley, stressed the danger of attempting to enforce the election,[45] but the commissioners went ahead, with Alfred Power appointed as returning officer. Amid considerable excitement, a board was elected, but the new guardians were all former vestrymen and refused even to elect a chairman. After conferring with Lord John Russell and taking legal counsel, the commissioners applied for a writ of mandamus to compel the guardians to perform their duties.[46]

St. Pancras fought back in the courts, winning an important victory in the Court of King's Bench in January 1837. The judges

42. Mott to PLC, May 28, 1836, MH 32/56.
43. Ibid., July 28, 1836.
44. PLC Minutes, March 22, 1836, MH 1/5.
45. PLC Minutes, April 16, 1836, MH 1/6.
46. PLC Minutes, July 9 and 25, October 11 and 31, 1836, MH 1/7.

ruled that the commissioners were not empowered to direct parishes relieving their poor under local acts or Hobhouse's Act to elect guardians according to the 1834 law.[47] This reverse caused no end of trouble at Somerset House, where hostile deputations and petitions increased markedly. Tottenham, Edmonton, Woolwich, Mile End Old Town, St. Andrews Holborn, St. George the Martyr, and Lambeth all sought either exemption from the voting system based on the St. Pancras decision or changes in the composition of the poor law unions.[48] Some of these parishes sought a judicial remedy, but few were as successful as St. Pancras.[49] Nonetheless, the spirit of resistance manifested by some London parishes, along with the opposition in the north and elsewhere, contributed to the modification of the law during the course of 1837 and 1838.[50]

The appointment of a select committee at the beginning of 1837 grew not only out of dramatic encounters in the streets and courts but also out of a growing stream of critical petitions presented to Parliament and the activities of the law's opponents in Parliament. In 1835, petitions and questions criticising various parts of the law, often citing the separation of man and wife in the workhouse, were presented by A. J. Roebuck, Charles Hindley, William Cobbett, John Walter, Sir Samuel Whalley, Lord Teynham, and the duke of Buckingham.[51] The last of these was taken quite seriously by the government because of the high standing of the duke and his heir,

47. The King v. the Poor Law Commissioners for England and Wales, January 30, 1837, *Law Journal Reports,* N.S., VI, 114-18. The humiliation of this defeat for the commissioners was underscored when they had to apply to the treasury to pay the printer for the nomination and voting papers after St. Pancras refused to pay the bill. PLC Minutes, April 29, 1837, MH 1/10.

48. PLC Minutes, April 8, 1836, MH 1/6; February 11, 1837, MH 1/9; April 18, 1837, MH 1/10; May 18, 1837, May 26, 1837, MH 1/11.

49. On the issue of uniting parishes, the judges of King's Bench declared that the commissioners could indeed "unite parishes having local acts for the government of the poor, without the consent of the trustees or guardians or rate-payers of such parishes." The King v. the Poor Law Commissioners for England and Wales (in re the Whitechapel Union), *Law Journal Reports,* N.S., VI, 232.

50. In 1838, James Kay complained that in many London parishes the board members were "Pickwickians"—the old parochial vestry transformed into a board of guardians. Consequently, he concluded: "The administration of the law in London is . . . as unsatisfactory as it can well be. The remedy is—the reeducation of the Board of Guradians—at least in the principles and details of parochial management. This is a most difficult task!" Kay to Lefevre, September 21, 1838, MH 32/50.

51. *Hansard,* 3rd ser., 26(1835):596-602 (March 6); 26(1835):1056-73 (March 17); 26(1835):154-55 (March 24); 27(1835):357-59 (March 27); 27(1835):1025-28 (May 12); 27(1835):1052-54 (May 13, 1835); 27(1835):1194-96 (May 19); 29(1835):426-30 (July 10); 29(1835):715-20 (July 20, 1835).

the marquis of Chandos, among gentry and farmers throughout the country. He presented a petition from the Buckinghamshire parish of Stoke Poges, which objected to being included in a union and protested against splitting married couples in the workhouse. The assistant commissioner in Bucks, W. J. Gilbert, stressed the need for a good reply to his petition,[52] but the cabinet's response dismayed many poor law officials. Russell wrote to Somerset House to emphasize the "great importance" of the petition, and the commissioners replied that while Stoke Poges must remain in the union, the aged and infirm "should be treated with care and tenderness and not of necessity be forced into the Workhouse, as they now generally are, in preference to the sturdy and able-bodied Pauper."[53] This spirit of concession informed the reply given by Lord Brougham that evening, in which he denied it was the intention of the act's framers to separate man and wife.[54] While Gilbert believed such a conciliatory spirit had some effect in moderating Lord Chandos' view of the act, neither the duke nor the duchess (the "gray mare," as Gilbert called her) was won over.[55]

Similar petitions continued during 1836 and began to affect some previously favorable opinion.[56] Richard Hall wrote that in the east midlands the complaints of severe administration in Bucks were evoking an unfavorable response from staunch friends of the measure. Earl Howe was about to write Somerset House while the countess sent Hall a lengthy letter detailing cases of hardship and suffering. Lord Howe's close connection with the king might also cause a reversal of royal approval for the act, which so far had been an important factor in securing acceptance for the new system. Hall concluded:

> I confess I am apprehensive that friends will cool and foes revive, unless some proof is given, that it was the intention of the framers of

52. Gilbert to Lewis, March 15, 1835, MH 32/26.
53. PLC Minutes, March 17, 1835, MH 1/2.
54. *Hansard,* 3rd ser., 26(1835):1061-73 (March 17). For the dismayed reaction of some of the assistant commissioners to Brougham's speech, see pp. 95-96.
55. Gilbert to Lefevre, June 14, 1835, MH 32/26. Two years later, the duke wrote assistant commissioner W. H. T. Hawley that "every hour's experience increases my objection to the principle of the measure and the mode of administering it." Duke of Buckingham to Hawley, October 6, 1837, MH 32/39.
56. See, for example, *Hansard,* 3rd ser., 31(1836):943-46 (February); 31(1836):1136-38 (March 2); 34(1836):1289-91 (July 6).

our Act, and is the endeavour of those to whom its execution is committed, to mitigate as much as possible the hardships which cannot altogether be avoided.[57]

Fortunately for the commissioners, neither the king nor any of the favorable magnates became outright opponents. This steadiness was reflected in the leadership of the Conservative party. Sir Robert Peel continued to give his support to the act, and his reception of the assistant poor law commissioner in Warwickshire was courteous and helpful. Peel invited Richard Earle to dinner at Drayton Manor to meet the local magistrates and delivered a "formal, though *very* kind and business-like speech," in which he stressed the advantages of poor law unions but "studiously avoided any eulogy" of the poor law commission.[58] The duke of Wellington was an even stronger partisan of the law and sometimes responded more fervidly to attacks in the House of Lords than any members of the government.[59] But in an age before mass party organization and discipline, the attitudes of party leaders could not prevent considerable anti–poor law politicking by Tory gentry and farmers in many parts of the country. Henry Goulburn, who had served as home secretary in Peel's short-lived government of 1834-35, expressed his concern that the poor harvest of 1836 would stimulate further opposition:

> There is everywhere a strong party opposed to this Poor Law. They make but little noise at present but they are acquiring strength. To espouse the cause of the Poor is naturally popular and it is difficult to make people see the advantage of the ultimate result while every one can see the immediate sacrifice. . . . I should not at any time be surprised if the approval or disapproval of the Poor law were to be made generally as it has been made at Warwick a test for Parliamentary representation.[60]

57. Hall to Nicholls, March 1836, "Private," MH 32/34.
58. Earle to Lefevre, January 16, 1836, MH 32/21.
59. See his reply to Bishop Philpott's presentation of hostile petitions from the north alleging the cruelty of the law. *Hansard*, 3rd ser., 37(1837):851-52 (April 7). The assistant commissioner had worked very closely with the duke's steward in Hampshire respecting the inclusion of the fifteen parishes of the Strathfield Saye estate in the Basingstoke union. Colonel A'Court to Lefevre, March 3 and 19, May 10, 1835, MH 32/2.
60. Goulburn to Peel, September 2, 1836, Peel Papers, B.M. Add. MSS 40,333, ff. 360-63.

In a contest that was an embarrassment for the leaders of both parties, the two candidates in the Warwick by-election of 1836 opposed the New Poor Law.[61]

By the beginning of 1837, the uneasiness of the country's political leaders disposed them to grant a hearing to the complaints of the opponents. In February, John Walter moved the appointment of a select committee, a motion that received considerable advance publicity in the *Times*. From Cornwall, Gilbert wrote that the hostile newspapers had been briefed by Walter and pressure was being brought on all the local M.P.s and guardians.[62] In South Wales, Clive was taunted by many guardians with the prospect of humiliation of the poor law commission by the committee.[63] In the debate on Walter's motion, the government's defense of the law was based on the assertion that the New Poor Law was not an act of centralization but rather one that strengthened local control. Furthermore, the new system was said to be one in which the character of applicants was an important consideration. In a statement that deserves to be quoted at length, Lord John Russell declared that all talk of the destruction of local government

> was a gross misrepresentation of the Poor-law Act, the real object of which was to establish self-government—a principle found to be so useful in all matters of local concern. What was the case formerly? The idle labourer, complaining of the overseer who refused him relief, went to some distant magistrate and made out his false tale of distress. The magistrate, knowing nothing of the matter, made an order for relief, ignorant of what the effect would be. But what was now the case? The magistrate was now a member of the Board of Guardians; he met his brother guardians at the board, where they conferred together as to the actual facts of each case; and where the pauper merited relief they granted it to him, while the impostor was detected and turned adrift. . . . The consequence was, that a kind of local government was established, acting certainly under such general rules and general directions as the intelligence and experience of

61. The Tory, Charles Canning, narrowly defeated the Liberal candidate, Henry Hobhouse. Canning, son of the former prime minister, was to attain cabinet office under Peel, a peerage, and the post of governor general of India. His opponent was the brother of Sir John Cam Hobhouse, at that time serving as president of the board of control in Melbourne's cabinet. For a predictably gleeful interpretation of this contest, see *The Times*, August 24, 1836.
62. Gilbert to Lefevre, February 18, 1837, MH 32/27.
63. Clive to Lewis, March 9, 1837, MH 32/12.

the Poor-law Commissioners had prescribed, but with respect to details, acting according to the judgment of the magistrates, country gentlemen, the farmers, and the ratepayers connected with the district.

Russell agreed to the select committee but insisted that the house amend Walter's motion, which had simply specified an inquiry "into the operation of the Poor-law Amendment Act." Russell's amendment called for inquiry into the administration of relief "under the orders and regulations issued by the Commissioners appointed under the provisions of the Poor-law Amendment Act."[64] Walter's motion would have permitted a direct probe of the actions of boards of guardians, but under Russell's amendment attention was to be directed when necessary toward the regulations emanating from Somerset House. If Cobbett had still been living, he might well have repeated his charge that the commissioners were "three red herrings."[65]

The twenty-one members of the select committee were appointed on February twenty-seventh, but Walter complained that seventeen of them were known advocates of the law and "there was not a single Member who was personally connected with the manufactures of the country." He suggested the addition of six members, including Thomas Attwood and Major Beauclerk, to which Russell offered to replace himself with one of the six.[66] In spite of the pro-law composition of the committee, Walter hoped to use it to publicize the cruelties of the law. Walter was reportedly dismayed on inspecting the Abingdon workhouse to find such "order, regularity, and *comfort*," but said that "no facts" would alter his opinion.[67] Poor law officials were understandably nervous about the coming ordeal. Gulson, in obvious anxiety over his pending appearance as a witness, appealed to Nicholls:

64. *Hansard*, 3rd ser., 36(1837):1032–34 (February 24). In supporting Russell, Joseph Hume agreed that the act was one of local government, the only drawback to which was the system of plural voting and ex officio guardians, ibid., c. 1052.

65. See p. 63. Cobbett had died in June 1835.

66. *Hansard*, 3rd ser., 36(1837):1280–87 (March 6). One of those on Walter's list, James Freshfield, was added to the committee March twenty-first on another member's retirement.

67. Gulson to Nicholls, March 1837, MH 32/28. Earlier in the year, Richard Hall had reported that Walter was "much disappointed" to find no flagrant abuses during an inspection of the Berkshire workhouses. Hall to Nicholls, January 16, 1837, MH 32/35.

Pray do not let us lose credit—or allow the cause to suffer from any want of *effort* on the part of *the whole staff*. We only require *the truth* to be shewn—but we ought to have the *whole truth*. I would rather sit up for these two months day and night—and travel from one end of the kingdom to the other over and over again—than that any portion of the *whole truth* should be lost to the detriment of the great cause in which we are engaged. No effort should be spared.[68]

Chadwick was concerned with more than his own performance as a witness. After three weeks of hearings, he expressed his anxiety about Russell's relative lack of knowledge about "the details of the proceedings under the Poor Law Commission" to Lord Howick, wishing that Howick were on the committee.[69] Howick agreed that hostile witnesses were not being pressed hard enough and hoped that Chadwick could produce some "industrious labourers" who would attest to the benefits of the new system.[70]

Among the sixty-four witnesses who gave testimony during the next three months were sixteen laborers, though not all of them were favorable to the law. The remaining witnesses included Chadwick, three assistant commissioners (A'Court, Hawley, and Gulson), and an assortment of guardians, union clerks, workhouse masters, relieving officers, clergy, and others.[71] The topics investigated included the formation of poor law unions, the effect on wages of prohibiting outdoor relief to the able-bodied, medical relief, pauper burials, workhouse dietaries, separation of man and wife in the workhouse, and charges of abuse or neglect by workhouse masters and relieving officers. An example of the inquiry that touched on several of these topics involved the Westhampnett union in Sussex, of which the duke of Richmond was chairman. One witness charged that control of the board by the Richmond interest was ensured since the vice chairman, the deputy chairman, and seven other guardians were the duke's tenants, while the union clerk was his solicitor and agent. Sir James Graham, later described by Peel as the chief defender of the New Poor Law on the committee, forced the witness to admit his dislike of ex officio

68. Gulson to Nicholls, March 1, 1837, MH 32/28.
69. Chadwick to Lord Howick, March 28, 1837, Grey MSS, Department of Palaeography and Diplomatic, UD.
70. Howick to Chadwick, March 31, 1837, Chadwick Papers, UCL.
71. *Sess. Papers* (Commons), "Report from the Select Committee on the Poor Law Amendment Act," 1837, 17(pt. 2):555-645, hereafter cited as "Index to the Report."

guardians generally.[72] Graham blunted some further hostile testimony after the committee had been told by a Westhampnett guardian, William Field, that when the children of one Charlotte Legg died in the workhouse, the duke refused to allow her to leave the corpses there till the next day. Field quoted the duke as saying "he could not let the living go without the dead." But Graham got Legg herself to testify, and she denied that Field had been present and stated that the duke had spoken kindly to her.[73]

While other damaging testimony was not countered quite so effectively, the impression created was that the abuses were isolated examples of mismanagement by workhouse masters and local paid officers. Russell's insistence on investigation of poor relief under the orders of the commissioners proved its usefulness. It provided a more complicated chain of authority and responsibility which made it possible to absorb even proven cases of cruelty without harsh criticism of the local boards. The poor law commission was there to buffer the shock. For this reason, Walter again tried to change the terms of the investigation. When Russell moved to continue the inquiry after Sussex to Hampshire, Wiltshire, Kent, Staffordshire, and Gloucestershire, he was careful to include the expression "under the Poor Law Commissioners." Walter moved to amend it to "the operation of the Poor Law Amendment Act."[74]

The committee's further investigations were cut short by the death of William IV on June twentieth, 1837. The king's passing, in addition to removing one of the strongest proponents of the New Poor Law, necessitated a dissolution of Parliament and new elections in which the anti-poor law movement was certain to play a role. It also required the hasty drawing up of the select committee's report. When the report was nearly complete, Walter moved four resolutions that he realized had no chance of passing but hoped would influence the elections:

1. That outdoor relief shall be administered at the discretion of the Guardians.

---

72. Ibid., QQ. 16509-36. Peel to Croker, December 13, 1838, C. S. Parker, *The Life and Letters of Sir James Graham,* 2:435.

73. *Sess. Papers* (Commons), "Report from the Select Committee on the Poor Law Amendment Act," 1837, 17(pt. 2): QQ. 14232-319.

74. Ibid., pt. 1, p. 223. Walter's amendment was defeated by twelve to four.

2. That the Committee do recommend a limitation of the size of the unions; and that no union shall extend beyond the distance of eight miles from the centre, or from the place where the board of guardians meet.

3. That the officiating clergyman in every Parish be ex officio a Guardian.

4. That the discretion allowed to Magistrates of ordering outdoor relief to aged persons shall be extended also to the amount of relief to be given.[75]

To no one's surprise, the committee reported favorably on the act; but the report did allude to cases of hardship and called for closer vigilance to prevent cruelties, and greater flexibility in granting outdoor relief. They also mentioned without censure the practice of some boards of admitting children into workhouses without compelling their able-bodied parents to enter—a practice in violation of commission orders. The highest praise was bestowed on the boards of guardians—"boards so constituted must bring to the consideration of cases connected with the circumstances and character of the poor, a degree of intelligence and experience utterly unknown before, except in a few rare instances."[76] The allusion to the "character" of the poor recalls Russell's speech in agreeing to the investigation, and further underlines the difference from the Benthamite idea of poor relief, which was to be self-acting and to exclude the consideration of character. The central board was mentioned only briefly at the end of the five-page report:

> The authority of the Poor Law Commissioners has, in the opinion of Your Committee, and as far as they have had an opportunity of observing it, been exercised with great discretion. A more difficult task could scarcely have devolved on any department of government.[77]

Before the report was in print, the election campaign was well under way. The commissioners were anxious about the political

75. Ibid., pp. 3-4. The third resolution recalls the identical provision in Chadwick's original bill. See p. 33.
76. Ibid., p. 11.
77. Ibid., pp. 11-12.

impact of the anti-poor law movement and carefully monitored the reports of their assistants. For Chadwick, the election was doubly eventful, for Earl Fitzwilliam promised him the reversion of the family borough of Malton in Yorkshire.[78] That he would consider leaving his post at Somerset House indicates the frustrations of serving under the commissioners (especially Frankland Lewis) as well as his persistent ambition for recognition and advancement. Gulson, who was chiefly responsible for making the arrangements with Fitzwilliam, teased Chadwick with "how shall I describe your politics? Shall I say you are a Tory?" Chadwick's sense of humor, thin at the best of times, completely deserted him. He replied stiffly and indignantly that he was certainly not a Tory, though he preferred the Tories "over the Radicals of the Cobbettite school."[79] The plan came to nothing when Fitzwilliam's heir, Lord Milton, lost in Northamptonshire and had to fall back on Malton.

Despite the fears of the government and the poor law commissioners, the New Poor Law did not figure prominently in the election. In most areas, candidates of both parties had little or nothing to say about the law, and the Tory attack centered on such issues as O'Connell, tithes, and the malt tax. Nonetheless, there was a spirited use of anti-poor law sentiment by candidates in some places. In certain other constituencies, even when the candidates tried to remain silent on the issue, the crowds around the hustings (often composed mostly of nonvoters) shouted their hatred of the law. The timorous Colonel A'Court wrote that such sentiments were strong in Portsmouth, Weymouth, and Shaftesbury. Some hostile post boys overturned his coach in Wiltshire, but he was "lucky enough to escape with trifling injury."[80] Sir Harry Verney, a Whig M.P. for Buckingham and chairman of the Buckingham poor law union, complained to Lefevre that he nearly lost the election because of his ardent support of the measure: "Alas—alas—your conservative friends have indeed forgotten themselves in this anti Poor Law

78. Finer, op. cit., pp. 133-34. Finer incorrectly states the constituency to be "South Molton."

79. The correspondence begins with Gulson to Chadwick, July 15, 1837, Chadwick Papers, UCL. Gulson had to explain that calling Chadwick a Tory had been a joke, "fancying that it was so out of the question that you would not suppose it possible I should thus estimate your opinions."

80. A'Court to Lefevre, July 19, 1837, MH 32/3; July 15, August 1 and 4, 1837, MH 32/4.

cry."[81] The voters of Maidstone elected Benjamin Disraeli after he had delivered one of the most forceful speeches of the campaign in which he declared that "this Act has disgraced the country more than any other upon record."[82] In East Cornwall, Sir Charles Lemon and E. W. W. Pendarves, the Liberal M.P.s who were also chairmen of poor law unions, noted the anti-poor law placards used by the Tories in the election and lamented that some of their own powerful supporters were hostile to the law.[83]

These instances were unusual in southern England—most elections in rural constituencies were more like those in Northamptonshire. In south Northants, the two Tory M.P.s, Sir Charles Knightley and W. R. Cartwright, were returned unopposed, and both were firm supporters of the new law.[84] In the northern half of the county, neither of the Tory winners, T. P. Maunsell and Viscount Maidstone, was anti-poor law. In the borough of Northampton, the losing Tory, Charles Ross, spoke as warmly in favor of the law as the two Liberal victors, Robert Vernon Smith and Raikes Currie.[85] Berkshire is another case in point: The first county to be unionized, it was also the seat and constituency of John Walter, the act's most vocal critic. But Walter chose not to run in 1837. Chadwick later claimed that he withdrew because a canvass had revealed that "the determination to vote against him on account of his conduct on the Poor Law Question was so extensively prevalent that he stood no chance of being returned."[86] During the election, Russell used this taunt in an address to the voters of Stroud, where he and Poulett Scrope won handily over an anti-poor law Tory.[87] Stung by such charges, Walter published a letter to the voters of Stroud in *The Times* denying the charge and asserting that in the Berkshire election "the New Poor Law was no more the object of discussion,

---

81. Verney to Lefevre, August 10, 1837, Shaw Lefevre MSS, HLRO. Verney had previously urged the government to exclude anti-poor law magistrates from the new commissions of the peace to be issued on Victoria's accession, thus removing them from the boards of guardians. Verney to Lefevre, July 1837.

82. W. F. Monypenny and G. E. Buckle, *The Life of Benjamin Diaraeli,* 1:374.

83. Pendarves to Lefevre, September 3, 1837, Shaw Lefevre MSS, HLRO.

84. Brundage, "The Landed Interest," pp. 36-37.

85. *Northampton Mercury,* July 22 and 29, August 4, 1837.

86. Chadwick to Lord John Russell, October 12, 1837, Chadwick Papers, UCL.

87. By 1837, Scrope was a supporter of the New Poor Law and, like Russell, a member of the select committee. Russell's speech had been punctuated with cries of "No Poor Law Act," and he stated his willingness to accept any change that "would render the condition of the poor less uncomfortable." *The Times,* July 25, 1837.

and had no more to do with the issue of the election, than the Alcoran or the laws of the Gentoos."[88] Even this was an admission that his fellow gentry did not share his concerns about the law's cruelties. Furthermore, it should be noted that the Conservatives replaced Walter with Viscount Barrington, who was strongly pro-poor law and a vigorous chairman of the Faringdon union.

As was expected, the noisiest electoral challenge to the act came in the north, but it was not as widespread or successful as the government had feared. In Westmorland, while two Lowthers stood unopposed, their proposer "most violently attacked the Poor Law," responding to which E. W. Hasell, the pro-poor law chairman of the West Ward union, "merely coldly acknowledged" that he approved "some parts of the law."[89] This was typical of many northern constituencies—vituperation from the law's enemies, lukewarm endorsement by its friends. There was, naturally, a more heated atmosphere in the manufacturing areas, but the results were hardly a mandate against the act. Richard Oastler failed twice in 1837 to win the Huddersfield seat. In May, he narrowly lost a by-election to Edward Ellice and in the general election was beaten by W. R. C. Stansfield, both of them pro-poor law Whigs. The results were close, but the Whigs triumphed in spite of wholesale intimidation of the voters by excited anti-poor law crowds.[90] A close west Riding election occasioned considerable violence on both sides, but a Tory opponent of the law, J. S. Wortley, lost to the Whig candidates, Lord Morpeth and Sir George Strickland. It is true that Morpeth proclaimed the act was inapplicable to the manufacturing areas, but Strickland declared the law "founded on humanity and kind feeling."[91]

A major reason why opponents of the New Poor Law could not make significant gains in the election was that the alliance between the Tories and the radicals, which had given the movement formidable strength, was already beginning to crumble. While it still held together in places like Huddersfield (but was nonetheless

88. Ibid., August 8, 1837. In the election of 1835, Conservative party leaders had been reluctant to secure support for Walter. Wellington to Peel, January 2, 1835, B.M. Add. MSS, 40,310.
89. Voules to Lefevre, August 3, 1837, MH 32/73.
90. Driver, op. cit., pp. 344–50, 357–60.
91. *The Times,* July 20, 1837. At Huddersfield, the two Whigs were hissed and booed, and bread and cheese (the exact quantity specified in one of the commission's workhouse dietaries) were thrust at them on the end of a fork.

unable to secure Oastler's return), it had disintegrated at Leeds. The radical *Leeds Times* commended Oastler as a kindly and well-meaning man but pointed out that he was "a fanatical Churchman and a Winchelsea Tory" and called for support of the Liberal candidates Baines and Molesworth.[92] The result was that the antipoor law Tory banker, Sir John Beckett, who headed the poll in the 1835 election, finished last. Northern radicals were becoming increasingly aware of the absurdity of the Tory-radical alliance, since most Conservatives (including party leaders) did not share their views on such topics as the New Poor Law, while those who did (like Oastler) held unacceptable views on other issues. When this perception was coupled with a full realization that most voters under the 1832 franchise did not embrace radical principles, Chartism was the consequence. The Chartist movement in turn created an impassable barrier between radicals and anti-poor law Tories, leaving men like Oastler isolated—discountenanced by the leaders of their party and ignored by the masses they once led.[93] It is true that anti-poor law Liberal M.P.s like John Fielden, who was elected again for Oldham, retained an important role in opposing the act, but Chartism also eroded their position somewhat.

An assessment of the overall importance of the 1837 general election must distinguish between the government's loss of seats in the House of Commons and the more diffuse effects of the campaign on the policies of the boards of guardians and the government's support of the poor law commission. The Whigs lost an estimated twenty-three seats, the majority of them in English counties, and maintained control in Victoria's first Parliament only with the support of Irish and Scottish M.P.s.[94] Few of these losses were directly attributable to the anti-poor law cry. Chadwick argued that only a handful of seats had been lost for that reason, and Russell agreed that it was probably not more than one or two.[95]

---

92. Driver, op. cit., p. 347.

93. Ibid., pp. 390-414. In 1839, Charles Mott described a conversation with Oastler in which the latter reiterated his opposition to the law but admitted that the Conservative party wouldn't change it. The duke of Wellington told Oastler that "he was determined to support the New Law." Mott to PLC, May 9, 1839, P.R.O. HO 73/55, "Private."

94. Norman Gash, *Reaction and Reconstruction in English Politics, 1832-1852*, p. 164.

95. Chadwick to Russell, October 12, 1837, Russell to Chadwick, October 16, 1837, Chadwick Papers, UCL. *The Times,* which would heve been only too happy to show that the New Poor Law had hurt the Whigs, made no such claim.

The home secretary was nonetheless furious with the opposition, whose "cry against the Poor Law exceeds anything in Tory profligacy known before."[96] While this was unfair as a general indictment, it is true that Tories in some districts had used the cry to their advantage. The effects in such places are to be seen not in Whig losses but in candidates shunning the act at the hustings. As Alfred Power reported from Manchester: "I fear the elections may have done us some mischief—as many of the Whig candidates have spoken of the law not being applicable to the north."[97] Although such opposition was often perfunctory and made only to assuage public clamor, the fact that a number of Whigs had publicly criticized the act created some uncertainty as to the degree of support the poor law commission might expect from the new Parliament.

More serious than a slight erosion of support in Parliament was the effect on boards of guardians. From York, John Revans reported that practically all poor law work had ceased because "the clerks to the Unions have been engaged as election Agents."[98] In Cheshire, assistant commissioner R. D. Neave reported considerable backsliding in all the poor law unions and spent ten days "meeting the mischief stirred up by the Election Committees."[99] In itself, the election turmoil would have had only a temporary impact on the policies of the local boards, but in conjunction with the report of the select committee and an expectation of that body being reappointed when the new Parliament met in November, the effect was significant—and not only in the north. Chadwick, who gave little importance to the election, complained to Lord Howick that the committee's report

has revived the hopes of the abettors of the allowance system; and in many of the unions in Berks, Bucks, Kent, and Gloucester a tendency to an increase of expenditure is now manifested. The assistant com-

---

96. Russell to Howick, August 16, 1837, Grey MSS, Department of Palaeography and Diplomatic, UD. He told the prime minister that the conduct of the Tories in using the anti-poor law clamor was "the most disgraceful of which any party was ever guilty." Russell to Melbourne, August 13, 1837, Russell Papers, P.R.O. 30/22/2F, fo. 10.

97. Power to Nicholls, July 27, 1837, MH 32/63.

98. Revans to Chadwick, August 6, 1837, MH 32/65.

99. Neave to Lefevre, September 17, 1837, MH 32/59. By year's end, however, Neave reported that the "ground recovered since the General Election is greater than I anticipated." Neave's quarterly report ending December 31, 1837.

missioners who have great difficulty in withstanding it ascribe the increase to the tenor of the Committee's report.[100]

In a letter to the duke of Richmond, Chadwick claimed that while the anti-poor law cry affected only a handful of close contests in the election, the committee's report "has been a severe blow."[101]

Chadwick and other advocates of a strict construction of the order prohibiting outdoor relief found more than the tone of the report discouraging. Even more disturbing was the action taken by the poor law commissioners in revising the order to meet some of the concerns of the select committee. On August sixteenth, a new circular was drafted at Somerset House that gave wider discretion to boards of guardians. While reiterating the general ban on outdoor relief to the able-bodied (including women) and their families, it provided exceptions based on the policies already adopted by many boards of guardians for (1) cases of sudden and urgent necessity, (2) sickness, (3) unavailability of workhouse accomodation, (4) widows, and (5) able-bodied laborers married before August 1834, some of whose children might be admitted to workhouses. The circular pointed out that the poor law commission had already, in many instances, sanctioned the admission of some of the children of able-bodied laborers into workhouses, a concession which "has induced them [boards of guardians] to support more willingly the general principle of the Rule." The commissioners stated they would feel "more confident" in explicitly sanctioning these exceptions because of the select committee's report.[102] The assistant commissioners were asked for their opinions on the draft of the

100. Chadwick to Howick, September 7, 1837, Grey MSS, Department of Palaeography and Diplomatic, UD. Howick's reply disagreed with this harsh verdict and ended with the hope that "the worst is now over and that firmness on the part of the Commissioners united with discretion will secure to the country the inestimable benefits the act is calculated to produce." Howick to Chadwick, September 15, 1837, Chadwick Papers, UCL.

101. Chadwick to the duke of Richmond, September 4, 1837, Goodwood MSS, 1585, fo. 72, West Sussex Record Office.

102. PLC Minutes, August 16, 1837, MH 1/12. The chief pressure on the select committee for allowing boards of guardians to admit some children of able-bodied laborers into workhouses came from William Miles, Tory M.P. for Somerset and chairman of quarter sessions. So powerful was his influence in the west country that assistant commissioner Robert Weale refused Chadwick's request that he attempt to get the Somerset and Gloucestershire boards to denounce Miles' resolution. Weale to Chadwick, June 4, 1837, Chadwick Papers, UCL.

circular, and not all were pleased with it. Daniel Adey called the exemption for widows a "serious departure from correct principle"; on receiving children of the able-bodied into workhouses, he presumed the commissioners would not have "entertained it for a moment" but for the committee's report.[103]

On October twenty-fourth, the commissioners reviewed their draft circular in the light of the assistants' comments. They rejected the latter's advice that the "sudden and urgent necessity" exception for outdoor relief to the able-bodied be available to overseers only, not boards of guardians. They did follow the recommendations that the exception on sickness be restricted to heads of families and that on unavailability of workhouse space be deleted as unnecessary. Most assistants accepted the wisdom of an exemption for widows, but strongly criticized allowing some children of able-bodied laborers to be admitted into workhouses while their parents received outdoor relief. Many assistants and guardians in the south and midlands, where the peremptory order had been in force for nearly two years, expressed "the strongest reluctance to yield the ground which has with so much difficulty been gained." Most of the assistants in other areas, however, thought the exception essential, recognizing the "necessity of yielding to public opinion." The commissioners decided to omit this exception for unions already operating under the order but apply it elsewhere. They also followed assistant commissioner Wade's suggestion in making commission approval a condition precedent rather than a condition subsequent, and by having the exception operate only through the end of 1839.[104]

Despite this partial restoration of some degree of rigor to the new order, Chadwick was convinced the effect of the circular would be ruinous. In a lengthy and ably argued memo to the home secretary, he claimed the exemptions constituted relief in aid of wages and signaled a return to the abuses of the Old Poor Law. He concluded:

> But the greater question after all is one of principle. Is the statute of the 43 Elizabeth still binding and operative? Or have the Commissioners the right to extend the practice of giving relief in aid of wages to persons who do not use an ordinary and daily trade of life to get their living by?—or to persons who have some means to maintain

103. Adey to PLC, August 23, 1837, MH 32/6.
104. PLC Minutes, October 24, 1837, MH 1/13.

them? This is the largest question which they perhaps had brought before them for consideration.[105]

Russell agreed, at least in regard to the exception on able-bodied laborers' children and got the commissioners to suspend the issuing of the order.[106] Assistant commissioner Hawley congratulated Chadwick,[107] but this turned out to be premature. Several weeks later, Colonel Wade pointed out that in Essex the boards were increasing outdoor relief to the able-bodied and quoted the most zealous of the Essex chairmen, a clergyman, that "the Report of the Commons Committee is rung in my ears by all my Clerical Friends.[108]

The attitude of the poor law commissioners during these proceedings might appear unduly timorous unless the political constraints under which they were operating are considered. First of all, their five-year term would expire in 1839, and they were anxiously contemplating the fate of a renewal bill. Furthermore, they thought that if they did not moderate the prohibition of outdoor relief, Parliament would do it instead. Describing the genesis of the circular of August 1837, Nicholls said that he and Lefevre had worked it up and gotten Frankland Lewis' approval, thinking it "well to yield a little to the pressure." Their fear, according to Nicholls, was that if Parliament enacted the exceptions in statutory form, the poor law commission's influence would be destroyed.[109] From the start, the commissioners were denied the wholehearted support of the Whig government. This can be seen in the earlier reluctance to sanction the appointment of more assistant commissioners.[110] It was also evident in the government's unwillingness to introduce remedial legislation requested by the commissioners on such matters as increasing their power to dissolve Gilbert Unions, dissolve or add to existing poor law unions, change the numbers of guardians for parishes in a union, or compel the building of workhouses.[111] This lack of support was more painfully manifested by a

105. Undated memo by Chadwick, P.R.O. HO 73/53.
106. PLC Minutes, November 6, 1837, MH 1/13.
107. Hawley to Chadwick, November 5, 1837, Chadwick Papers, UCL.
108. Wade to PLC, November 26, 1837, MH 32/74.
109. Nicholls to George Cornewall Lewis, July 26, 1839, Russell Papers, P.R.O. 30/22/3c, ff. 381-82.
110. See p. 84.
111. PLC Minutes, June 2, 1836, MH 1/6; February 24, and March 2, 1837, MH 1/10. A'Court to Lefevre, January 19, 1837, MH 32/4.

refusal to alleviate the desperately overcrowded, uncomfortable, and unhealthy conditions at Somerset House. Somerset House was a labyrinth of chambers, many connected only by long and convoluted routes. Intraoffice communications often involved traversing several flights of steps to accomplish the most routine task. Many of the clerks were confined to garrets—freezing in winter and stifling in summer—and consequently a great many fell ill. The commissioners made repeated requests for better accomodation, and in a memo of August 1837, Chadwick claimed that several cases of consumption among the clerks (one of them fatal), were due to the conditions of the office and that rooms and passageways were so cluttered with papers that it was impossible to classify them.[112] The absolute refusal of the government to correct these conditions was not likely to make the commissioners feel optimistic about their long-term prospects.

Finally, the commissioners were fearful that the select committee, which had been reestablished when the new Parliament met in November, might produce a report even more detrimental than the last. Considerable gloom prevailed in the early months of 1838, both at Somerset House and among the assistant commissioners. Hawley reported from Sussex that relief was becoming increasingly lax, "in a great measure from the anomalous position in which the Commission is placed by the appointment of a Committee of inquiry, and their consequent inability to act with the firmness and decision they could desire."[113] Hall reported a similar erosion in Leicestershire and concluded: "I am convinced that every new Board of Guardians will be found to be worse informed and less tractable than that which preceded it, and that the intelligent and firm supporters of sound principle will be a decreasing minority."[114] William Day passed on to Somerset House a despairing letter from a pro-poor law magistrate in Montgomeryshire which declared that rates were not being collected, none of the

112. PLC Minutes July 19, 1836, MH 1/7; August 25, 1837, MH 1/12.
113. Hawley to Lefevre, January 18, 1838, MH 32/39. He expressed to Nicholls his fear that the select committee would bolster the doctrine of discretionary power, "which once granted gives a death-blow to the Poor Law." Hawley to Nicholls, January 24, 1838, MH 32/39.
114. Hall to Nicholls, February 2, 1838, MH 32/35. He told Lefevre: "Already I perceive that the Administration is becoming a matter of tradition, and is not supported by a constant reference to the written law. Principles are not safe under such circumstances." Hall to Lefevre, March 27, 1838, Shaw-Lefevre MSS, HLRO.

other magistrates would act, and that all chairmen would have to be made "Government responsible officers—or the whole concern will go off in smoke and turn to deeper dust than before."[115] In the north, the act was advancing on a grueling union by union basis, with the commissioners suffering some sharp reverses, particularly at Todmorden.[116]

Spirits revived somewhat with the crushing defeat of John Fielden's motion to repeal the New Poor Law on February twentieth. First to reply for the government in the debate was Lord Howick, who ably recapitulated the arguments of the royal commission and reminded the house of the horrors of the Swing riots.[117] Russell and Peel also made good speeches, and the division was 309 to 17.[118] Of the nineteen repealers (including the tellers), twelve represented northern and midlands industrial towns. Not a single county member was in the minority, and only one from London.[119] Two other developments in Parliament during the session served to bolster morale at Somerset House. The first was the passage of the Irish Poor Law (1 and 2 Vict., c. 56), which established a system there similar to that of England and Wales. Its enactment not only implied a vote of confidence in the English Poor Law but also could be expected to mitigate somewhat the problem of destitute Irish in England, hitherto without any system of public relief in their own land to fall back upon. The second welcome development was the complete exoneration of various administrators from charges of cruelty by a House of Lords select committee chaired by Lord Wharncliffe. This committee investigated allegations of cruelty made by Earl Stanhope, the Reverend G. S. Bull, and others, and declared the commissioners and boards of guardians blameless, though they did suggest that relieving officers have less discretion in the granting of relief.[120]

Still, the House of Commons select committee attracted the great-

115. Captain Thruston to Day, January 24, 1838, MH 32/14.
116. Midwinter, op. cit., Chapter 7.
117. *Hansard,* 3rd ser., 40:(1838):1374-89 (February 20).
118. Ibid., cc. 1408-10, 1413-16.
119. This was Thomas Wakley (Finsbury) who, after Walter's retirement from the select committee, was the most vigorous anti-poor law voice on that body.
120. *Sess. Papers* (Lords), "Report from the Select Committee on the Poor Law Amendment Act," 1837-38, 19(Pt. 1):3-12. For a recent debate on the "cruelty" issue, see David Roberts, "How Cruel Was the Victorian Poor Law?"; Ursula Henriques, "How Cruel Was the Victorian Poor Law?"

est attention, and poor law officials continued to worry about the investigation and the report. Although the majority of its members were favorable to the law, John Fielden, Thomas Wakley, and T. L. Hodges were among the most able and energetic opponents. Even among the pro-poor law committee members were men of a critical cast of mind and considerable influence—G. Poulett Scrope, Edward Baines, and William Miles. Chadwick was pleased that Lord Howick was on the committee, but this gain was offset by the absence of Sir James Graham. Moreover, the investigation this session was to turn to implementation in manufacturing districts. An array of witnesses similar to those called the year before, including four assistant commissioners (Gulson, Hall, Power, and Kay), were closely questioned on the workings of the new system. The report, issued on August second, praised the performance of the poor law commissioners and their assistants but called for "a less strict construction of the words 'general rule.'" The report declared the implementation of the law in the manufacturing areas to be satisfactory, but the evidence to support this noted that in Nottingham, strict rules had been relaxed when necessary and an outdoor labor test substituted. The prohibition of outdoor relief to the able-bodied was supported "subject to such occasional departures from the general rule, under the pressure of special circumstances, as it appears that the local boards have been ready to adopt, and the Commissioners to sanction, in cases of real necessity." The committee approved the practice of allowing the aged and children to leave the workhouse to visit friends and exercise, and gave a qualified approval to taking some of the children of able-bodied laborers on outdoor relief into workhouses. Also recommended were changes in contracting for medical service, drawing medical and relief districts within unions (inconveniently large in some cases), and bastardy ("with a view of inflicting some punishment for the crime of seduction"). Finally, there were two items the commissioners had been trying to get the government to deal with by remedial legislation—their power to appoint district auditors and to reconstitute poor law unions without the consent of two-thirds of the guardians (but with the consent of the parishes to be transferred).[121]

Somerset House wasted no time in drafting new bills to carry out

121. *Sess. Papers* (Commons), "Report of the Select Committee on the Poor Law Amendment Act," 1837–38, 18(pt. 1):11–40.

these two recommendations, but the government once again refused to introduce them.[122] Despite the appearance of support by the committee, the tenor of the report and some of the specific recommendations further undermined the position of the advocates of a rigid workhouse test. Two days after the publication of the report, assistant commissioner Daniel Adey pointed out that the protracted inquiry "has occasioned our best friends to relax considerably in their attention to particular cases as well as to sanction a higher rate of relief to the outdoor aged and infirm and the sick."[123] The chairman of the select committee, J. N. Fazakerley, wrote Lefevre about the "utmost jealousy" felt in some quarters regarding the commission's authority and suggested bestowing "a little flattery and condesencion" on the boards of guardians. "It is most important," he warned, "that this feeling should subside before the mention of the renewal of your Powers comes on in Parliament."[124]

As this ordeal approached, the Somerset House establishment was in considerable disarray. Nicholls was sent to Ireland in the summer of 1838, and Frankland Lewis, worn out by the cares of office and shattered by his wife's death, was to resign in December. Both of these changes seemed an opportunity for Chadwick to gain a board post at long last. In July, he sent off a lengthy memo to Russell setting forth his claims and reminding the home secretary of the promises made at the time of his appointment as secretary.[125] To bolster his case, Chadwick argued that, contrary to Nicholl's assertion that six more assistant commissioners were needed for Ireland, these could be spared from England. In fact, he went on, with larger districts in England (and the appointment of district auditors), perhaps eight or nine could be eliminated, at a saving of nearly £10,000 per annum.[126] Evidently, this memo was the basis of Russell's refusal to sanction Nicholls' request, for he told the commissioners that the number of assistants in England was "at present rather larger than necessary."[127] Probably Chadwick be-

122. PLC Minutes, August 14, 1838, MH 1/15.
123. Adey to PLC, August 4, 1838, MH 32/6.
124. Fazakerley to Lefevre, August 26, 1838, Shaw-Lefevre MSS, HLRO.
125. Chadwick to Russell, July 2, 1838, Chadwick Papers, UCL.
126. Chadwick to Russell, July 27, 1838, Russell Papers, P.R.O. 30/22/3B, ff. 217-22. S. E. Finer cites this letter (op. cit., p. 185) to support his claim that Chadwick was fighting to prevent a reduction in the number of assistant commissioners, but Chadwick's intent was clearly the opposite.
127. Russell to PLC, August 11, 1838, Chadwick Papers, UCL. Four assistants were reassigned from England to Ireland—Gulson, Hawley, Earle, and Voules.

lieved that such an economy-minded approach would increase his chances of securing a commissionership from the hard-pressed government, but he was disappointed. No fourth commissioner was named—Lewis and Lefevre were to carry on their duties in London while Nicholls operated out of Dublin. Chadwick's hopes revived with Frankland Lewis' retirement in December, only to be dashed again. The appointment went to George Cornewall Lewis, a man who came to share his father's intense dislike of the secretary and reluctance to embrace strict principles of poor law administration.

The "Chartist Year" of 1839 was not propitious for a poor law commission renewal bill to be brought forward by any government, especially one as feeble as Lord Melbourne's. The strength of the ministry had been sapped by electoral losses in 1835 and 1837, by Althorp's retirement to the country as Earl Spencer, Brougham's exclusion from the cabinet, defections over Church issues, wrangles with restive radical and Irish supporters, and the vexations of coping with an economic depression and rising militancy of the laborers. The government's spirit was broken; ministers went through the motions, sustained in power principally by the young queen's infatuation with Melbourne. This was demonstrated clearly by the ludicrous "Bedchamber Crisis" of May 1839, in which Victoria alone prevented the assumption of power by the Conservatives.[128]

In the hopes of making the continuation bill more palatable, the government introduced it late in the session, and in conjunction with one to mitigate the rigors of the bastardy clauses by restoring affiliation proceedings before petty sessions.[129] It nonetheless encountered stiff resistance. During the second reading in the House of Commons, most speakers opposed the bill, the strongest denunciations being delivered by Colonel Sibthorp, Wakley, Fielden, Duncombe, and Thomas Attwood.[130] But while these men all wanted complete repeal of the law, most opponents of the bill agreed with W. S. Blackstone, a Tory M.P. for Wallingford, who alleged that the law worked well when the guardians enjoyed complete discretion. Even some of those arguing for the bill, like L. W. Buck, Tory M.P. for North Devon and chairman of the Bideford

128. Elie Halevy, *The Triumph of Reform 1830-1841*, pp. 240-44.
129. Henriques, "Bastardy," p. 117.
130. *Hansard*, 3rd ser., 49(1839):353-68 (July 15).

poor law union, declared that guardians should enjoy discretion in administering outdoor relief.[131] Russell delivered a very short, lackluster speech in which he agreed to shorten the time extension to one year (the original bill would have extended the commission's life nearly three years). The only spirited defenses of the law and the commissioners' policies were delivered by two northern Liberal M.P.s—Mark Philips of Manchester and Philip Howard of Carlisle.[132] Many opponents were persuaded to vote for the second reading by Russell's concession.

Further onslaughts against the measure were made during the committee stage. Henry Liddell, a Tory member for North Durham, voiced the sentiments of many when he declared that the poor law commissioners had been useful in establishing the boards of guardians, but "now that the machinery had been organised and put in motion all over the country, he could not conceive that the central board was necessary for any good purpose."[133] An instruction to the committee to add a clause that legalized taking the children of able-bodied laborers married before 1834 into workhouses was carried against Russell's opposition, and he declared it "a matter of such importance" as to require a delay of over a week.[134] When proceedings resumed, Russell introduced the clause, but a stronger amendment, to allow such relief to those married after 1834 as well, was carried, with Lord Howick and Graham in the majority and Peel voting with Russell in the minority, although this was shortly reversed.[135] Pressed by Nicholls not to enact the exemption, Russell asked Cornewall Lewis if the commissioners would publicly acknowledge their willingness to sanction such a departure from their rule and to put this in the form of a circular to the boards of guardians. Lewis agreed, as did Nicholls.[136] Armed with this concession, Russell was able to counter what would certainly have been a successful attempt to carry the clause. The seconder on this occasion was a Tory M.P. for East Norfolk, H. N. Burroughes, whose poor law union James Kay had praised before the select

131. Ibid., c. 358.
132. Ibid., cc. 357, 366.
133. Ibid., c. 555 (July 20).
134. Ibid., c. 584.
135. Ibid., cc. 965-72 (July 29).
136. Nicholls to Lewis, July 26, 1839, Lewis to Russell, July 31, 1839, Nicholls to Lewis, August 3, 1839, Russell Papers, P.R.O. 30/22/3C, ff. 381-82, 391-92, 395-96.

committee as "one of the best managed in the County of Norfolk."
Burroughes asked Russell to drop his opposition to the clause since
"the peremptory order of the commissioners had never been acted
upon in that union [and] the guardians had always exercised the
discretionary power now asked for."[137] Russell refused, but managed to mollify Burroughes and others and secure the defeat of the
clause by telling them of his communication with the commissioners, who "had no objection to relax their peremptory order whenever it should be represented to them by the guardians, that they
wished to take one or more children of able-bodied labourers into
the workhouse."[138]

Thus the essence of the 1837 circular, which Chadwick with great
difficulty had succeeded in delaying, was promulgated, but its
importance was more symbolic than real. From the beginning,
most boards of guardians had operated with a high degree of
autonomy, exploiting the loopholes provided in the statute and the
prohibitory orders, as well as the commissioners' reluctance to
enforce anything unacceptable to "respectable" public opinion. The
assertion that the failure of the law lay in the inability of Somerset
House to draft workable orders and the reluctance of local boards to
apply them begs the question.[139] This impasse was inherent in the
structure and operation of the English political system: Leaders of
the landed interest, who controlled most boards of guardians, also
dominated Parliament. They made the law, they were implementing the law, and they had the power to change the law whenever
they saw fit. They created the poor law commission to establish the
local machinery and to provide a means of disseminating information and encouraging greater strictness during the first years of the
new law, when the process of disciplining the laborers and lowering the rates would prove most difficult. Once this initial period was
successfully completed (as it was in the south by 1836 or 1837), the
value of a central commission in the eyes of many proponents of
the New Poor Law was considerably lessened. Parliament grudgingly extended the commission's life, for a year in 1839 and in

137. *Hansard*, 3rd ser., 50(1829):101 (August 8). Burroughes also quoted Kay's
testimony about the need to permit discretion to the local boards. Kay had emphasized this in his reports to Somerset House. See p. 124.

138. Ibid., c. 103.

139. These are the reasons assigned for the continuation of outdoor relief and the
allowance system after 1834 by Michael E. Rose, "The Allowance System under the
New Poor Law."

1840 and for five years in 1842, most members recognizing some residual utility in the commission, while for party leaders there was the added motive of the patronage afforded to the government.

Although there would be additional disputes over the wording of the commissioners' orders through the 1840's, the pattern of the relationship between central and local government was clearly defined by 1839. With more than 90 percent of the country operating under the New Poor Law, it was obvious that the initiative and active working of the law lay with the local boards. Poulett Scrope, who had criticized the bill in 1834, noted approvingly in the *Quarterly Review* ten years later:

> We believe the Amended English Poor Law to work well for all classes, but especially for the poor themselves, *when well administered by its officials.* And by this term we do not mean the much-abused 'Somerset House Triumvirate;' but the guardians and their paid subordinates, the relieving officers, workhouse governors, and medical officers.[140]

Chadwick, whose doctrinaire approach to the poor laws was offset only intermittently by the gleam of political reality, was excluded from real power, though his talents and roles as a scapegoat were exploited by the government. The rejection by government, Parliament, and country, of the doctrinal nostrums of the 1834 report and bill was best explained by assistant commissioner Edward Twistleton in 1839. The major impediment, he declared, was

> the peculiar character of the English people. Of all nations which have been remarkable in the history of the world, they have manifested the most singular backwardness in carrying out principles to their remote legitimate consequences. They always stop short, and rest content with realizing a moderate practical good, leaving it to men whom they call theorists to point out greater advantages within their reach. . . . I see in this peculiarity of character a practical difficulty which will embarrass the Poor Law Commissioners in every further measure which they may recommend; and which will prevent the future progressive improvement of the Unions from corresponding with the sanguine anticipations of many benevolent men.[141]

---

140. [G. Poulett Scope], "Poor Laws for Scotland," p. 126. This article, a review of the report of the royal commission on the poor laws in Scotland and other works, has been reprinted in A. W. Coats, ed., *Poverty in the Victorian Age,* vol. 4.
141. Twistleton to PLC, November 4, 1839, MH 32/72.

Chapter VII

Conclusion

Any summation of the findings of this book must take into consideration a larger historical process of which the New Poor Law is considered a part—the nineteenth-century "revolution in government." In addition to poor law reform, the 1830's and 1840's saw major parliamentary initiatives in reforming and regulating such other activities as factories, mines, asylums, education, public health, police, and the emigrant passenger trade. Attempts to analyze this process and to explain its origins have produced a vigorous controversy among historians. A marked features of this debate is the assumption that the New Poor Law, along with the other reforms of the period, was an act of centralization, and the argument has principally turned on whether the dynamic was supplied by Benthamism, Evangelicalism, or humanitarianism.[1]

One way to approach these questions is by analyzing the differences between poor relief and other governmental functions. Clearly, some activities, by their very nature, were amenable to central government control. These were the technical problems attending rapid industrialization and urbanization, including some

---

1. The major contributors to this debate are A. V. Dicey, J. B. Brebner, S. E. Finer, Oliver MacDonagh, David Roberts, Henry Parris, Jenifer Hart, L. J. Hume, Robert Gutchen, and William C. Lubenow, whose books and articles are listed in the bibliography. It is true that Lubenow, in his *Politics of Government Growth,* rejects both Benthamism and centralization as features of the New Poor Law. But his concept of politics is confined entirely to the words and deeds of members of Parliament, and he is thus unable to explain the dynamics of reform other than as the "incrementalist politics" of cautious government leaders.

problems of industrial pollution and activities like the emigrant passenger trade, and their solution did not come into conflict with powerful entrenched interests. Regulation of factories, mines, railways, and public health did have some important interests standing in the way of central control, but not to the same degree as poor relief, which was the area of the greatest involvement by the dominant interest group in society. The poor laws, which were vitally important in maintaining the economic ascendancy of peers and gentry, had been a major field of legislation and administration for centuries. Some areas, like control of factories, were newer, and in others, like public health, earlier governmental activity only remotely foreshadowed nineteenth-century practice. Another factor is the amount of technological and scientific expertise required for the solution to a problem—from this viewpoint, poor relief appears to be on the opposite end of the spectrum from control of industrial pollution. These considerations suggest the need for a typology of areas of government growth, incorporating the factors mentioned, to replace the explicit or implied models of government growth now in use. Using such criteria as whether an activity was a traditional area of government involvement, the amount of technological expertise required, and above all its relationship to the power centers of the society, some problems appear to have been amenable to a centralized solution based on Benthamism. These same perspectives suggest why the New Poor Law was nonrevolutionary and owed little to Benthamism. Its purpose and result were to reorganize and strengthen the power of the country's traditional leaders over their localities.

That such a reorganization of social control became necessary and possible in the 1830's testifies to the serious crisis in the relationship between rich and poor, particularly in the countryside, that was evident by 1815. From the viewpoint of landed leaders, this crisis took the form of an increasingly numerous, truculent, and work-shy peasantry who sent poor rates spiraling at a time of agricultural depression. When thwarted in their demands for relief, the poor responded by appeals to liberal magistrates, intimidation of parish officers, and, most ominously, attacks on property. Reforming magistrates and parishes seemed powerless to make much headway against dense and discontented nests of pauperism, while such optional administrative expedients as select vestries were of limited effectiveness. By the 1830's, there was a new willingness to accept a comprehensive reform, the need for which was underscored by the Swing riots.

The system fashioned by parliamentary and local leaders between 1832 and 1839 was indeed effective in restoring social cohesion and labor discipline and lowering the rates, though not without some violent confrontations with the poor. This restoration was due almost entirely to the effectiveness of the new boards of guardians, rather than to the central commission or the operation of such doctrinaire prescriptions as the workhouse test. The latter was never applied comprehensively. Local boards, many of whose leaders were members of Parliament, insisted on the freedom to use the workhouse as one of many options in their case-by-case dealings with pauper applicants. This was occasioned in part by their discovery that outdoor relief to the able-bodied and their families was cheaper than institutionalization and in part by the survival of a certain degree of paternalist sentiment. In the last years of the Old Poor Law, paternalism had often seemed to emanate from the disruptive wilfulness of some "poor man's J.P.," who defied the policies of fellow magistrates and parish overseers alike. Under the New Poor Law, there was corporate activity—granting a traditional form of relief, albeit at lower levels and partly in bread, to the "deserving poor" of a district by a board composed of the leading landowners and farmers. This continuity of outdoor relief was one of the major factors in winning over many who had initially adopted a hostile attitude toward the law because of its supposed interference with paternalistic discretion.

These considerations left very little room for theorists and officials to maneuver. All were obliged to play the political game, which is to say operate within the constraints of the power structure. Edwin Chadwick was no exception to this rule, though his recognition of it was intermittent. As a royal commissioner, he certainly displayed a willingness to bring some of his Benthamite doctrines into conformity with the policies of an aristrocratic government, particularly with the constitution of the boards of guardians. He apparently believed that such an accomodating posture would both secure his appointment as a poor law commissioner and give him a free hand to abolish outdoor relief with the workhouse test, a policy he never ceased to embrace. For years he endured the vexations of serving as the commissioners' secretary, in the vain hope of receiving the next appointment to the board. Chadwick was a curious blend of dedicated social reformer, ambitious political intriguer, and inflexible doctrinaire, who grievously overestimated the government's need for his services.

The profile of relief policies and the lines of authority remained remarkably constant throughout the nineteenth century. In towns as well as rural districts, four-fifths of those supported wholly or partly out of the poor rates were on outdoor relief. The union workhouse was relegated to the status of a general asylum for the very old, the very young, and the infirm. It was also useful as a residual deterrent against insubordination. It does seem that in many unions the early active involvement of peers and gentry tended to decline, leaving the routine tasks of administration to the elected guardians, who were drawn chiefly from the ranks of the better-off tenant farmers:[2] But the disengagement of the ex officio guardians did not entail a loss of control. Because poor law unions had often been drawn in conformity with their estate boundaries and the property qualifications and plural voting system ensured the return of "respectable" elected guardians who were often their tenants, the magistracy continued to exercise a corporate domination of relief policies.[3] Moreover, landed magnates continued to benefit from the system of parish chargeability, which the 1834 act did not change. Nor were they adversely affected by the Union Chargeability Act of 1865 (28 and 29 Vict., c. 79), which spread the burden of poor relief evenly on all ratable property in a union. The very effectiveness of the New Poor Law in reducing the "surplus population" by 1865 led to a rural labor shortage—a situation in which the financial advantages of owning close parishes were superseded by the need for a more efficiently dispersed labor force.[4]

Significant alterations in the system began only at the end of the century. The Local Government Act of 1894 (56 and 57 Vict., c. 73) abolished ex officio guardians and eliminated property qualifica-

2. Anne Digby, "The Rural Poor Law," p. 153.
3. I develop these points at greater length in "The Landed Interest and the New Poor Law: A Reply," a response to a critism of my 1972 article made by Peter Dunkley, "The Landed Interest and the New Poor Law: A Critical Note."
4. For the operation of the system of settlement and removal up to its final elimination in 1948, see Michael E. Rose, "Settlement, Removal, and the New Poor Law."

tions, plural voting, and proxy votes for elected guardians. It thus ended the formal control of boards of guardians by landed magnates, but it by no means deprived them of all influence, nor did it fundamentally alter the policies pursued by most boards since 1834.[5] More important than this change in the constitution of boards of guardians was the gradual supplanting of the poor laws by new social legislation. The ultimate dissolution of the system described in this book was effected during the half-century between the first Workmen's Compensation Act of 1897 and the full-fledged welfare state adopted after World War II. This period witnessed continued population growth and urbanization along with the revolutionary impact of modern transportation and communications. England's landed leaders, their powers eclipsed as a result of these processes, were no more capable of preventing the establishment of new structures of "poor relief" than they were of preventing the new forms of national political organization which replaced the hierarchical localism of the nineteenth century.[6]

5. See Brundage, "Reform of the Poor Law Electoral System, 1834-94." For an interesting discussion of powerful but unsuccessful efforts to inject a spirit of deterrent vigor in the waning years of the New Poor Law, see Rachel Vorspan, "Vagrancy and the New Poor Law in late-Victorian and Edwardian England."
6. D. C. Moore, *The Politics of Deference.*

Bibliography

Primary Sources

Manuscript Materials

London, Public Record Office

Russell Correspondence. Correspondence of Lord John Russell, 1834-39.

Home Office Papers. HO 73/51-55. Correspondence with poor law commissioners.

Poor Law Commission Papers

Commissioners' Minute Books:

MH 1/1-16—Official Minutes, 1835-39.

Correspondence with boards of guardians:

MH 12/5279—Milton union.

MH 12/6581—Market Harborough union.

MH 12/6629—Boston union.

MH 12/6657—Bourn union.

MH 12/8828—Peterborough union.

MH 12/9228—Basford union.

MH 12/9411—Newark union.

MH 12/16727—Potterspury union.

Assistant Commissioners' correspondence:

MH 32/1-4—Charles Ashe A'Court.

MH 32/5-6—Daniel Adey.

MH 32/12—George Clive.

MH 32/14—William Day.
MH 32/21—Richard Earle.
MH 32/26-27—W. J. Gilbert.
MH 32/28—Edward Gulson.
MH 32/34-35—Richard Hall.
MH 32/39—W. H. T. Hawley.
MH 32/48-50—James Kay.
MH 32/56—Charles Mott.
MH 32/59—Sir Richard Digby Neave, Bart.
MH 32/60—Sir William Parry, K.C.B.
MH 32/63—Alfred Power.
MH 32/65—John Revans.
MH 32/66—Edward Senior.
MH 32/68—Thomas Stevens.
MH 32/69—E. C. Tufnell.
MH 32/72—Edward Twistleton.
MH 32/73—W. J. Voules.
MH 32/74—Colonel Thomas Wade.
MH 32/76—Sir John Walsham, Bart.
MH 32/85—Robert Weale.

Althorp

Spencer Papers.

Bedfordshire Record Office

Russell Estate Correspondence.
Lieutenancy Correspondence.

Oxford, Bodleian Library

Russell of Swallowfield MSS.

London, British Museum

Peel Papers.
Place Papers.

London, House of Lords Record Office:

Shaw-Lefevre MSS.

Aberystwyth, National Library of Wales

Harpton Court MSS.

Northamptonshire Record Office

Fitzwilliam MSS.
Peterborough Union Minute Book

University of Durham, Department of Palaeography and Diplomatic

Grey of Howick MSS.

University College, London

Brougham Papers
Chadwick Papers

University of London, Goldsmith's Library

Nassau Senior's MS Diary of the passing of the Poor Law Amendment Act

West Sussex Record Office

Goodwood MSS.

Printed Sources

Sessional (Parliamentary) Papers

1819, vol. 2, "Report from the House of Commons Select Committee on the Poor Laws."
1830, vol. 4, "Report from the House of Commons Select Committee on Select and Other Vestries."
1834, vol. 27, "Report from His Majesty's Commissioners for Inquiring into the Administration and Practical Operation of the Poor Laws."
1834, vols. 28-29, Appendix A, "Reports of Assistant Commissioners."
1834, vols. 30-34, Appendix B1, "Answers to Rural Queries."
1834, vols. 35-36, Appendix B2, "Answers to Town Queries."

1834, vol. 37, Appendix C, "Communications."

1834, vol. 38, Appendix D, "Labour Rate"; Appendix E, "Vagrancy"; Appendix F, "Foreign Communications."

1835, vol. 35, "First Annual Report of the Poor Law Commissioners."

1836, vol. 29, "Second Annual Report of the Poor Law Commissioners."

1837, vol. 31, "Third Annual Report of the Poor Law Commissioners."

1837-38, vols. 17-18, "Report from the House of Commons Select Committee on the Poor Law Amendment Act."

1837-38, vol. 19, "Report from the House of Lords Select Committee on the Poor Law Amendment Act."

1837-38, vol. 28, "Fourth Annual Report of the Poor Law Commissioners."

1839, vol. 20, Fifth Annual Report of the Poor Law Commissioners."

1840, vol. 17, "Sixth Annual Report of the Poor Law Commissioners."

Miscellaneous

Becher, J. T. *The Anti-pauper System.* Second edition. London: W. Simpkin and R. Marshall, 1834.

[Chadwick, Edwin.] "The New Poor Law." *Edinburgh Review* (July 1836):487-537.

Cowell, J. W. *A Letter to the Rev. John T. Becher.* London: James Ridgeway and Sons, 1834.

Day, William. *An Inquiry into the Poor Laws and Surplus Labour.* Second edition, enlarged. London: James Fraser, 1833.

Dod, Charles R. *Electoral Facts from 1832 to 1853 Impartially Stated* (1853). Reprinted with an introduction and bibliographical guide to electoral sources, 1832-1885 by H. J. Hanham. Hassocks, Sussex: The Harvester Press, 1972.

Extracts from the Information Received by His Majesty's Commissioners as to the Administration and Operation of the Poor Laws. London: B. Fellowes, 1833.

Garnier, Thomas. *Plain Remarks upon the New Poor Law Amendment Act, More Particularly Addressed to the Labouring Classes.* Winchester: Jacob and Johnson, 1835.

Glyde, John, Jr. *Suffolk in the Nineteenth Century.* Ipswich: J. M. Burton, n.d. [1856?].

[Head, Francis Bond.] "English Charity." *Quarterly Review* 53(April 1835): 473–539.

Kay, James. *The Moral and Physical Condition of the Working Classes Employed in the Cotton Manufacture in Manchester.* London: James Ridgway, 1832.

Knight, Charles. *Passages of a Working Life during Half a Century.* 3 vols. London: Knight & Co., 1873.

Martineau, Harriet. *Biographical Sketches.* London: Macmillan, 1869.

Martineau, Harriet. *Harriet Martineau's Autobiography.* Edited by Maria Weston Chapman. 2 vols. Boston: J. R. Osgood, 1877.

Martineau, Harriet. *Illustrations of Political Economy.* London: Charles Fox, 1832–34.

Pratt, John Tidd. *The Act for the Amendment and better Administration of the law relating to the Poor, in England and Wales.* Second edition. London: B. Fellowes, 1834.

[Scrope, G. Poulett.] "The New Poor Law." *Quarterly Review* 52(August 1834):233–61.

[Scrope, G. Poulett.] "The Poor Law Question." *Quarterly Review* 50(January 1834):347–73.

[Scrope, G. Poulett.] "Poor Laws for Scotland." *Quarterly Review* 75(December 1844):125–48.

Walter, John. *A Letter to the Electors of Berkshire on the New Management of the Poor, proposed by the Government.* London: J. Ridgway & Sons, 1834.

Whitbread, Samuel. *Substance of a Speech on the Poor Laws: Delivered to the House of Commons on Thursday, February 19, 1807.* London: J. Ridgway, 1807.

White, John Meadows. *Remarks on the Poor Law Amendment Act as it affects Unions, or Parishes under the Government of Guardians or Select Vestries.* London: B. Fellowes, 1834.

Secondary Works Cited

Ashby, A. W. *One hundred years of Poor Law administration in a Warwickshire village.* Oxford studies in social and legal history. Edited by P. Vinogradorf. Oxford: At the Clarendon Press, 1912.

Blaug, Mark. "The Myth of the Old Poor Law and the Making of the New," *Journal of Economic History* 23(1963):151-84.

Blaug, Mark. "The Poor Law Report Reexamined," *Journal of Economic History* 24(1964):229-45.

Brebner, J. Bartlett. "Laissez-faire and State Intervention in Nineteenth-century Britain." *Journal of Economic History* 8(1948): Supp., pp. 59-73.

Brock, Michael. *The Great Reform Act*. London: Hutchinson, 1973.

Brundage, Anthony. "The English Poor Law of 1834 and the Cohesion of Agricultural Society." *Agricultural History* 48(July 1974):405-17.

Brundage, Anthony. "The Landed Interest and the New Poor Law: a Reappraisal of the Revolution in Government." *English Historical Review* 87(January 1972):27-48.

Brundage, Anthony. "The Landed Interest and the New Poor Law: A Reply." *English Historical Review* 90(April 1975):347-51.

Brundage, Anthony. "Reform of the Poor Law Electoral System, 1834-94." *Albion* 7(Fall 1975):201-15.

Chambers, J. D., and Mingay, G. E. *The Agricultural Revolution 1750-1880*. New York: Schocken Books, 1966.

Clokie, H. M., and Robinson, J. W. *Royal Commissions of Inquiry*. Stanford Cal.: Stanford University Press, 1937.

Coats, A. W. "Economic Thought and Poor Law Policy in the Eighteenth Century." *Economic History Review* 2d. ser. 2(1958-59):39-51.

Coats, A. W., ed., *Poverty in the Victorian Age*. 4 vols. Farnborough, Hants: Gregg, 1973.

Cowherd, Raymond G. "The Humanitarian Reform of the English Poor Laws from 1782 to 1815." *Proceedings of the American Philosphical Society* 104(1960):328-42.

Dicey, Albert Venn. *Lectures on the Relation between Law and Public Opinion in England during the Nineteenth Century*. London: Macmillan and Co., 1905.

Digby, Anne. "The Rural Poor Law." In *The New Poor Law in the Nineteenth Century*, edited by Derek Fraser. London: Macmillan, 1976.

Driver, Cecil. *Tory Radical: The Life of Richard Oastler.* New York: Oxford University Press, 1946.

Dunkley, Peter. "The Landed Interest and the New Poor Law: A Critical Note." *English Historical Review* 88(October 1973): 836-41.

Edsall, Nicholas C. *The Anti-Poor Law Movement 1834-44.* Manchester: Manchester University Press, 1971.

Finer. S. E. "The Transmission of Benthamite Ideas 1820-50." In *Studies in the Growth of Nineteenth-century Government,* edited by Gillian Sutherland. London: Routledge & Kegan Paul, 1972.

Finer, S. E. *The Life and Times of Sir Edwin Chadwick.* London: Methuen, 1952.

Fraser, Derek, ed. *The New Poor Law in the Nineteenth Century.* London: Macmillan, 1976.

Fraser, Derek. "The Poor Law as a Political Institution." In *The New Poor Law in the Nineteenth Century,* edited by Derek Fraser. London: Macmillan, 1976.

Fraser, Derek. "Poor Law Politics in Leeds, 1833-1855." *Publications of the Thoresby Society* 53(1970):23-49.

Gash, Norman. *Reaction and Reconstruction in English Politics, 1832-1852.* Oxford: At the Clarendon Press, 1965.

Gutchen, Robert M. "Local Improvements and Centralization in Nineteenth Century England." *Historical Journal* 4(1961): 85-96

Halevy, Elie. *The Triumph of Reform 1830-1841.* Translated by E. I. Watkin and D. A. Barker. Second edition. London: Benn, 1950.

Hampson, E. M. *The Treatment of Poverty in Cambridgeshire, 1597-1834.* Cambridge: At the University Press, 1934.

Hart, Jenifer. "Nineteenth Century Social Reform: a Tory Interpretation of History." *Past and Present* 31(July 1965):39-61.

Henriques, Ursula. "Bastardy and the New Poor Law." *Past and Present* 37(July 1967):103-29.

Henriques, Ursula. "How Cruel Was the Victorian Poor Law?" *Historical Journal* 11(1968):365-71.

Hobsbawm, E. J., and Rudé, George. *Captain Swing.* New York: Pantheon Books, 1968.

Holderness, B. A. "'Open' and 'Close' Parishes in England in the Eighteenth and Nineteenth Centuries." *Agricultural History Review* 20(1972):126-39.

Hume, L. J. "Jeremy Bentham and the Nineteenth Century Revolution in Government." *Historical Journal* 10(1967):361-75.

Levy, S. Leon. *Nassau W. Senior 1790-1864.* Newton Abbot: David & Charles, 1970.

Lewis, R. A. "William Day and the Poor Law Commissioners." *University of Birmingham Historical Journal* 9(1964):163-96.

Lubenow, William C. *The Politics of Government Growth: Early Victorian Attitudes toward State Intervention 1835-1848.* Newton Abbot: David & Charles, 1971.

MacDonagh, Oliver. "The Nineteenth Century Revolution in Government: A Reappraisal." *Historical Journal* 1(1958):52-67.

MacDonagh, Oliver. *A Pattern of Government Growth.* London: MacGibbon, 1961.

Marshall, Dorothy. *The English Poor in the Eighteenth Century.* London: George Routledge and Sons, 1926.

Marshall, J. D. "The Nottinghamshire Reformers and Their Contribution to the New Poor Law." *Economic History Review* 2d ser., 13(1961):382-96.

Martin, E. W. "From Parish to Union: Poor Law Administration, 1601-1865." In *Comparative Development in Social Welfare,* edited by E. W. Martin, pp. 25-56. New York: George Allen & Unwin, 1972.

Midwinter, E. C. *Social Administration in Lancashire 1830-1860: Poor Law, Public Health and Police.* Manchester: Manchester University Press, 1969.

Monypenny, W. F., and Buckle, G. E. *The Life of Benjamin Disraeli, Earl of Beaconsfield.* 6 vols. New York: Macmillan, 1914.

Moore, D. C. *The Politics of Deference. A study of the Mid-Nineteenth Century English Political System.* Hassocks, Sussex: The Harvester Press, 1976.

Neuman, Mark Donald. "Aspects of Poverty and Poor Law Administration in Berkshire, 1782-1834." Ph.D. dissertation, University of California, Berkeley, 1967.

Neuman, Mark Donald. "A Suggestion Regarding the Origins of

the Speenhamland Plan." *English Historical Review,* 84(1969): 317-22.

Nicholls, Sir George, and Mackay, Thomas. *A History of the English Poor Law.* 3 vols. First edition, 1854. Revised edition, 1898. Reprint (revised edition). London: Cass, 1967.

Oxley, Geoffrey W. *Poor Relief in England and Wales 1601-1834.* Newton Abbot: David & Charles, 1974.

Parker, C. S. *The Life and Letters of Sir James Graham.* 2 vols. London: Murray, 1907.

Parris, Henry. "The Nineteenth Century Revolution in Government: A Reappraisal Reappraised." *Historical Journal* 3(1960):17-37.

Poynter, J. R. *Society and Pauperism: English Ideas on Poor Relief, 1795-1834.* London: Routledge & Kegan Paul, 1967.

Roberts, David. "How Cruel Was the Victorian Poor Law?" *Historical Journal* 6(1963):97-107.

Roberts, David. "Jeremy Bentham and the Victorian Administrative State." *Victorian Studies* 2(1959):193-210.

Roberts, David. *Victorian Origins of the British Welfare State.* New Haven: Yale University Press, 1960.

Rose, Michael E. "The Allowance System under the New Poor Law." *Economic History Review* 2d ser., 19(1966):607-20.

Rose, Michael E. "The Anti-Poor Law Movement in the North of England." *Northern History* 1(1966):70-91.

Rose, Michael E., ed. *The English Poor Law 1780-1930.* Newton Abbot: David & Charles, 1971.

Rose, Michael E. "The Poor Law in the North." In *The Industrial Revolution,* edited by R. M. Hartwell. New York: Barnes & Noble, 1970.

Rose, Michael E. "Settlement, Removal, and the New Poor Law." In *The New Poor Law in the Nineteenth Century,* edited by Derek Fraser, pp. 25-44. London: Macmillan, 1976.

Styles, P. "The Evolution of the Law of Settlement." *University of Birmingham Historical Journal* 9(1963):33-63.

Taylor, James Stephen. "The Impact of Pauper Settlement 1691-1834." *Past and Present* 73(November 1976):42-74.

Taylor, James Stephen. "The Mythology of the Old Poor Law." *Journal of Economic History* 29(June 1969):292-97.

Vorspan, Rachel. "Vagrancy and the New Poor Law in Late Victorian and Edwardian England." *English Historical Review* 92(January 1977):59-81.

Wallas, Graham. *The Life of Francis Place.* London: Geo. Allen & Unwin, 1918.

Webb, R. K. *The British Working Class Reader 1790-1848.* London: Geo. Allen & Unwin, 1955.

Webb, R. K. *Harriet Martineau: A Radical Victorian.* New York: Columbia University Press, 1960.

Webb, Sidney, and Webb, Beatrice. *English Poor Law History: Part I, The Old Poor Law.* London: Longmans and Co., 1927.

Webb, Sidney, and Webb, Beatrice. *English Poor Law History: Part II, The Last Hundred Years.* 2 vols. London: Longmans and Co., 1929.

Webb, Sidney, and Webb, Beatrice. *English Poor Law Policy.* London: Longmans and Co., 1910.

Webb, Sidney, and Webb, Beatrice. *The Parish and the County.* London: Longmans, Green and Co., 1906.

Index